WEST CEMETERY—PAYNE KENYON KILBOURN

# Litchfield and Morris Inscriptions

A Record of Inscriptions upon the
Tombstones in the Towns of
Litchfield and Morris,
Connecticut

Transcribed by
*Charles Thomas Payne*

HERITAGE BOOKS
2015

# HERITAGE BOOKS

*AN IMPRINT OF HERITAGE BOOKS, INC.*

**Books, CDs, and more—Worldwide**

For our listing of thousands of titles see our website
at
www.HeritageBooks.com

A Facsimile Reprint
Published 2015 by
HERITAGE BOOKS, INC.
Publishing Division
5810 Ruatan Street
Berwyn Heights, Md. 20740

International Standard Book Numbers
Paperbound: 978-0-7884-0560-0
Clothbound: 978-0-7884-6128-6

Limited Edition

No._____

# Publisher's Notice

THE publishing of this book is the result of a wish I have long entertained of placing in permanent form and thus preserving the rapidly disappearing inscriptions upon the tombstones of my native town.

Mr. Charles Thomas Payne, of New York City, a descendant of a number of the families who founded the Town of Litchfield, cordially seconded my desires, and spent several summers transcribing them. This he has faithfully done for all prior to 1900, and many later inscriptions have been gathered.

I am pleased to acknowledge the hearty response to my circular for subscribers.

The cuts were photographed by Sherry and Karl, and engraved by the Hartford Engraving Co. The mechanical work was done by the Waterbury Blank Book Mfg. Co., and it is all as nearly possible a local undertaking.

With a hope that it will be a valuable addition to our Town's history, and of interest to all it is now presented to the public.

DWIGHT C. KILBOURN.

Litchfield, October 9, 1904.

# Contents

# Illustrations

# Preface

**T**HIS book is merely a collection of the inscriptions on gravestones and monuments in all the cemeteries of that area comprising what was Litchfield Town before 1859. In that year nearly half of the Township, then known as the Society or Parish of the South Farms, was formed into the Town of Morris. The purpose of such a book is necessarily directed toward increasing knowledge of the past of Litchfield. So from the standpoint of the historian or the genealogist, any comprehensive data of this sort must include what may be known of Morris as well as Litchfield as it is now. The inscriptions contained here are believed to be complete to the year 1900, and a number have been added from tombs and monuments erected since that date.

Before each list of inscriptions found in the several graveyards I have inserted something of their history; and nowhere is the quaintness of old New England life better shown than in these dealings of man concerning his dead.

Enough has been said in other books, of the good and the great who lie sleeping here; they need not my hand to point their names or celebrate their virtues.

To Dwight Canfield Kilbourn, Esq., I confess my deep obligation; and credit is due him not only for publishing this book but for many suggestions which I have followed in its preparation.

CHARLES THOMAS PAYNE.

August, 1902.

# West Burying Ground

This is the earliest of the burial places in Litchfield, and its establishment was nearly contemporaneous with the founding of the Town. The first notice of it appears in Volume One of the Land Records, as follows:

"An acompt of the High Ways In Litchfield In 1723.... the 2ᵈ high Way Runing East and West between Samuel Smedly his home Lott and the Widow allens home Lott of twenty eight Rods in bredth Sixty Rods West and then is twelue Rods Wide down to the swamp and then is laid out but six rods Wide thorou the swamp Which highway runs on the West side of the letle plain buting north upon Land Laid out to John Gay to make up the fifteen acres for his home Lott and so continuel a West Line until it comes to the swamp or flooded Lands and all the Land upon the letele playn South of said highway to the swamp or flooded land which is not yet Laid out is Resarued and Laid out for a burying place Which highway at the West End of the litle plain or burying place runs six Rods Wide throro the swamp and acrose the hill called buck's Neak With the same corce and bredth until it comes to the pine plain Which high Way is Called by the name of Middiel Street."

Here were interred nearly all of the pioneers of Litchfield, and the yard remained the principal burial ground of the Town until the Revolution.

Early in the Nineteenth Century a large tract was added on the western side.

# INSCRIPTIONS

In memory | of the | Hon. Andrew Adams, Esq., | Chief Judge of the Superior Court, | who died Nov. 27, A D 1797, in the 62ᵈ year of his Age. | Having filled many distinguished offices with | great Ability and Dignity, he was promoted to | the highest Judicial Office in the State, which he held | for several years, in which his eminent Talents shone | with uncommon Lustre, and were exerted to the great | Advantage of the Public and the Honor of the High | Court in which he presided. He made an early Pro | fession of Religion, and zealously sought to promote | its true Interests. He lived the Life and died the | Death of a Christian. His filial Piety and pater | nal tenderness are held in sweet Remembrance | Here also lies interred | the body of Mrs. Eunice Wife of the Hon. Andrew Adams Esq | Who died June 4, 1797 aged 51 years |

Mrs. Minerva Adams | Wife of Mʳ Elijah Adams | Died July 1ˢᵗ A D 1800 in the | 19ᵗʰ year of her age |

Mʳ· | Andrew Adams Jr. | died Dec 9, 1804 | in the 38ᵗʰ year | of his age |

In | Memory of | Mrs. Abbey D. | **wife of** | Thomas Addis | who died | April 14, 1813 | **aged 40 years** |

Thomas Addis | died | July 22, 1853 | Æ 85 |

Mrs. | Thomas Addis | died | June 20, 1854 | Æ 86 |

Thomas Addis | Died | July 8, 1871 | Æ 68 |

Catharine S. | daughter of | William & Julia Ann Addis | died | Mar 23, 1839 | **aged 8 ye'rs** |

In | memory of | Samuel Addis | who died | March 18, 1845 | aged 49 years |

Amy Adam | wife of John Adam | deceased | Sept 4, 1833 | Aged 43 |

Chester Addis | 1824-1883 |

Charles Percy | Adcock | born | Apr. 6, 1890 | died | Aug 29, 1891 |

U. L. A. |

Our Mother | Laura | wife of | Lucius S. Buell | died | June 21, 1874 | æ 55 |

James B. Beach | Co. F 23 Regt. C. V. | wounded | at Lafourche, La. | June 19, Died in | St. Louis Hospital N. O.| Aug 21, 1863, aged 34 |

Wesley E. | died Dec 8, 1861 | æ 6 yrs. 9 mo's | Mary A. | died Dec 13, 1861 | æ 8 yrs. 5 mo's | Children of | J. B. & V. E. Beach |

William L. | son of Ellas & | Clarissa Briggs | died | Mar 10, 1838 |

In memory of | Roxana Bliss | daughter of | Aaron & Anna Bliss | who died Sept 6th 1824 | in the 24th year | of her age |

Frank E. | son of Ezra & Miranda C. | Buell | died | Oct 10, 1859 | Æ 8 y'rs 2 mo. | & 16 d's |

Ezra Buell | died | Dec 26, 1865 | Æ 53 y'rs & 8 mo | His wife | Miranda C. French | died May 4, 1890 | Æ 80 y'rs & 6 mo. |

Almira | wife of | Vincent Belden | died | Aug. 25, 1868 | Æ 50 |

Nancy Buell | died | May 10, 1879 | Aged 72 |

Susannah | wife of | Miles Buell | died | May 7, 1855 | Æ 78 |

Miles Buell | died | Jan 4, 1858 | Æ 85 |

In | memory of | Ebenezer G. Buell | who died | Aug 19, 1853 | Æ 41 |

In memory of Hannah | relict of | Ebenezer Buell | who died | Sept 6, 1835 | aged 86 years |

In | memory of | Ebenezer Buell | who died | May 26, 1823 | aged 76 years |

John Buell | died June 12, 1824 | aged 73 years |

Lydia Buell | died March 7, 1823 | aged 75 years |

Lois Ann | Daughter of | Capt Samuel & Anne | Buell 2nd | died April 27, 1848 | aged 36 years |

John W. | son of | Cap. Samuel & | Ann Buell | Died Feb 20, 1819 | æ 2 ye | Also their Daughter | Lydia Died Jan | 22, 1820, æ 1 yr. |

Lois | wife of Cap. Samuel Buell | Died Aug 12, 1809 | Æ 21 |

BUELL | Samuel Buell | Born March 28, 1783 | Died Nov 20, 1863 | Annie Wadhams | his wife | Born July 11, 1777 | Died May 27, 1865 || John W. Buell 2nd | Born May 13, 1821 | Died April 30, 1864 || Children of | Samuel & Annie W. Buell | Lois A. | Born Feb 27, 1812 | Died April 27, 1848 | John W. | Born Jan 14, 1816 | Died Feb 20, 1818 | Lydia | Born Feb 13, 1819 | Died Jan 22, 1820 |

In memory | of Ashbel Buel son | of Deacon Peter | Buel he Departed | this life Septembr | ye 7th A. D. 1753 in ye | 7th year of his | age |

In memory | of Anne Buel 3rd | Daughter of Deacn | Peter Buel who | Departed this | Life Sept ye 11th 1753, | in the 4th year of | her age.

In memory of | Asa Bull | who died | April 14, 1805 | in the 54 year | of his age |

In memory of | Tamar wife of | Asa Bull | who died Sept 13, 1801 | in the 45 year | of her age |

Harvy | son of | Henry B. & | Lucy S. Barney ] died | Sept 9, 1879 | aged 8 mo. |

In memory of | Ira Brown | who died | May 28, 1820 |aged 42 years | Catharine his wife | died April 27, 1809 | in her 26 year |

Here lies Interr'd | the Body of | Mrs Avis Bewell wife | of Capt Peter Bewell | who Departed this | Life Novembr the 1st A. D. 1754 in | the 41st year of | her Age |

BUELL | Dea. John Buell | first settler of | Litchfield |Born Feb 17, 1671 | Died April 22, 1746 | Andrew Buell | Born March 8, 1794 | Died March 9, 1876 | Lamira his wife | Born Feb 18, 1799 | Died Feb 19, 1853 || Children of Andrew & Lamira | Buell | Marian C. | Born Dec 17, 1822 ¦ Died May 15, 1872 | Melinda A. | Born Nov 30, 1829 | Died July 14, 1841. ||

Marian C. Buell | daughter of | Andrew & Lamira ⌐ Buell | Born Dec 17, 1822 ] Died May 15, 1872 |

Melinda A. | daughter of | Andrew & | Lamira Buell | died | July 14, 1841 | aged 11 y'rs | & 7 mo's |

In | memory of | Lamira Catlin | wife of | Andrew Buell | who died | Feb 18, 1853 | æ 53 |

A. B. |

Sarah M. Buell | daughter of | Elias & | Cynthia Buell | born | Jan 17, 1836 | died Aug 26, 1854 |

Cynthia M. | daughter of | Elias & Cynthia Buell | born May 1, 1840 | died | Aug 30, 1848 |

Elias W. | son | of | Elias & | Cynthia Buell | born Feb 4, 1831 | died | Dec 25, 1842 |

Mary A. | daughter | of | Elias & | Cynthia Buell | born Mar. 3, 1833 | died June 13, 1842 |

Cynthia W. | wife of | Elias Buell | died | Mar 28, 1863 | aged 57 |

Elias Buell | son of | Obed Buell | born Nov 16, 1790 | died | Aug 14, 1855 |

In memory of | Uncle William | William E. Buell | died April 25, 1872 | Aged 65 |

In | memory of | Honour M. Buell |daughter of Obed | & Honour Buell | died | Aug 28, 1855 | æ 54 y'rs |

Charles H. Buell | born Nov 28, 1809 | died | March 23, 1840 | aged 30 |

In | memory of | Almira Buell | daughter of | Obed & Honour Buell | who died | July 19, 1829, aged 26 | years |

In | memory of | Honour Buell | wife of Obed Buell | who died | April 28, 1824 | aged 57 |

> Mortals, how few among your race
> Have given this thought its weight
> That on this fleeting moment hangs
> Your everlasting state.

In | memory of | Obed Buell | who died | July 16, 1848 | aged 79 y'rs |

Melinda | daughter of | Obed & | Honour Buell | died | Aug 27, 1819 | aged 21 y'rs|

WEST CEMETERY—MARY BUELS

In |memory of | Silas Son of | Obed & | Honour Buel | who died | Dec 1, 1795 | æ 5 months | & 11 days |

In | memory of | Belinda | daughter of M$^r$ Obed | & Mrs. Honour Buel | who died Sep$^t$ 9, 1791 | æt 1 year 9 months & 27 days |

In memory of | Ebenezer Buel | who died | Feb 25, 1801 | æ 88 |

Here lies Interr'd | the Body of Capt John Buel, Esq$^r$ who | served in the Office | of a Deacon of the Church in Litchfield | and Departed this | Life April the 3$^{rd}$ 1746 | in the 75$^{th}$ year | of his age |

Here lies the Body | of M$^{rs}$ Mary wife of | D$^n$ John Buell Esq | she died Nov 4$^{th}$ | 1768, ætat 90 | Having had 13, Children | 101 Grand Children | 274 Great G. Children | 22 Great G. G. Children | 410 Total | 336 survived her |

Here lies Interd y$^e$ | Body of Mr$^s$ | Dorothy y$^e$ wife | of M$^r$ Ebenezer | Buell who Died | June y$^e$ 24$^{th}$, 1767 | & in y$^e$ 57$^{th}$ year of | Her Age |

In memory of | Ruth Buell | who died Sept 19, | 1796 | Aged 67 | Consort of | Ebenezer Buell |

Here lies the Body | of M$^{rs}$ Eunice wife | of Capt Solomon | Buell she Departed | this Life Aug 7$^{th}$ | 1771·in the 51$^{st}$ year of her Age | she was the first | English person ever | Born in Litchfield |

Here lies the | Body of Capt Solomon | Buel who | Departed this | life March the 22$^{nd}$ 1795, in the | 80$^{th}$ year of his | Age |

In memory of | M$^r$ Salmon Buel | who Departed this life | Dec 18, 1811 | Aged 75 years |

In memory of | Mrs Margaret Buel | who Departed this | Life Dec 18, 1812 | aged 71 years |

David Buel | Died | Feb 9, 1820, æ 38 |

Gen. Frederick Buel | died Oct 23, 1863 | Aged 66 |

Julia | wife of | Gen. Frederick Buel | Died Aug 29, 1860 | æ 60 |

In | memory of | Jerusha | wife of Capt Solomon Buel | who departed this life | Oct$^r$ 30th, 1798 in the 63$^{rd}$ year | of her age |

This Stone is Erected | In Memory of Mrs | Anne Baldwin Relict of M^r John | Baldwin who departed | this life June the 5^th | 1788 in the 88^th year of her age |

Here lies the Body of M^r John | Baldwin who Di'd | Oct y^e 17 1762 in | The 70^th year | Of His Age |

Capt Salmon Buel | died | Jan 3, 1868 | Aged 100 Years | 6 M's & 24 D's |

In memory of | Mrs. Lydia Buel | wife of | Capt. Salmon Buel | who departed this life | Oct 18, 1807 | Aged 36 years |

Jerusha | wife of | Capt. Salmon Buel | died June 28, 1845 | aged 64 |

Stephen C. Buel | died July 28, 1823 | aged 6 months | also Harriet Buel | died April 14, 1825 | aged 8 months | son & daughter of | George M. & | Marilla Buel |

Uriel H. Brace | Born | Dec 13, 1822 | Died April 21^st 1828 |

James Brace | died Apr 7, 1833 | æt 65 | Susan Brace | His wife died | June 3, 1830 | æt 68 |

In memory of | Olive | daughter of Norman & Lois Barber | who died | Feb 20, 1835 | aged 24 y'rs |

Norman Barber | died | April 20, 1862 | æ 82 |

Lois | wife of | Norman Barber | died | Oct 12, 1854 | æ 74|

Anna Birge | widow of | Harvey Birge | Born Nov 4, 1795| Died Mar 28, 1868 |

Mrs. | Rachel Bishop | wife of | Jonathan Bishop | and Daughter of | Cap't. | John Stoddard | Died August 15 | 1793| Aged 25 years |

Silvanus Bishop | died | May 15, 1862 | Aged 70 |

Clarinda | wife of | Silvanus Bishop | Died Feb. 11, 1868 | Aged 70 |

In Memory of | M^rs Abigail | Wife of Cap^t Miles Beach | who Died Nov | ye 28^th 1781 in ye | 35^th year of her | Age

Joseph Barber | died May 21, 1821 | aged 70 |

In Memory of | M^r James Belden | a Member of Yale College | & Son of Col. Thomas | & Mrs. Abigail Belden | of

Wethersfield | who Departed this life | the 27ᵗʰ of Novʳ | An. Dom. 1779 | and in the 20ᵗʰ year | of his Age | The Bloom and Vigor of youth | are no Security against the | Arrests of Death |

Harriet M. Barney | died | Oct 15, 1835 | æ 23 | by her son W. Barney |

Mary | Jennett | daughter of | Mylo & | Rhoda P. Beach | died Nov 29, 1824 | aged 8 d's |

Rhoda P. | wife of | Milo Beach | died | July 7, 1851 | æ 47 | In the belief of a speedy resurrection |

Lucretia D. | wife of | Milo Beach | died | July 22, 1856 | æ 39 |

> Here sweet be thy rest
> Till He bid thee arise
> To hail him in triumph
> Descending the skies.

Betsey E. Barnard | Daughter of George | & Lois Barnard | died August 30ᵗʰ | 1800 in the 14th year | of her age |

Samuel Beach | died | Apr 14, 1873 | æ 81 |

In memory | of | Elizabeth | wife of | Noah Beach | who died | April 10, 1808 | æ 44 | Also | Sarah | wife of | Noah Beach | who died | Aug 25, 1850 | æ 66 |

In memory | of | Noah Beach | who died | April 12, 1851 | æ 87 |

Here lies Interrd the | Body of Mrs. Elizabeth | Barnes wife of Capt. | Amos Barnes; Departed | this life June the 27ᵗʰ | A D 1777 in the 40ᵗʰ | year of her age |

In memory of | Norman Son of | Capt Amos Barns | who Died Sept | the 4ᵗʰ A D 1777 | in the 4ᵗʰ year | of his age |

In Memory of | Betty Daughter of | Capt Amos Barns | who Died Sept | the 10ᵗʰ A D 1777 | in the 6ᵗʰ year of | her age |

Ann | wife of | Calvin Bishop | and relict of ] Lewis Kilborn | died | Aug 10, 1839 | aged 80 |

In Memory of | Mʳ Joel Bissell | He Died January ⌈ yᵉ 15ᵗʰ A D 1757 | Aged 48 years |

Mrs. Mary | wife of | Archelaus Bissell | died ⌈ Oct 12, 1826 | æ 64 |

Archelaus Bissell | died | April 26, 1846 | aged **88** |

Thalia Bissell | died | Dec 10, 1850 | æ 60 |

Elias Bissell | died July 28, 1863 | æ 71 |

Clarissa Bissell | died | April 9, 1877 | æ 79 |

Calvin Barnum | died | Feb 20, 1867 | æ 58 |

In | memory of | Parmelia | late relict of | Anson Beach |
who died | Aug 2, 1849 | æ 67 |

> Our last earthly Parent has left us and gone
> Weary Pilgrims, to travel this earth all alone
> No resting place sure while encumbered with clay
> Dear Jesus could find and shall we fear the way.

Enos Beach | died | March 25, 1848 | æt 77 yrs |

Susannah | wife of | Enos Beach | died | June 10, 1847 |æt
70 years |

Caroline | wife of | Mills Barnum | died at the | Insane re-
treat | Hartford, Ct. | Mar 10, 1853 | æ 46 yr. 9 mo. | 24 d's |

> Pass a few swiftly fleeting years
> And all that now in bodies live
> Shall quit like me the vale of tears
> Their righteous sentence to receive.
>
> But all before they hence remove
> May mansions for themselves prepare
> In that eternal house above
> And Oh, my God, shall I be thier.

Lewis M. | son of | Mills & | D. A. Barnum | died | Aug 27.
1853 | æ 10 w'ks |

Died | Jan 13, 1858 | Eddie S. | son of | Mills & | D. A.
Barnum | æ 13 mo |

Cromwell Buell | Died Jan 30, 1859 | æ 81 | His wife |
Sally | Died July 29, 1872 | æ 88 |

In Memory of | Lyman Buell | who died | Mar 1, 1852 |
æ 43 |

Fanny | wife of | Charles C. Buell | died | Feb 6, 1851 |
Aged 49 |

Weep not my friends, my friends weep
not for me, All is well, All is well.

Elizabeh Bissell | died || Oct. 19, 1860 | æ 28 | She was beloved and fell asleep | Lyman Bissell | died | Nov 28, 1838 |
æ 1 year || Lydia B. Hall | wife of | Amos Bissell | died | June
12, 1863 | æ 61 | My Children, love God, love Jesus | love one
another ; that God | may love you and dwell in you and you in
him | BISSELL || Amos Bissell | died | Jan 29, 1888 | æ 87 |

Allan | son of | Dwight & | Elizabeth Bissell | died Sept 24,
1872 | Aged 5 w'ks |

Lyman | son of Amos & | Lydia Bissell | died | Nov 28,
1838 | aged 1 year |

Esther | Relict of | Benjamin Bissell | died | Dec 27, 1840 |
æ 83 |

M^r | Benjamin Bissell | died Feb 28.th, 1825 | æt 71 |

Abigail Benton | died | July 21, 1829 | æ 70 |

In memory of | M^r Nathaniel Benton | who was Born August 25^th | 1726 & Died Sept^r 30^th | 1800 Aged 74 years |

Eunice Bissell | 1790-1877 |

Catharine E. | wife of | Philip S. Beebe | died | Nov 29,
1843 | aged 21 yr's |

Philip S. Beebe | died | April 12, 1891 | æ 79 | Lucy Robbins | his wife died | April 27, 1876 | æ 60 |

William Beebe | died | Nov 18, 1861 | Aged 80 | Clarissa |
his wife | died | April 12, 1860 | Aged 74 |

In Memory of Sarah Beebe | Daughter of Bezaleel and |
Elizabeth who Died | February 1st, 1800. of | Consumption
Aged 35 Years |

Col. | Bezaleel Beebe | died | May 28^th 1824 | æt 83 |

M^rs | Elizabeth Beebe | wife of Col. B. Beebe | died | April
12^th, 1825 | æt 80 |

Harriet M. | daughter of | William & | Clarissa Beebe |
died | April 21, 1837 | aged 22 years |

In Memory of | Ormond G. Burge | died May 30, 1816 | æt 3 yrs | Orrin, died May 7, 1814 | æt 1 yr | sons of Orrin & | Anna Burge |

David Booth | died | June 2, 1845 | aged 46 |

In | memory of | Lydia wife of | David Booth | who died | April 7, 1838 | aged 43 years |

Mr. | Zebulon Bissell | died | May 16th 1824 | æ 72 |

Our father's grave | Luther Bissell | died Jan 26, 1858 | æ 54 |

Calvin Bissell | died Oct 28, 1837 | æ 84 years | also | Elizabeth | wife of | Calvin Bissell | died March 29, 1830. | æ 69 years |

Henry Bissell | died | Feb 18, 1876 | æ 83|

Henry Wessells Brown | Grand-son of | Wm & Anna Ward| died | June 9, 1846 | aged 21 y'rs |

Maria C. Brown | wife of | Frederick W. Brown | died | June 20, 1855 | æt 37 |

Frederick Henry | son of | Frederick W. | & Maria C. Brown | died | Apr. 16, 1852 | æ 13 mo. |

> This lovely bud so young & fair
> Call'd hence by early doom
> Just came to show how sweet a flower
> In Paradise would bloom.

Emiline M. | daughter of | Frederick W. & | Maria C. Brown | died July 3, 1854 | aged 10 mo. |

Phebe L. | wife of | Heman Beach | died | Sept 9, 1858 | æ 84 |

Ethan O. Barber | died | Dec 9, 1873 | Aged 64½ |

Frances A. Gray | wife of | Ethan O. Barber | Died Jan 24, 1871 | Aged 60 |

Francis E. Barber | of Co E. 8, Regt. C. V. | died | on board a Hospital Ship | off Hatteras | Jan 30, 1862 | Aged 19 |

> "Death has no terror for me."

Corp | Geo. F. Booth | Co. E. 8. Regt. | Conn Vols | died | Sept 17, 1862 |

Sarah E. Brown | wife of | Samuel E. Brown | died | Aug 22, 1883 | Aged 57 |

James H. | Son of | Eugene & Ella | Banker | died | Mar 16, 1885 | Aged 2 m'o |

William H. | son of | Herbert E. & | Harriet E. Banker |died June 12, 1874 | æ 2 Y'rs & 6 Mo |

George B. | son of | Herbert E. & | Harriet E. Banker | died | Feb 3, 1863 | æ 8 mo |

Willie | son of | Herbert E & | Harriet E. Banker | died | Mar. 11, 1863 | æ 4 Y'rs & 3 Mo |

Abby || Abby Jane | daughter of | Jacob W. & | Sarah K. Bigelow | born Feb 14, 1865 | died | June 18, 1869 |

Seth Farnam Benton | Jan 13, 1832 | Sept 18, 1839 | BENTON ||`George B. Benton | July 6, 1805 | Sept 11, 1854| Harriet B. Farnam | Wife of | G. B. Benton | Sept 8, 1809 | May 18, 1888 |

Seth F. | son of | George B. & | Harriet B. Benton | died | Sept 18, 1839 | aged 8 years |

Nelson H. Barnes | died | ——— | Abby J. | wife of | Nelson H. Barnes | died | Dec 21, 1884 | Aged 44 |

Infant son of | Chauncey J. & Maggie M. | Buell | died | Mar 3, 1877 | Æ 2 Mo. & 10 D's |

Etta E. | daughter of | William A. & | Kate L. Buell | died | May 7, 1880 | Aged 22 Y'rs | As thy days thy strength shall be.

Roland | Son of | Frank & | Estella Beyer | died | Jan 10, 1888 | aged 2 Y'rs |

Louise M. | daughter of | Ferdinand & Almeda | M. Buell | Oct 11, 1880 | aged 35 |

Florence A. Buell | died | Jan 13, 1877 | Aged 27 |

Ida E. Buell | Apr 7, 1874 | aged 20 |

Ferdinand Buell | died | June 18, 1886 | aged 68 |

Isabella M. | daughter of | Ferdinand & | Almeda M. Buell | died | May 26, 1859 | æ 1 y'r & 7 mo |

David C. Buell | died | Sept 6, 1885 | aged 60 yrs. | & 11 m'o. |

Truman Buell | died | Jan 31, 1867 | aged 81 | Nancy Hinman | his wife | died Nov 27, 1866 | aged 81 |

David M. | died | Aug 28, 1890 | aged 6 mo. | son of A. E. & | Ella E. Buell |

Bessie Eva | died | Jan 30, 1880 | aged 1 y'r | & 7 mo's | Daughter of A. E. & | Ella E. | Buell|

Our baby | died | May 31, 1876 | (*In Buell lot*)

George D. | died | Mar 7, 1861 | æ 3 Y'rs & 4 Mo |

Nancy J. | died | July 21, 1849 | æ 16 Da's | Children of David & Betsey B. | Buell |

In | memory of | Sylvia, wife of | Tobias Cleaver | who died | Aug. 25, 1816 aged 52 |

Julia Ann | wife of | Raynolds C. Crandall | died | Jan 12, 1840 | aged 27 |

Dyer Coe | died | Apr 18, 1866 | aged 72 |

Olive M. W. Coe | Daughter of Levi | & Deborah Coe | Died | May 24, 1833 | æ 26 yrs |

In Memory of | Deborah | wife of | Levi Coe | who died | April 29, 1843 | aged 74 |

In | memory of | Levi Coe | who died | Feb 28, 1832 | æ 71|

In memory | of | Mrs. Lois Collins | relict of Capt Daniel Collins | of Guilford | who died | Jan 4, A. D. 1768 | aged 66 years | This monument was | re-established in 1825 | to the virtuous mother | of a numerous family | by her | Grandson | Oliver Wolcott |

Died | Feb. 4, 1768 | *Original footstone of Mrs. Lois Collins*)

Here lies the | Body of Mʳ Lew | is Collens 3ʳᵈ son | of Timothy Collens, Esqʳ who | died July yᵉ 16ᵗʰ | A D 1753 in yᵉ 24ᵗʰ | year of his Age |

In memory of | William M. | Collins who | departed this life | Feb'y ye 26ᵗʰ A. D. 1788 | in the 2ⁿᵈ year of | his age |

In | memory of | Rhoda wife of | Lot Chase | died | April 10, 1844 | aged 66 |

In | Memory of | Lot Chase | who died | Feb 10, 1836 | in his 78, year |

Timothy Childs | died March 1, 1831 | in the 72$^d$ year of his age | His berieved friends has erected this monument, | to his memory.|

Julia Childs | Wife of | Col. H. W. Childs | died Nov'r 9, 1830, | aged 23 years |

It may not be : it will not last
The vision of enchantment's past.
Rest here my body, till the cries
Of Gabriel's trumpet bids thee rise.

In Memory of | Augustin Child | Son of Timothy & | Nancy Child | Who died Feb 3$^d$ | 1810 | in the 6$^{th}$ | year of his age |

Here lieth Interr'd | y$^e$ Body of M$^r$ | John Catlin | he Departed this | Life December y$^e$ | 25$^{th}$ 1768 in y$^e$ ⌈ Sixty Six year | of his age |

In | memory of Mrs. | Margret Catlin Who | Departed this life | October 5$^{th}$ A. D. 1792 | in the 83$^d$ year of | her age | Wife to Mr. | John Catlin |

Here li$^e$s y$^e$ Body of | Mr. Thomas Catling | Who Di'd Nov y$^e$ | 14, 1754 In the 49$^{th}$ | year of his age |

In | Memory of | Emeline Churchill | who died | Mar 15, 1848 | æ 25 y'rs |

In | memory of | Timothy Churchill | who died | Aug 11, 1842 | aged 66 |

Charles | son of Timothy & | Dotha Churchill | died | April 27, 1842 | aged 16 | In life beloved | in death lamented |

In | memory of | George Churchill | who died | May 28, 1833 | aged 27 years |

In memory of | Sarah Jane | Daughter of | Luman & Mary | Curtis. Died | Sept 2, 1836 | æ 1 year & 4 mo-s |

In memory of | Mary Eliza | Daughter of Luman ⌈ & Mary Curtis | Who died | Aug 6, 1831 | æ 4 —— |

(*Kenney*) || George Kinney | only son of | Samuel P & | Mary E. Camp. | Died Sept 17, 1882 | aged | 3 Yrs. 7 Mos 15 Ds |

William Campbell | died | Dec 18, 1876 | æ 77 |

Nancy | wife of | Wᵐ Campbell | died | Aug 10, 1883 | æ 70|

James | son of | Ezekiel & Elvira | Campbell | died | April 4, 1868 | æ 1 y'r & 9 mo |

Marina Kilbourn | wife of | Walter Coe | Died Oct 20, 1876| æ 77 | Not dead, but gone before |

.Walter Coe | died | Mar. 14, 1871 | æ 73 | A successful life, a ripened age, | a peaceful end |

C | Henry L. Coe | 1827- | Cornelia A. Griswold | his wife | 1831-1867 | Julia A. Page | his wife | 1831-1902 | COE || Mary L. Coe | wife of | Walter D. Smith | 1853-1888 |

Charles Culver | Of Co. E 8 C. V. | died | Aug 14, 1867 | æ 40 | Erected by his children |

Henry T. Cable | Born 1818 | Died 1902 | Melissa Brown | his wife | Born 1821 |——| CABLE || William H. Cable | Born 1844 | Died 1865 | Buried in Bantam, C. T. | George E. Cable | Born 1849 | Died 1855 || Helen Louise | wife of Carroll Jeness | Born 1857 | Died 1879 | Buried in | Deerfield, N. H. ||

In memoriam | Thomas | son of John & | Caroline Cox | of Ibstone | Oxfordshire, England | Born Dec 21, 1856 | Died Nov 15, 1875 | He that believeth on the Son hath everla | sting life |

Levi Coe | born Sept 14, 1810 | died Nov 1, 1881 | Lavinia M. McNeil | wife of | Levi Coe | born Sept 30, 1815 | died July 27| 1896 | COE || Frederic L. | son of | Levi & Lavinia M. Coe| born Sept 20, 1842 | died June 1, 1883 ||
Lᴀᴜɪɴɪᴀ ᴍ. Cᴏᴇ| ʙᴏʀɴ ᴍᴀʀ 6 , 1848|ᴅɪᴇᴅ Dᴇᴄ .3, 1863|

In memory | of | Philo de Forest | who died | April 6, 1855| æ 72 |

In memory | of | Mahitable | wife of | Philo De Forest | who died | June 7, 1855 | Æ 70 |

In Memory of | Mʳ Ebenezer Dickinson Who | died Nov yᵉ 21ˢᵗ | 1774 in —— 85ᵗʰ | year of his age |

In | memory of | Harvy | son of Amos & Anna Dean | who died | Sept 13, 1827 | aged 16 y. 14 d. |

Relations & friends behold & see
Prepare in time to follow me.

Angeline M. | wife of | Theodore E. Dean | died | Jan 3, 1847 | aged 22|

In Memory of two | Daughters of M^r | Benjamin Doolittle | & Mrs Hannah Doolittle |

Nancy Died | June 20^th A D 1798|in the 18^th | year of| her age |    Phebe Died | Feb^ry 19^th | A D 1798 | in the 16^th year of her | age |

David D. Deforest | —— | his wife | Fidelia J. | died Sept. 16, 1877 | æt 54 |

Little | Ruth | daughter of | L. D. & M. J. | Deforest | died | Dec. 22, 1890 | Age 3 y'rs |

Edward J. | son of | Alvin B. & Sarah T. | Dickinson | died| Mar. 17, 1856 | æ 2 yr. & 6 mos. |

This lovely bud that's nipt so soon,
Will rise and bloom beyond the tomb.

Myron J. | son of | Harvy & Anna | Dickinson | whose remains are | interred in the Milton | burying grounds | died | Sept 18, 1840 | æ 13, mo. & 6 ds. |

So fades the lovely
blooming flower.

In | memory of | Anna | wife of | Harvey Dickinson | who died | May 21, 1871 | æ 74 |

In | memory of | Harvey Dickinson | who died | May 1, 1855| Aged 57 |

He sleeps in Jesus and is blest
Let none his loss deplore
But those who view his place of rest,
Go hence and sin no more.

Lucius B. | Infant son of | Thos. & Sarah J. | Elliott | died July 22, 1864 | æ 3 Mo. & 2 Ds. |

William Elder | Co. D. 29 Regt | Conn. Vols. | died | Sept 4, 1882 |

Deborah | wife of | Abner Everett | & daughter of | Capt. Solomon Marsh | died | Jan 10, 1851 | æ 77 |

John Elliott | Born a slave | at Charlottesville, Va. | Nov. 27, 1836 | died | June 14, 1887 | Aged 50 Y'rs 6 M'os | & 17 D's |

Mabel M. | daughter of | John W. & Emma L. | Ferris | died| Oct 9, 1878 ] Æ 1 y'r & 10 M's |

George F. S. Fisher | Co. D. 11, Regt | Conn. Vols. | died | June 18, 1872 |

William S. Fisher | died | Feb 3, 1863 | aged 73 |    There is rest in Heaven |

In memory of | Mary K. wife of | Wᵐ S. Fisher | who died| Dec 13, 1852 | Æt 63 |

> A wife, a mother slumbers here
> Her soul has left this earthly sphere
> And when the last Angel's trump shall sound
> May she with endless life be crowned.

Edward E. Fisher | Co I 13 Reg't. C. V. | died | Dec 19, 1875 | æ 50 |

Annie Louise Fuller | died | Oct 5, 1874 | æ 11 W'ks |

Jonathan E. Fuller | born | March 23, 1805 | Died May 8, 1875 | his wife | Julia A. | Born Nov 22, 1804 | Died Aug 13, 1889 |

Mary L. Fenn | born | Nov 17, 1804 | died | Feb 23, 1890 |

Henry E. Fenn | died | Feb 13, 1877 | æ 40 | His wife | Rosalinda Fenn | died Dec 24, 1882 | æ 41 | FENN |

William Fisher | Co. A. 8, Regt. | Conn. Vols. | died | July 24, 1884 |

George H. Fellows | born | Nov 13, 1802 | died Apr 17, 1857|

Jane Ferguson | his wife | born Sept 8, 1805 | died July 1, 1892 |

Sarah | our darling | æ 6 yrs |    (*In Fellows' lot*).

In Memory of | Capt Nathaniel | Goodwin who | Died With| Small Pox May | yᵉ 18 ( ?)ᵗʰ 1777; in | yᵉ 50ᵗʰ Year of | his Age |

Elisha Galpin |

Clarissa Galpin |

In Memory of | Mʳˢ Jane Wife | of Mʳ Amos | Galpin who dieᵈ | April ye 30ᵗʰ | 1783, in the 27 | year of her Age |

In | memory of | Amos Galpin | who died | Dec 7, 1843 | aged 89 |

In | memory of | Sybil wife of | Amos Galpin | who died | May 15, 1838 | æt 77 |

Betsey Galpin |

Fanny Galpin | Aged 11 years |

In| memory of | Clarissa Galpin | who died | Aug 29, 1840 | æ 49 |

Tallmage Son | of Leonard & | Mary Ann Goodwin died | Dec 12, 1820 |

In | memory of | Leonard Goodwin | who died | July 27, 1831 | aged 42 | Also Mary Tallmage Goodwin | died | Nov 10, 1825 | aged 8 months |

Here lies Interr'd | the Body of Cap$^t$ | Thomas Grant | who departed | this life August | y$^e$ 16$^{th}$ 1753 in | y$^e$ 43$^{rd}$ year of | his Age |

Here lies Interr$^d$ | the Body of | M$^r$ Abraham Goodwin | who departed this | Life January 6$^{th}$ | A D 1771 | Æ 72 years |

In-memory-of- | M$^r$-Benjamin Gibbs | who-died-May-y$^e$-10-1767- | in the 93 year | of-his-age |

In-memory-of-|-M$^{rs}$-Abigail-Gibbs | Who-Died January | the 20, 1767,-and-| 80-years of-age |

In memory of | Honor | daughter of Lucy & | Roger Marsh, Esq | & wife of Solomon Gibbs | who died | March 12, 1829, aged 69 | Also | Caroline Gibbs | died Dec 13, 1812 | aged 24 |

In | memory of | Solomon Gibbs | Dec 6, 1842 | æ 82 | Also | Idea Gibbs | Died Feb 2, 1871 | æ 73 | The memory of the just is blessed |

Lois | Daughter of | Ruth & Charles Dudley | and wife of | Frederick Gibbs | Died March 2, 1861 | Aged 59 |

Frederick Gibbs | February 20, 1803 | October 25, 1893 |

In | memory of | Hannah Goodwin | relict of | Ozias Goodwin | who died | Nov 5, 1822 | aged 82 |

In | Memory of | Mr. Ozias Goodwin | who died | March 1$^{st}$, 1788 | aged 55 years |

Frederick Augustus | Son of | Capt Micah & | Mrs. Sally Goodwin | died Dec 10<sup>th</sup> 1802 | aged 2 years |

Augustus Michael | Son of | Capt Micah & | Mrs. Sally Goodwin | died Jan 16, 1810 | aged 14 months |

In | Memory of | Capt. Micah Goodwin | who died | April 4, 1815 | Æt 45. |

Mary Goodwin | widow of | James Guthrie | died | in Litchfield | April 13, 1865 | æt 62 |

James N. | son of | James & Harriet C. | Ganung | died | Oct 17, 1859 | aged 4 Yrs | & 2 Mo |

In | memory of | James Griswold | who died | Jan 30, 1827 | aged 72 |

In | memory of | Desire Griswould | who died | Nov 27, 1839 | æ 76 |

Abigail Griswold | 1792-1886 |

In Memory of | Elizapeth Garitt | Widow of Joshua Garitt | & Daughter of Bezaleel | & Elizabeth Beebe who | Died March 29, 1802 | of Consumption | Aged 34 Years |

In | memory of | Clarissa S. | wife of | Sylvester Galpin | who died | July 8, 1840 | æt 42 |

In| memory of | Sylvester Galpin | who died | Dec 12, 1841 | æ 48 |

Lillian E. | daughter of | David C & Olive J. | Goodwin | died | Dec. 9, 1871 | æ 18 Y'rs 4 Mo | & 9 D's. |

Olive J. | wife of | David C. Goodwin | & daughter of Major| David & Rachel Marsh | died | Nov 16, 1863 | æ 35 |

Henry S. Gillett | died | July 17, 1895 | aged 72 | Laura A. Baldwin | his wife | Born Nov 25, 1825 | Died March 11, 1901 || GILLETT |

Harris B. Gibbud | died | Nov 6, 1882 | aged 66 |

Ruth | daughter of | Charles M. & Loda J. | Ganung | died | May 4, 1884 | Aged 6 M's |

Albert Homer | died | Dec 19, 1855 | Aged 59 |

Charles B. Hurlburt | died | Nov 25, 1846 | aged 28|

Harriet Almira | daughter of Drew | & Almira Hall | died June 10, 1840 | aged 14 |

WEST CEMETERY—JOSEPH HARRIS

Drew Hall | died | Nov 16, 1837 | Aged 40 |

Almira Hall | wife of | Drew Hall | died July 22, 1837 | Aged 36 |

Dorcas | wife of Isaac Hammond | died Oct 14, 1854 | æ 77|

Isaac Hammond | died | Aug 2, 1854 | æ 97 |

Mary S. | wife of | Thaddeus Hungerford | died [ Oct 15, 1861 | Aged 77 |

In Memory of | Joseph Harris | who was murder | ed by the Indians | in the year 1721. | While plowing in | his Field in the vi | cinity of the Alms | House, he was shot | by the Indians concealed in Am | bush. He was found | dead Sitting on the Ground, his | Head and Body reclining against | the Trunk of a Tree. || To record the fir- | st Death among the | original Settlers of | this Town & to per- | petuate the Memory | of a worthy but unf | ortunate Citizen | this Monument | is erected 1830 by | the voluntary Ben- | efactions of individual Subscribers |

Levi W. | son of | Elliot & Mary A. | Hitchcock | died Nov 17, 1871 | aged 31 |

Elliot Hitchcock | died | Sept 16, 1849 | æ 43 |

Julia S. | daughter of | Elliot & Mary A. | Hicchcock | died| Apr 28, 1860 | Aged 26 ]

Mary A. Preston | wife of | Elliot Hitchcock | Died Jan 23, 1885 | aged 73 |

Harriet Bissell | wife of | Curtis Hallock | born July 12, 1803| died | Feb 9, 1895 |

To the Memory of | Miss Ellen Taggert | was born in Hill Hall | Co. Down Ireland | June the 11, 1832 | was a wife of | Harcourt Lee Hull | for 42 y'rs | Entered into rest | Apr 11, 1896 | Age 63 y'rs & 10 m's |

I trust her soul in Heaven
With Angels that's on High.

H. G. L. Hull.

Anna E. | daughter of | Cyrus & | Adeline Hurd | died | Sept 30, 1855 | Æ 16 y'rs & 8 mo |

Capt | Lorenzo Hart | died | Aug 31, 1829 | æ 37 |

Irene Hadsell | died | Feb 27, 1887 | Aged 75 || Lewis Hadsell | died | Aug 31, 1878 | Aged 61 |

Our Grandmother | Sally French | wife of | Harlow Humphrey | died | Jan 11, 1890 | Aged 83 |

Louisa Homer | died | Nov 2, 1881 | Aged 46 |

Charlotte H. Hall | died | Aug. 18, 1866 | Aged 32 |

Henry W. Hotchkiss | Co A. 2 Regt. | H'v'y Art'y C. V. | died | Jan 23, 1896 |

Clarissa | Daughter of Orrin | & Asenath Judd | Died | Sept 29th, 1822 | aged — mon | & 17 days |

Elizabeth A. | daughter of Orrin | & Asenath Judd | died | Feb 24, 1833 | æ 24 |

Orren Judd | Died | June 5, 1830 | æ 59 |

Clarissa A. Judd | born Jan 17, 1825 | died | March 17, 1892|

Miranda | died | Aug 30, 1883 | Aged 4 m's | Children of | George H. & | Jane Jackson || Ethil A. | died | Aug 29, 1883 | Aged 1 Y'r | & 10 M's |

> Weep not for the little ones,
> Their jentle spirits' fled
> They sweetly sleep in Jesus
> Among the silent dead.

Jane | wife of | Geo Jackson | died | May 21, 1866 | Aged 45|

Payne Kenyon Kilbourne | July 26, 1815—July 19, 1859 | Elizabeth Cone | wife of | P. K. Kilbourne | afterwards wife of | James H. Hoyt | of Stamford, Conn. | July 27, 1816—Nov. 1, 1900 || KILBOURNE || Lelia K. Kilbourne | May 1, 1850 | May 9, 1861 |

Lelia Kenyon | Kilbourne | born May 1, 1850 | died May 9, 1869 |

Julia Rebecca | only daughter of | Edward W. & | Mary Ann King | died | April 25, 1854 | aged 10 y'rs | & 6 mo. |

> Ere sin coud blight or sorrow fade
> Death came with friendly care
> The opening bud to Heaven conveyed
> And bade it blossom there.

Henry E. | son of | Edward W. | & Mary Ann | King | died|
Nov. 12, 1840 | æ 2 y'rs | & 11 mo's |

Thou destroyest the | hopes of man |

Edward E. | son of | Edward W. & | Mary Ann | King: died|
Feb 10, 1837 | æ 13 mo's |

Rebekah King | wife of David King | died July 17, 1821 |
aged 42 years |

Here lies Interr'd | the Body of M^rs | Hannah Kilborn | late
wife of M^r | Benjamin Kilborn | she Departed this | life Oct
y^e 3^d 1756 | in the 24 year of | her Age |

In Memory of Cap | Lewis Kilborn | Who Departed this |
Life August 30^th 1804 | in the fiftieth Year of | His Age |

> By nature taught
> Not school'd by feigning art
> His was a generous
> And a human heart.

Benjamin Kilbourn | died | Sept 28, 1862 | Aged 63 |
Amanda Kilbourn | his wife | died | Sept 25, 1861 | Aged 62 |

Gertrude | wife of Lewis S. Kilbourn |

In Memory of Mr. | James Kilborn | Who Dece's'd | March
the 9^th | 1762. In the 55^th | Year of His Age |

Here lies Interr'd | the Body of C.... | Joseph Kilborn | he
Departed this | life September y^e | 14^th 1756 in the 57 | year of
his | Age |

Solomon Kilbourn | Died July 30, 1806 | æ 70 | Ann Kil-
bourn | Wife of | Solomon Kilbourn | Died Aug 20, 1816 |
Æ 80 |

Charles son of | Cap^t | Joseph & Mrs. Abi | gail Kilborn he |
was Kil'd by a Cart | May 25^th ( ?) 1756 in the 17^th | year of
his Age |

> Deth Conquers all
> Both .... .. ....

Here lieth | the Body of M^rs | Mary Kilborn ^the | wife of M^r
Elisha | Kilborn she died | June y^e 3^d ( ?) 1754 | in the 28^th
year of | her Age |

Here lies Interr'd | the Body of M^rs | Abigail Kilborn | late
wife of Cap^t | Joseph Kilborn | she died May y^e | 23^rd A D
1748 in y^e 48^th year of her | Age |

M<sup>r</sup> Giles Kilbourn died | Sept. 13, 1797 aged 69 | M<sup>rs</sup> Cloe his wife died | Oct 10, 1824 aged 95 | Near this stone lies Sabra| Kilbourn daughter of | Giles & Cloe Kilbourn | who died Oct 5, 1798 | aged 30. Chauncey | Kilbourn son of Giles & | Cloe Kilbourn died | June.. 1819 |

Chauncey Kilbourn | died | June 9, 1819 | æ 47 | Hannah Kenyon | his wife | afterwards the wife of | Dea. N. C. Bates | died in Salisbury | Feb 26, 1848 | æ 64 |

The memory of the just is blessed

In Memory of | Mehala Kilbourn | Daughter of John & | Lois Kilbourn who | died January 9<sup>th</sup> | 1826, Aged 25 |

Mary Kilbourn | died Nov 10, 1826 | aged 23 | also | Thirza Kilbourn | died July 22, 1828 | aged 32 | daughters of | John & Lois Kilbourn |

In memory of | Lois Kilbourn | wife of John Kilbourn | Died æ 61 | John Kilbourn | Died | Feb 6, 1835 | æ 69 |

Mary | wife of Henry Kilbourn | died | April 12, 1880 | æ 87 |

Harry Kilbourn | died | Nov 20, 1851 | Æt 53 y'rs |

Lois S. | daughter of | Harry & | Mary Kilbourn | died | Jan 21, 1851 | æ 27 |

Friends, nor physician could not save
Her mortal body from the grave
Nor can the grave retain it here
When Christ her Saviour doth appear.

Laura J. | daughter of | Harry & | Mary Kilbourn | died Jan 17, 1852 | æt 24 y'rs | David J. | son of Harry & | Mary Kilbourn | died June 4, 1837 | æt 5 y'rs |

Clarrissa A. | daughter of | Harry & | Mary Kilbourn | died | July 9, 1859 | æ 34 |

Harriet A. | daughter of | Philip S. & Catharine E. | Beebe | wife of Rev Henry S. Kelsey | Born Feb 17, 1840 | Died Aug 3, 1865 | Catharine Beebe | daughter of | H. S. & H. A. Kelsey | Born Sept 4, 1864 | Died May 1, 1866 |

In | Memory of | Julia Maria | daughter of | James & | Diantha Kilbourn | who died Dec 18, 1819 | aged 10 years |

KENNEY || (*see Camp, G. K.*)

Lottie Emeline | Daughter of | Geo. & C. M. Kenney || Lottie Died | Aug 14, 1866 | æt 5 |

Theron Kent | died | Dec 20, 1867 | æ 69 |

Sacred to the Memory of | Anna C. | wife of | Theron Kent | died | Feb 24, 1860 | æ 53 |

Corp. | Robert Lampman | Co C. 29, Regt | Conn Vols | died | Dec 26, 1875 |

L. L. | Lynde Lord Esq^r | died June 16, A. D. 1801 | aged 68 years | He was 3 years Sheriff of the | County of Litchfield and | discharged the duties of that | High office with great ability | & Integrity. | Upright & Exemplary | in Life, | His Memory | is blessed of the | Just.

This Monument is erected | In Memory of Mrs. Lynde Lord | consort of Lynde Lord Esq^r | who departed this life August | the 2nd 1792, in the 55^th year of | her age | Epitaph |

> By nature taught, not School'd by feigning art:
> Hers was a generous and a human heart:
> Nor Small the praise for charity and love,
> From the pure passions of the saints above.

In Memory of | Rufus son of Lynde | and Lois Lord | who di'd July 11^th, 1765, aged 7 | weeks & 6 days |

Lynde Lord Jr | born Oct 21, 1761 | died Feb 12, 1813 | Æt 52 years |

This monument is erected | to his memory. |

Mary Lyman Lord | born | Feb. 26, 1764 | died | May 13, 1843. |

Joseph Lynde Lord son of | M^r Lynde Lord Jun^r and Mrs. Mary Lord born the 2^h | of Sep^r 1788 and died the | 4^th of Oct^r 1789 thirteen | Months and two days Old | Epitaph |

> Ye whose afflicted spirits know
> For a lost child a parent's woe
> Here drop the tender tear
> For Innocence from being born
> In infant beauty's opening morn
> Serenely slumbers here.

In Memory of Mrs. | Mary Landon wife | of David Landon | & Daughter of M^r Thomas Osborn of | Long Island in East | Hampton | She died | June the 16, 1754 | Aged 35 Years |

Sacred | to the Memory of | David Landon | who departed this life | May 4th 1804 | in the 86th year of his age |

Emogene | (*Landon*)

Julia Landon | died | Feb 11, 1866 | Aged 46 |

Died | Oct 18, 1843 | Seth Landon Jr. | Aged 66 |

Died Aug 2, 1860 | Sally wife of Seth Landon | Æt 81 |

Lemira Landon | died | Oct 14, 1829 | Aged 19 | Elizabeth Landon | died | Nov 26, 1829 | Aged 17 | daughter of | Seth & Sally Landon |

In | memory of | Edward Langmaid | who died | Mar 16, 1838 | aged 28 years |

> There is a rest for those who weep
> A rest for weary pilgrims found
> They gently lie they sweetly sleep
> Low in the ground

In memohy of | Nathan Landon | Who Died | April 27, 1833 | in the 81 year | of his age |

Sarah | wife of | Nathan Landon | died | Dec 30, 1838 | aged 78 |

In memory of five Children |
of John and Abigail Landon, viz: |

Micah Landon, Born Dec | 11, 1769 & died the 29 of | the same Month |

Micah Landon, 2d Born | Oct 22, 1770 & died | Oct 3, 1776 |

Orange Landon Born | May 1, 1772 & died | Oct 5, 1776 |

Joseph Landon Born | Dec 27, 1775 & died | Oct 9, 1776|

Rhoda Landon Born | Jan 2, 1784, & died | Jan 15, 1787 |

> Beneath this stone lies children five
> Endearing objects when alive
> Though long in silence here they've lain
> They certain will revive again

> At that blest hour may they be found
> Clad in Christ's vestments all divine
> Rising triumphant from the ground
> May they like constellations shine

Sacred to the Memory | of | Capt Daniel Landon of Litch-
field who | Died July the 11ᵗʰ 1790 aged 73 Years | who Served
as Clerk of the Episcopal | Church in Litchfield 40 Years |

His God he served with pious zeal
The sacred dome was his delight
Far distant from that holy hill
Has took his everlasting flight.
Composed by himself.

So here I leave this earthly clay
And fly beyond etherial blue
Unchained into eternal day
To sing yᵉ praise of God anew.

Mʳ Zophar Landon died | May 5, 1814 | Æ 40 |

In Memory of | Joseph Landon | Youngest Son of | Capᵗ
Daniel & Mʳˢ | Martha Landon | Who Died August | yᵉ 24ᵗʰ |
1775 in yᵉ | 18ᵗʰ Year of his Age |

Beneath yᵉ Ground
his dust must Lay
Until yᵉ Resurection
Day.

In memory of | Mrs. Eunice | 2 Wife of | Seth Landon,
Esq: | Died | March 4, 1832 | Æ 81 |

In | memory of | Mrs Anne Landon | Consort of | Seth Lan-
don, Esqʳ | who died | Nov 10, 1800 | æt 47 |

She has gone to learn that wisdom
Which this world can never teach

In memory of | Seth Landon, Esq. | Died | Feb 4, 1832 |
æ 82 |

Corrina M. | daughter of | Erastus A. & Charlotte D. Lord |
Born Aug 4, 1818 | Died Oct 1, 1865 | aged 47|

Charlotte D. | wife of | Erastus Lord | died Oct 30, 1878 |
Aged 88 |

Erastus A. | son of | Lynde & Mary Lord | Born Oct 16,
1792 | Died Dec 6, 1860 | aged 68 |

William R. Lord | Son of Erastus A. & | Charlotte D. Lord |
Born Apr 29, 1827 | Died Nov 21, 1883 | Aged 56 |

William Landon | Died Nov 23, 1878 | Aged 69 | Mary |
His Wife | Died Mar 30, 1881 | aged 69 |

Mary A. | wife of | George W. Loomis | died at | New Haven, Conn. | July 25, 1878 | æ 32 | Daughter of E. O. & Lois
P. Peck |

Mrs | Sarah M. | wife of | Charles Matthews | Died | April
14, 1837 | æ 28 |

Here lies | the Body of | M^r Isaac Marsh Jun^r | who Departed this | Life Aug^st the 9^th | 1779 in the 43^d | year of his
Age |

> Behold & see as you pass by
> As you are now so once was I
> As i am now so you shall be
> prepare for death & follow me.

Elisha Marsh | 1779, 1841 | Rhoda Kilbourn | his wife | 1773,
1850 | Myron Marsh | 1814, 1867 | Clarissa A. Bradley | his
wife | 1825 ...... | MARSH || Mary Marsh | 1804 ...... |
Rhoda Marsh | 1806, 1882 | Elisha Marsh | 1808, 1840 | Lewis
Marsh | 1810, 1865 | Elias Marsh | 1812, 1820 | George
Marsh | 1816, 1817 |

To the memory of | George H. son of | Jonothan & Lorane |
Marvin, who died | by the cars passing | over him, while in
an | excursion to Bridgeport | July 6, 1852 | aged 20 y'rs 11
mo's | & 21 d's |

Orpah | wife of | Robert Matthews | died | April 13, 1845 |
æ 65 years |

Lyman Matthews | died | May 30, 1881 | æ 58 |

The Body | of | Elisha Marsh | lies here | He Died January
20,^th | 1804 in the 62 Year | of His Age |

In | memory of | Honour, wife of | Elisha Marsh | who died |
Sept 16, 1809 | æ 64 |

In | Memory of | Isaac Marsh | who died | Mar 8, 1788 |
æt 78 |

In | memory of | Susanna wife of | Isaac Marsh | who died
Apr 6, 1788 | æ 73 |

In | memory of | William Marsh | who died May 5, 1835 |
aged 95 |

Esther wife of | William Marsh | died | Aug 19, 1830 | aged 62 |

Capt | William Marsh | died | Aug 6, 1798 | aged 92 |

Susannah | wife of | Capt. William Marsh | died July 21, 1803 | aged 93 |

In Memory of | Capt. Solomon Marsh | who died | May 30th A. D. 1804 | in the 70th year | of his age |

Here lies the Body of Mrs | Jerusha wife to | Mr Solon Marsh | who Died Octor | ye 20th 1759 In | the 24th Year | of Her Age |

Mrs | Elizabeth Marsh | widow of Capt | Solomon Marsh | Died June 29, 1835 | In the 94 year | of her age |

Solomon Marsh | died | June 10, 1857 | æ 80 |

David F. | son of | Major David & | Anna Marsh | died | Oct 1, 1856 | æt 35 |

Capt Solomon Marsh | son of | Major David & | Anna Marsh | died | July 6, 1859 | Æ 39 |

Henry son of | Mr David & | Mrs. Anna Marsh | died | Nov 15, 1826 | aged 2 years | & 3 months |

Solomon | Son of | Cap. David & Anna | Marsh | Died Aug 23, 1820 | æ 7 ye. |

An Infant | son of David | & Rachel Marsh | died | March 10, 1827 | æ 3 months |

Happy infant early blessed
Rest in peaceful slumbers, rest.

Mrs. Anna | wife of | Maj. David Marsh | died Sept 3rd 1824 | æt 39 |

Behold we see while here we look
The dearest ties of friendship broke
Tho' grief & sorrow pierce the heart
The dearest friends we see must part.

Mrs Rachel | Wife of | Maj. David Marsh | Died | March 1, 1831 | æ 41 |

Maj. David Marsh | died | Dec 28, 1869 | æ 86 | The last of his generation. |

William M. | son of | Maj. David & | Anna Marsh | died | Dec 25, 1838 | aged 29 years |

Elizabeth Ann | daughter of | Maj. David & | Mrs Anna Marsh | Died | April 10, 1834 | æ 19 yrs |

Harriet M. | wife of | Solomon S. Mase | died | Oct 6, 1847 | æ 37 |

Ellen H. | daughter of | Solomon S. & | Harriet M. Mase | died | Dec 17, 1842 | aged 1 year |

Julia M. | daughter of | Solomon S. & | Harriet M. Mase | died | Sept 3, 1842 | aged 4 years |

Ervin C. | son of | Solomon S. & | Harriet M. | Mase died | April 14, 1837 | Æ 2 y's |

George | son of Solomon & | Elenor D. Mase | died | April 30, 1861 | Æ 4 y's |

Sheldon | Munger | born august 17$^{th}$ 1794 died | Oct 5, 1794 | Sheldon | Munger | born july | 31, 1801 died | june 29, 1802 |

Amy Munger | died | Jan 27, 1842, aged 19 | Almira Munger | died | Mar 1, 1843 | aged 24 |

Truman Munger | died | Mar 2, 1844 | aged 46 |

Morris M. | son of | Rufus & | Fanny Munger | died | Sept 27, 1847 | æ 2 years | & 2 mo's |

A. A. Monroe | Died May 24$^{th}$ 1890 |

Jonathan Marvin | died | Feb 4, 1870 | æ 70 | Loraina Buell | his wife | died | July 13, 1885 | æ 80 |

> Home is not home for mother is not there
> Dark is her room—empty is her chair
> Now will she rest from her labor and care
> Till that morning so fair.

Farewell | Stephen | son of | Stephen & Elizabeth J. | McCarthy | died | April 4, 1879 | æ 8 y'rs & 2 m's |

Enos Melanson || died | Oct 14, 1866 | Aged 23 Y'rs |

Christopher | son of Jacob & | Jane Morse | died | Sept 27, 1859 | aged 7 mo |

Ella O. Morse | Thy will, O Lord, be done. || daughter of | Jacob & | Jane Morse | died | Oct. 26, 1857 | æt 5 y'rs |

Nancy | wife of | Col. Isaac Morse | Died May 17, 1887 | æ 82 Y'rs | & 4 Mo's |

Col. Isaac Morse | died | July 8, 1869 | æ 63 |

M | Jacob Morse | 1827-1901 | Mary J. Wheeler | his wife | 1825 | MORSE || M | their children | Ella Orinda | 1852-1857 | Christopher Wheeler | 1859-1859 | Dermot Levi 1865-1866 |

Sheldon Munger | died | May 15, 1889 | æ 65 | MUNGER || George W. | son of | S. & Jane C. | Munger | died | July 24, 1889 | æ 38 |

Charlie A. | son of | Charles & | Emeline | Merriman died | Feb 2, 1874 | Aged 10 W'ks |

Una Louisa | daughter of | Joseph & | Catharine | Merriman | died | Feb 19, 1877 | æ 5 y'rs | & 7 m's |

Lemuel O.Meafoy | born | May 27, 1804 | died | Apr. 22, 1888 | Aged 84 | MEAFOY |

Erastus P. Moulthrop | — | Mary E. | his wife | died | Jan 16, 1892 | aged 75 Y'rs | MOULTHROP |

S. J. N.  (*footstone*).

Benjamin | son of | John & Harriet Negus | died Nov. 22, 1832 | aged 1 year | & 3 months |

My Father | Joseph Negus | died | Apr 20, 1845 | æ 32 | Erected by his daughter | Mary |

My Sisters | Mary Jane | and | Elizabeth | Infants of Joseph & Mary Ann Negus | Erected by Sister | Mary |

Ella E. | daughter of | Henry & Abby J. Neal | died | Aug. 29, 1854 | aged 3 mo |

Diadama | wife of | Abram W. Neal | died | May 6, 1854 | aged 55 years |
Rosanna | wife of | James B. Newcomb | died | Apr 10, 1885 | Aged 64 |

Rossa | Aged 5 Mo's | (*In Newcomb lot*)

Simon Norberg | born in Sweden Jan 25, 1849 | died in Litchfield, July 15, 1883 | Mina wife of Simon Norberg | born in Sweden Oct 12, 1853 | died in Providence, R. I. Mar 29, 1895 | NORBERG || Bertha E. | born in Hartford Aug 14, 1877 | died in Providence R. I. Aug 11, 1891 | Arvid W. | born in Litchfield April 27, 1879 | died in Providence, R. I. Dec 7, 1896 | Children of Simon & Mina Norberg |

Here lies the | Body of Gideon | Orton he Di'd | May yᵉ 12, 1753 In | yᵉ 22 year of his | Age |

In Memory of | Submit wife of | Dea. Isaac Osborn | who died | Dec 24, 1784 | æ 33 yrs |

In | memory of | Dea Isaac Osborn | who died | March 25, 1826 | æ 82 yrs |

Mʳˢ | Hannah Osborn | wife of | Dea. Isaac Osborn | Died March 28, 1833 | in the 77 year | of her age |

Elizabeth Odell | died | Oct 11, 1863 | Aged 73 |

Ethan | son of | Capt Eliada & | Sally Osborn | born Aug 22, 1793 | died Feb 8, 1795 |

Dianthe | wife of | William Oxx | died July 24, 1839 | aged 30 |

Wᵐ Lyman | son of Wᵐ & | Dianthe Oxx | died Aug 30, 1840 | aged 1 year & | 2 months |

Abigail Stoddard | wife of | Heman Osborn | died | Feb. 20, 1876 | æ 81 |

Heman Osborn | died | Jan 15, 1852 | æt 65 |

John W. | son of Heman | & Abigail | Osborn Died | Jan 23, 1832 | Aged 1 year | and 6 mo's |

Died | June 6, 1827 | Sally. wife of | Heman Osborn | in the 37, year | of her age |

In memory of | Sally M. Osborn | Daughter of | Heman & Sally | Osborn who died | Dec 3, 1838 | æ 18 |

In memory of | Sally Osborn | who died | July 17, 1832 | æ 39 |

Mʳˢ Olive Osborn | Relict of John Osborn | died | March 21, 1832 | In the 77 year | of her age |

Mr. | John Osborn | Died | Feb 6, 1832 | In the 80 year | of his age |

In memory of | Jesse Osborn | who died | July 2, 1838 | æ 55 |

In | memory of | Clarissa, wife of | Jesse Osborn | who died | Nov 13, 1826 | aged 38 |

An Infant | of J. & C. Osborn | died | Nov 10, ] 1826 |

Mary Louisa | died | July 5, 1855 | æ 2 y'rs | & 11 mo | daughter of | James H. & | Esther Osborn |

In | memory of | Lucinda | daughter of | Heman & | Sally Osborn | who died | Dec 12, 1824 |in the 14 year | of her age |

Lois Osborn | wife of | Capt. John Osborn | died Nov 28, 1819 | Aged 87 |

Capt John Osborn | died Jan 7, 1814 | in his 87. yr. |

Eliada Osborn | Born | Aug 1, 1810 | Died | Feb 10, 1894 |

Nathan L. Osborn | died | July 11, 1878 | Aged 71 |

Mrs Abigail | wife of | Capt Eliada Osborn | died May 12, 1849 | æ 80 |

Capt. Eliada Osborn | died Dec 26, 1847 | æ 87 | A soldier of the Revolution |

Sally Osborn | wife of | Capt Eliada Osborn | died | Aug 28, 1793 | aged 33 |

In Memory of | Mr Benjamin | Osborn, who | departed this life | May 5th 1790 Aged 73 Years |

> Blessed are the dead
> who die in the Lord

In Memory of Mr | Benjamin Osborn | who Departed this | life July 26th 1762 | in the 70th Year of | his Age |

> Beneath this stone
> Death's Prisoner lies
> the stone shall move
> the Prisoner rise.

Died | Dec 10, | 1824 | (*Small stone in Osborn Lot*).

Chauncey S. | Son of | Heman & | Sally Osborn | died | June 20 | 1816 |

E. Goodwin Osborn | Sergt. Maj. 2 Conn Heavy Art'y |
Killed on the battlefield | near Petersburg. Va. | March 25,
1865 | aged 28 | OSBORN || Myron Osborn | died | April 12,
1893 | Aged 96 years | & 6 months | Emeline Goodwin | wife
of | Myron Osborn | died | Feb 23, 1885 | Aged 84 Yrs. ||
Elizabeth | Died July 10, 1837 | Aged 5 y'rs 10 M'o's | Myron
M. | Died Oct 1, 1842 | Aged 10 Mo's | children of | Myron &
Emeline Osborn |

James H. Osborn | died | Jan 22, 1896 | Aged 73 | Esther
Baldwin | his wife | Died Jan 22, 1896 | Aged 67 |

Chauncey J. | son of | James H. & | Esther B. Osborn |
died | Dec 11, 1874. | Æ 26 |

Ella M. | Died Aug 13, 1882 | Aged 28 | Esther M. | Died
Mar 2, 1884 | Aged 18 | daughters of | James H. & Esther B. |
Osborn | Asleep in Jesus! peaceful sleep |

Entered into rest | Jan 12, 1883 | George H. Osborn | Aged
32 |

Mabel Gertrude | Child of | Geo. H. & E. | Osborn | died |
June 20, 1880 | æ 11 Mo's |

Thomas Pilgrim | a revolutionary | pensioner | died April
24, 1843 | aged 89 |

In Memory of | M^rs Rachell | the Wife of | M^r Job Palmer |
who Died Aug 10 | 1787 in the 75^th Year of | Her Age |

In memory of | M^r Job Palmer | who departed this | Life
January y^e 24^th A. D. | 1798 in the 91^st year | of his age |

Henry A. Newell | son of | Dan'l L. & Cecelia A. | Potter |
died Sept 6, 1815 | aged 13 months

Samuel Palmer | died | Mar 29, 1812 | Aged 29 | Samuel B.
Plumb | died Aug 7, 1829 | Aged 53 | Dency Plumb | died Oct.
20, 1859 | Aged 70 |

Near this stone are | inter'd the remains of | Mrs Mary
Peirce | who died May 13, 1770 | æt 32 | Of Miss Ann Peirce |
who died Jan 25, 1802 | æt 44 | and of Mrs Mary Peirce | who
died May 1, 1803 | æt 59 |

Mary Pierce | died | June 22, 1863 | Aged 82 |

Sarah Pierce | died | Jan 19, 1852 | æt 84 |

James Pierce | died May 10, 1846 | aged 67 |

The grave of | Deborah | widow of John Plumb | who died | Nov 26, 1828 | aged 57 |

Permelia A..n Potter | died | June 21, 1866 | Æt 49 |

Ashbel Peck | died | Feb 6, 1837 | æ 74 |Anna | wife of | Ashbel Peck | died | Mar 9, 1847 | æ 82 |

In | memory of | Phebe, wife of | Ruel Plant | who died | Dec 24, 1839 | aged 53 years |

Ruel Plant | died | Feb 20, 1864 | æt 79 y'rs |

Death is the gate to endless joy
And yet we dread to enter there.

Huldah | wife of | Reuel Plant | died | Oct 8, 1851 | æ 66 |

Lillie R. Plant | died | Feb 3, 1864 | æ 8 y'rs & 7 mo |

Sleep on dear child & take thy rest.

Jane Ann | daughter of | Stephen & | Emeline Plant | died | Nov 23, 1853 | Æ 7 y'rs | Rebecca | their daughter died | Nov 24, 1853 | æ 5 y'rs |

Here lies our babes we once adore
They'v gone & cannot come no more
'Twas God that called them to depart
They was the darlings of our hearts.

Our Mother | Emaline | Wife of | Stephen Plant | died | Dec 26, 1876 | Æ 56 |

Our father | Stephen Plant | died | Oct 15, 1880 | æ 62 |

David Plant | died | Sept 26, 1878 | æ 57 | Oh, Lord, thou hast seen my wrong | judge thou my cause |

Charlotte | wife of | David Plant | died | Oct 2, 1881 | æ 61 | Erected by her daughter |

Caroline | daughter of David & | Charlotte Plant | died | Apr 21, 1853 | Æt 6 y'rs |

We miss thee, Caroline
Our hearts are filled with gloom
Twas hard in springtime to resign
Our loved one to the tomb

In | Memory of | David Parmele | who died | Nov 12, 1815 | aged 68 years |

Philo Peck | born Oct 3, 1752 | died Feb 13, 1831 | aged 78 years | 4 mo & 10 d's |

Hannah wife of | Philo Peck | born Sept 28, 1756 | died June 5, 1844 | aged 87 years | 8 mo & 7 d's |

Here lies y^e | Body of M^r Paul | Peck he died Dec^br ⎤ y^e 21^st 1751, in y^e 86^th | year of his age |

William B. | son of W^m & | Mary | Patterson of Roxbury | died | April 27, 1842 | aged 6 y'rs |

Frederick W. Plumb | Born Oct 28, 1801 | Died Sept 25, 1877 | Huldah S. Plumb ⎦ Born Dec 14, 1806 | Died July 19, 1854 |

Adaline Provost | died | Oct 18, 1851 | æ 16 |

| (see Ward, Wm) || Rev Solomon Palmer | the first Episcopal | Minister of this Town | died Dec 8, 1771 | aged 62 |

Edmund Peck | died | Apr 10, 1844 | Aged 31 years |

In | Memory of | Alvin Peck | who was born | Feb. 16, 1815 | & died | Feb 9, 1838 | aged 23 y'rs. |

Andrew Peck | died at | Galveston, Texas, | Nov 22, 1847 | æ 23 |

In | memory of | Doct. Walter Peck | son of Alfred and | Susan Peck | Nov 8, 1834 | aged 24 years | & 9 mo |

Alfred Peck | born | Feb 26, 1779 | died Mar 19, 1852 | æt 73. |

Susan | wife of | Alfred Peck | died | Dec 9, 1864 | æt 78 |

Seth F. Plumb | 1^st Sergt. of Co E. 8^th C. V. | Killed at Chapin's Farm, Va | Sept 29, 1864 | Aged 28 | Rest |

Florence A. | born | Feb 6, 1879 | Died Mar. 22, 1880 | An Infant Son | Died Oct 19, 1871 | Children of | William H. & Emma T. | Plumb |

Emma T. Buell | Wife of | W^m H. Plumb | died ⎦ April 11, 1882 | Aged 34 |

Little | Charlie | son of | Levi & Addie | Parmelee | died | Feb 24, 1879 | aged 4 y'rs & 11 M's |

Rufus Provost | Co I 13 Regt | Conn Vols | Died April 7, 1892 | Age 81 |

Almira | wife of | Andrew J. Pierpont | died | Aug 30, 1881 | Aged 63 |

Harriet A. | wife of | Edward W. Phelps | died at | South Egremont, Mass | Aug 19, 1879 | æ 25 | Daughter of E. O. & Lois P. Peck |

Edward Elijah | son of | Edward O. & Lois | Peck | died Jan 10, 1858 | aged 7 mos |

Edward E. | son of Edward O. | & Lois Peck | died | in Wethersfield | May 29, 1853 | aged 15 mo |

Oliver P. Peck | born | Feb 25, 1843 | died | Oct 25, 1888 |

Lois Pendleton | wife of | Edward O. Peck | born | Mar. 1, 1819 | died | Nov 2, 1890 |

Edward Ozias Peck | born | Apr 5, 1822 | died | Sept 17, 1894 | Capain Co K. 2, Conn Heavy Artilery |

Amanda K. | wife of | James B. Peck | died | Jan 22, 1876 | æ 64 |

James Baldwin Peck | born | Jan 28, 1808 | died | June 26, 1895 |

In Memory of | Ursula Daughter | of Mʳ Stephen | & Mʳˢ Margaret | Russel who Died | Septʳ ye 23ᵈ | 1777 in ye 2 | yeaʳ of her | age |

In Memory of | Maryann | Daughter of | Mʳ Stephen & | Mʳˢ Margaret | Russel who Died | Septʳ ye 18ᵗʰ 1777 in ye 3 | year of her | age |

In Memory of | Elijah son of Mʳ | Stephen & Mʳˢ Margaret Russel | who Died Septʳ | yᵉ 30ᵗʰ 1777 in ye 4 year of | his Age |

Mary E. | Infant | daughter of | Thomas H. & | Amelia C. | Richards | died June 9, 1852 |

This Monument | is erected to | perpetuate the memory | of the amiable Mrs | Margery, the wife of Mʳ Stephen Ranney | & the affectionate daughter of | Mʳ David Camp | She died May 5, 1790 in the | 20 year of her age |

Here lies yᵉ Body | of Mʳ Jonathan | Rosseter he died | Febʳʸ yᵉ 20ᵗʰ 1752 | in yᵉ 64ᵗʰ year of his | Age |

Here lies yᵉ Body of | Lucy. daugᵗʳ of | Mʳ Jonathan Rosseter | She died Aprˡ yᵉ 9ᵗʰ | 1753 in yᵉ 17ᵗʰ year | of her Age |

Vinetta M. | wife of | Walter Sills | died | Oct 2, 1872 | æ 37 |

Amelia | wife of | John Sawyer | died | May 23, 1869 | æt 78 |

Eligah G. | son of | John & | Amelia Sawyer | died | Feb. 12, 1828 | aged 15 years | also | Amelia | their daughter | died | Aug 5, 1829 | aged 3 years |

Julia A. | daughter of | Henry & Julia N. | Sawyer | died | Mar. 19, 1843, | aged 6 mo |

In | memory of | Abel Smith | who died | Aug 13, 1826 | aged 42 years |

In | memory of | Orilla Smith | who died | Oct 2, 1825 æt 39 |

In Memory of | Lorane Stoddard | wife of Ensign Dan.. | Stoddard who depa.... | this life november 10 A D | 1796 in the 34 year | of her age |

Miss | Jerusha Stoddard | daughter of | John Stoddard | died | March 29, 1840 | aged 82 years |

Miss | Irene Stoddard | Daughter of | Capt John Stoddard | Died Nov 30, 1828 | Aged 64 |

Capt. | John Stoddard | died | March 20, 1818 | æ 82 |

Mrs Eunice | wife of | Capt John Stoddard | died | Oct. 2, 1814 | æ 79 |

Clarissa | daughter of | Ephraim & | Sarah Spencer | died Sept 29, 1793 | aged 3 years |

In Memory of Mr | David Stoddard who | Departed this life May | 4th A D 1792 Aged 44 | Years |

> Upright, judicious & the
> Orphans friend
> Serious & Calm
> To sudden Death Resigned

Here lies the bo | dy of Deacon Moses | Stoddard who Died | Sept 2d A. D. 1777 Aged | 76 years |

> He liv'd beloved
> & respected
> Di'd Calm resigned
> lamented

Here lies the Body of | M^rs Ruth Stoddard | wife to Deacon Moses | Stoddard; who Died | Aug 20^th A D. 1777 in | the 70^th Year of her | Age |

HEAR LIETH THE | BODY OF EN^s JOHN | STODDOR WHO DE | CEASED IENVARY | 22          1727 |

HERE .... | ETH THE BODY | OF E..HA....TOD- ..R |(?) WHO DECEASED IVLY | 23 (?) 1728 |

In memory | of | Doc^r Reuben Smith | who died | on the 25^th day of August | 1804 | aged 67 years |

In M....... | Mary. D....... f | Elisha ......., Esq, (Sheldon?) | and E......th his | wife; Who departed | This Life August y^e 31^st | 1765 in the 22^nd year | Of her age.

This Monument is erected in memory | of The Hon. Elisha Sheldon Esq^r who | departed this life Sept the first | Anno Domini 1779 in the 70^th Year of | his Age | A Gentleman of extensive, ..o...mies and | Liberal Education, called in early | life to various public ..mp....s | both Civil and Military all which he | executed with punctuality and | fidelity; much respected for his Gener- | ossity and Benevolence, and greatly | lamented by his extensive acquaintance | In early life he made profession of the | Christian Religion and till Death | adorned by a very exemplary | Conversation | Blessed are the dead who die in the | Lord. |

Caroline M. wife of | Alva Stone | died | Dec. 9, 1842 | æ 21 | Frederick A. | their son | died Nov 25, 1842 | æ 11 Mo |

In Memory of Mr. | Sylvanus Stone Ju^r | Who Died April 1^st | A D 1793 in the 28^th | year of his Age |

In Memory of | Mrs. Anna wife | to M^r Silvanus | Stone who De- | parted this life Jan^r | 25^th A D 1789 in y^e | 58 year of her | age |

......ry of M^r | (*Sylvanus**) Stone Who | ....rted this life | Dec 13^th AD. 1785 in | The 73^h year of his age |

Wife and children 12
Behold and .. ee
Prepare ..n time
To follow ....

*From footstone.*

In Memory of M$^r$ | Truman Stone he | Departed this life | April 25$^{th}$ AD. 1791 | In the 25$^{th}$ Year of | his Age |

Gideon Stoddard | died | Apr 13, 1846 | aged 78 |

Anna wife of | Gideon Stoddard died | Nov 11, 1843 | in the 77 year | of her age |

William | son of | Philo C. & | Eliza Sedgwick | and grandson of | John Adam | died | March 12, 1835 | aged 4 months | & 5 days |

Mr. | Samuel Seymour | died | Nov 14, 1837 | æt 84 |

In | memory of | Mrs. Rebecca | widow of | Capt Samuel Seymour | who died | July 17, 1843 | aged 80 years |

This stone is | erected to the | Memory of Will- | iam Seymour | son to Cap$^t$ Sam- | uel Seymour & | Rebekah his | wife who depart- | ed this life the 30$^{th}$ day | of December A D | 1797 aged Six m.... |

Harriett Webster | Daughter of | Samuel & Rebecca | Seymour | Died May 4, 1854 | æ 65 |

Mrs | Lydia wife of | Mr. Isaiah Shepard | died April 12, 1818 | aged 58 |

Isaiah Shepard | died | Jan 21, 1823 | aged 64 |

Charles Stone | died | May 9, 1843 | aged 51 |

W$^m$ Beldin Smith | son of | Elizur B. & | Alma Smith | died | Mar 11, 1845 | æt 22 y'rs |

Could the tears of thy parents, the sisters who shared
All thy heart, and our hopes, thy life but have spared.
In vain, for death's signet sat pale on thy brow
And their hopes one by one fell like leaves from the bough
Thou hast passed from our eyes like a bright summer cloud
From thy brief happy day from thy home to the shroud.

Serg't Hiram S. Spencer | Co A. 2 Regt | H'vy Art'y | C. V. | died June 4, 1891 |

In | Memory of | widow Sarah Spencer | who died | June 8, 1830 | aged 66 years |

In | Memory of | Ephraim Spencer | who died | May 16, 1828 | aged 69 years |

In | Memory of | Aaron Spencer | who died | Oct 29, 1806 | aged 23 |

In | memory of | Ebenezer Spencer | who died | Oct 27, 1840 | aged 40 years |

Harry Lewis | Son of | F. M. & Sarah B. | Sanford | Died | July 20, 1863 | Aged 5 Mo's |

Our Baby. (*In Sanford lot*)

Garwood Sanford | died | Jan 5, 1876 | æ 82 | Diantha his wife | died Feb 24, 1881 | æ 81 |

Charlotte Plumb | wife of | Asa Slade | Born | Apr 25, 1799 | Died | June 27, 1894 |

Lorinda | wife of | Sampson Siddall | died | Aug 6, 1882 | Aged 39 |

Sampson Siddall | died | Feb 5, 1882 | Aged 57 |

Of such is the kingdom of Heaven | Ida || Ida E. | Youngest daughter of | A. B. & Fanny M. Shumway | Died Sept 6, 1866 | Æ 5 Y'rs & 7 Mo's |

Lyman J. Smith | Killed in Battle | at Cold Harbor, Va., | June 1, 1864 | æ 22 |

Lyman J. Smith | Born | Dec 22, 1798 | died | Feb 8, 1870 | Julia Bissell | wife of | Lyman J. Smith | born May 12, 1801 | died Apr 20, 1876 | SMITH || Lyman J. Smith, Jr. | Killed | in battle at | Cold Harbor, Va | June 1, 1864 | Aged 20 Y'rs | & 7 M. | Henrietta J.. Smith | born March 1, 1837 | died | Feb. 7, 1873 |

Mary L. || Mary L. Coe | wife of | Walter D. Smith | died | Apr 10, 1888 | Aged 34 Y'rs |

Frederick V. S. Sanford | died | Feb. 17, 1876, æ 73 | Miranda Palmer | his wife died | Oct 13, 1869, æ 64 | SANFORD || Susan Sanford | wife of Reuben Jenne | died | Sept 20, 1869 | æ 72 || Asa Sanford | died | Dec 7, 1856 | æ 91 | Susanna Baldwin | his wife | died | Mar 27, 1857 | æ 87 || George T. Sanford | died | Apr. 7, 1848 | æ 33 |

Father | Lyman E. Sweet | 1843-1893 | Mem. Co's-E. 8th | C. 14th F 20 H. A. | Conn. Vols. | Mother | Amelia Sweet | 1840-1890 | Their dau'r | Laura May | 1871-1892 |

Lucy M. | wife of | Alva A. Stone | died | Nov 14, 1890 | Aged 63 | at rest |

Almira | wife of | Purley Thomas | died | Mar 10, 1847 | æ 48 |

In | Memory of | Purley Thomas | who departed this | life Aug 18, 1827 | æ 32 years |

David Tallmadge | died | June 12, 1880 | Aged 70 |

Blessed sleep from which none ever wake to weep.

Emeline | wife of | David Tallmadge | Died May 14, 1872 | æ 59. |

> She sleeps in Jesus.

George B. Tyrrell | died | Sept 11, 1888 | Aged 76 | Mary A. | his wife | Born June 6, 1812 | Died Jan 22, 1894 |

P. S. Tyrrell | Co. I. 13ᵗʰ | Conn | Inf. |

In | memory of | Polly M. | daughter | of Reuben & | Ruth Tyrrell | who died | June 24, 1827 | aged 9 years |

> Come lovely youth
> Attend awhile & view
> And see what grace &
> piety can do
> They will disarm bold death
> the tyrant king
> And even in death will
> cause the saints to sing

Sarah Peck | wife of | Dea | Thomas | Trowbridge | born Apr 25, 1766 | died April 25, 1841 |

Deacon | Thomas Trowbridge | born Sept 14, 1764 | died Oct 6, 1837 |

Mr. | John Tryon | died May 19, 1816 | in the 88 year | of his age |

Mr James Tryon | died Nov 23, 1825 | æt 59 | Mrs Ruth 1ˢᵗ wife of | James Tryon | died June 1, 1795 | æt 34 | Mrs. Patty R. | 2nd wife of | James Tryon | died March 19, 1813 | æ 38 |

Harriet B Smith | wife of | Charles E. Tileston | died | Sept 30, 1855 | æ 28 |

> There! Mother, in the Savior's arms
> Forever undefiled,
> Among that little cherub band
> Is your beloved child.

Hatty B. S. | Daughter of | Charles & Harriet Tileston | died | Aug 30, 1856 | æ 10 mo & 7 d's | (?)

Henry P. Trowbridge | died | Aug 4, 1870 | æ 66 |

Maria Kilbourn | wife of | Henry P. Trowbridge | afterward wife of | Joseph Howard | Nov 15, 1823-Dec 21, 1894 |

Otis | Safe on the Saviour's | bosom resteth the little one || Otis H. | son of | George H. & Ellen A. | Trowbridge | æ 5 W'ks |

T | George H. Trowbridge | 1843—1896 | his wife | Ellen Gillette | 1845 - —— | TROWBRIDGE || Clara E. Trowbridge | 1871—1895 | Otis H. Trowbridge | 1874—1874 |

Leonard | (*In Trowbridge lot*)

Julia C. | daughter of | Stephen & | Eliza | Trowbridge | died | May 27, 1839 | aged 2 years |

Eliza | wife of | Stephen Trowbridge | died | May 5, 1841 | aged 38 years |

Stephen Trowbridge | Died Sept 6, 1884 | Aged 86 | Grace | his wife | Died Dec 26, 1873 | Aged 50 |

Jane | wife of | Chester Thomas | died | Oct 15, 1854 | æ 35 |

Gone to rest ! | Mary Jane | daughter of | Chester & Jane | Thomas | Died Apr 15, 1873 | æ 30 |

Almira | wife of | Jackson Tompkins | died | April 9, 1874 | æ 28 Y'rs & 1 Mo |

> Stop, my friend, and take another view,
> The dust that moulders here
> Was once alive like you.
> No longer then on future time rely
> Improve the present and prepare to die.

Jackson Tompkins | Co A. 19. Regt | Conn. Vols | died | Oct 28, 1892 | Aged 49 |

Marshall | L. Tompkins | died | Mar 25, 1894 | Aged 55 Y'rs | & 2 M'o || Jennie E. | wife of | Marshall L. | Tompkins | died May 17, 1888 | Aged 34 |

In Memory of Capt. Joseph | Vaill | who died | Aug 10, 1800 | aged 79 | || Jerusha | wife of Capt | Joseph Vaill | who died Feb 21, 1813 | aged 85 years |

Also | Jerusha Lydia & Sarah | daughters of Joseph & | Jerusha Vaill |

Benjamin L. | son of | Benjamin & | Sylvia Vaill | died Oct 26, 1829 | aged 19 years |

Benjamin Vaill | died Aug 17, 1852 | Aged 80 |

Jemina Vaill | wife of | Benjamin Vaill | died | Oct 7, 1848 | æ 78 |

In | Memory of | Sylvia wife of | Benjamin Vaill | who departed this life | April 13, 1813, | aged 41 |

Rev. Herman Z. Vaill | born Dec 7, 1794 | died Dec 29, 1870 | his wife | Flora Gold | born Sept 25, 1799 | ———— | Sarah Hopkins | born Oct 21, 1834 | died Sept 30, 1862 | VAILL || Charles B. Vaill | born Sept 11, 1826 | died Apr 30, 1881 | Charles H. Vaill | born Oct 26, 1856 | died July 21, 1876 |

Flora Gold | daughter of | Joseph H. & | Cornelia S. | Vaill | Born & died | Sept 18, 1872 |

Peleg Wheeler, Jr. | died | Mar 3, 1855. | æ 56 |

In | memory of | Henry W. Wheeler | who died | Apr 6, 1860 | æ 24 |

Edwin W. | Wheeler | died | Feb 5, 1890 | Aged 55 Y'rs |

In | memory of | Justus Webster | who died in the | year our Lord | 1776 or 77 |

In | memory of | Jerusha Webster | who died in the | year of our Lord | 1776 or 77 |

Lavina Wooster | Wife of | Lemuel Wooster | died Nov 11, 1831 | aged 72 years |

Judson Wooster | son of Lemuel | & Levina Wooster | died Dec 14, 1827 | Æt 24 |

R. W. | Here lies the Body of | Mrs Rebekah Wooster | wife of Mr Lemuel | Wooster, Daughter of | Mr Charles Gillet of | Sharon she Departed | this life Dec. 2d 1786 | in the 23d year of her age |

> Come all my living friends & see
> The place where you must shortly be
> This is the house that God hath chose
> But Christ hath sweetened this repose.

Lemuel Wooster | died | Oct 1, 1832 | Aged 75 years |

Here lies the | Body of Mrs. Tha | nkful Woodruff | the wife of Nathaniel | Woodruff she | died Jan 31, 1774 | in the 88 year | of her age |

In Memory of | M<sup>r</sup> Nathaniel | Woodruff, Cap<sup>t</sup> who | died November | the 13<sup>th</sup> A. D. 1758 | in the 72<sup>nd</sup> year of his Age |

Sacred | to the memory of | Inestimable worth, of | Unrivalled Excellence & Virtue | M<sup>rs</sup> Rachel wife of | Jerome B. Woodruff | & daughter of Norman | & Lois Barber, whose | etherial parts became | a seraph May 24, 1835 | in the 22 y'r of her age |

Rachel | daughter of | Jerome B. & Rachel Woodruff | died| Oct 10, 1836 | æ 1 y'r 4 mo's | & 16 days |

In Memory of M<sup>rs</sup> | Beate Wetmore | Wife of M<sup>r</sup> | Joseph Wetmore | who died March 23<sup>d</sup> A D | 1782 in the 40<sup>th</sup> year of| her age | A loving and beloved wife, a tender | and affecionate Parent, lamented by | her friends and acquaintance.

> Was every heart all love like hers
> Forgiving and forgiven
> This world might shine amidst the stars
> And earth become a heaven

This Monument | is Erected in Mem | ory of Oliver, Son | of Oliver Wolcott | Esq<sup>r</sup> & Lorrain his | Wife. Born Aug'st | 31st, 1757 & died | Sept 13 A D 1757 | Jesus Resuscitatio | et Vitas |

Here lies y<sup>e</sup> | Body of Dea<sup>cn</sup> Benjamin | Webster he died July y<sup>e</sup> 10<sup>th</sup> | 1755 in y<sup>e</sup> 58<sup>th</sup> year | of his Age |

Here lies y<sup>e</sup> Body of | Elijah Son of Dea<sup>cn</sup> | Benjamin & Elizabeth | Webster he died | Aug<sup>st</sup> y<sup>e</sup> 17<sup>th</sup>, 1754 in y<sup>e</sup> 22<sup>nd</sup> year of his Age |

Here lies y<sup>e</sup> Body of | James Son of Dea<sup>cn</sup> | Benjamin & Elizabeth | Webster he died Ju<sup>ly</sup> y<sup>e</sup> 30<sup>th</sup> 1754 in y<sup>e</sup> 21<sup>st</sup> | year of his age |

Williams Wadhams | died | July 7, 1882 | Aged 78 |

> There is rest for the weary.

David W. Wood | died Feb 24, 1875 | æ 74 |

Beulah | wife of | David Wood | died May 26, 1851 | æ 47 |

> She did strive in thought
> And word and feeling
> So to live as to make
> Earth next heaven

Delia C. Munson | widow of | David W. Wood | died | June 2ᵈ 1882 | æ 73 |

> "Her children rise up and call her Blessed
> Her works also they praise her."

William Ward | born | Oct 19, 1771 | died | July 22, 1854 | Charlotte | his wife | born June 25, 1784 | died | Aug 18, 1856| WARD |

Abbey Ward | died | Sept 20, 1835 | aged 29 |

Erwin Ward | died | Sept 2, 1834 | æ 14 |

Ambrose Ward | died | Oct 25, 1832 | æ 16 |

Harriet Ward | died | Sept 24, 1827 | æ 19 |

William Ward | died | Nov 5, 1824 | æ 11 |

In | memory | of | Curtis Woodruff | Born Nov 1, 1790 | died Sept 24, 1854 | and of his | wife | Sarah M. Trowbridge | Born Nov 11, 1791 | died Dec 6, 1851 | They rest from their labors |

Lucy Stone Whaples | Died | April 6, 1868 | æ 69 |

Dr. Ashbel Wessells | died | April 6, 1853 | æ 82 | Grace Ward | his wife | Died Nov 11, 1864 | æ 91 |

William Ward | died Nov 6, 1829 | aged 93 | Anna | wife of Wᵐ Ward | & daughter of | Rev. Solomon Palmer | died Nov 4, 1839 | aged 93 || (*see Palmer, Rev. Solomon*)

Lucinda B. | wife of | Charles B. Webster | died ] Jan 24, 1871 | Aged 40 |

Edwin Wadhams | Died Aug 14, 1865 | Aged 70 | Mary Lewis | His Wife Died | Mar. 15, 1879 | æ 72 |

WADHAMS | The battle is fought | The victory won | Rest Soldier, Rest || Lieut | Henry W. Wadhams | Co K 14 C. V. | Killed at North Anna, Va | May 26, 1864 | Aged 33 || Capt | Luman Wadhams | Co. A 2 C. V. A. | Wounded at the Battle Cold Harbor, Va | June 1 | Died June 3, 1864 | Aged 29 || Edward Wadhams | 1st Sergt. | Co E. 8 Regt. C. V. | Killed near Fort Darling, Va. | May 16, 1864, | aged 27 |

Hattie E. | daughter of | C. C. & Ella M. | Walker | Aged 6 W'ks |

Charles A. | son of | Austin & | Hattie Wheeler | died | June 17, 1882 | Æ 7 y'rs & 6 Mo's |

George C. Weed | Co K 91 Regt | N. Y. Vols | died | May 7, 1891 |

Charles Squire Wood | Surgeon, U. S. Army | born 27 February 1825 | died 1 February 1890 | WOOD || Walter Munson Wood | born 31 May 1880 |died 11 November 1882 | Sarah Hoffner Wood | born 7 October 1869 | died 18 July 1870 | children of | Charles S. and Cynthia A. Wood ||

---

ADDITIONAL INSCRIPTIONS.

R. Adele Smith | wife of David M. Goodwin | June 2, 1876 | June 18, 1899 | also twin daughter | June 18, 1899—June 18, 1899. |

Augustus A. Lord | Son of Erastus A. & | Charlotte D. Lord, | Born Nov 5, 1815, | Died Aug 4, 1903 | Aged 87 |

Mrs Leah wife | of Mr Paul Peck | deceased on the | 5th June 1767 in | the 87 year of | her age |

Lieutenant | Isaac Bissell | born in Windsor 22 September 1682 | died 6 November 1744 | Elizabeth his wife | daughter of Mr John Osborne of Windsor | born 19 December 1684 died 15 January 1761 |

# East Burying Ground

This has become the largest of the cemeteries in the township, although it was the third one to be established, and was at first, as it noted below, a part of the highway set apart for the purpose. It lies half a mile east of the Court-house. The following record in the first town book is of interest:

"Sept 26, 1754. .... At the same Meeting Mess^rs Samuel Colver Joshua Garritt & Edward Phelps were chosen com^tee to lay out a Burying Place in the East Side of the Town where & how much they shall think proper."

The laying out of this ground is recorded in the land records under date of Jan. 12, 1755:

"Whereas the town of Litchfield did at their annual Meeting choose and appoint us the subscribers to lay out some land in some of our Highways suitable for a burying Place pursuant to the abovesaid vote of the Town We have laid out one Acre wanting sixteen Rods upon the Plain upon the west side of the Mill River upon the North Side of the Path that leads to Chestnut Hill Beginning at a Heap of Stones about fifteen Rods West from said River from thence running West twelve Rods to a Maple Staddle with stones about it thence North twelve Rods to a Heap of Stones then East twelve Rods then a straight Line to the first Bounds and Buts North upon James Kilbourn's Pike Lot the same is to lye & remain for the Use of a burying Place laid out & bounded upon the Tenth Day of January 1755.

> Joshua Garritt
> Samuel Colver
> Edward Phelps Com^tee"

Dec. 15. 1767. "Voted That Timothy Marsh have the use and improvement of the burying place near the grist mill belonging to Col^l Eben Marsh during the towns pleasure."

EAST CEMETERY—NEW PART

In 1837 the yard was enlarged upon its western side by an addition of sixteen rods. The next year further extention was made on the northern side, and the town voted a part of the highway for the same purpose. The stone wall in front of the ground on East Street was built about 1850 by subscription.

Within fifteen years a corporation known as the Litchfield Cemetery Association has purchased a tract of land between the ancient yard and Torrington Road and has laid it out with much care. Many fine monuments have been erected upon the new ground.

In the southeast corner of the old burying yard lie a great number of Revolutionary soldiers who died during the war, and were buried here without any distinguishing marks.

# INSCRIPTIONS

To | the memory of the | Hon. John Allen, Esq. | many years, during a life of eminent usefulness | highly distinguished | for his | talents, integrity and patriotism, | as a member of the council and | Supreme court of Errors | of Connecticut | and no less distinguished | during a period interesting and critical | to his country | as a member of the | Congress of the United States | Born June 12, 1763 | Died July 31, 1812 | Aged 49 |

E. A. | Mrs. Esther Austin | relict of the late | David Austin, Esq. | of New Haven | and formerly of | Mr Daniel Allen | of G. Barrington | She died Sept 19th 1810 | aged 77 years | much lamented | by her numerous friends | and acquaintance | for her many virtues | and eminent piety. | This monument | is erected to her | MEMORY | by her affectionate | Son |

Abel F. Andrews | died | Sept 3, 1832, æ 49 | - His wife | Polly Rich | died | June 1, 1877 | æ 89 |

Barzilla Arntz | died | Dec 15 1879 | æ 79 | Susan T. his wife | died Feb 24, 1884 æ 82 | || ARNTZ ||

Here lies the Body | of Jeph Africa | servant of the Rev. | Judah Champion | who Died June | the 5th 1793 |

Jane Deborah | daughter of | Charles & | Julia M. Adams | died | June 27, 1832 | aged 13 mo's |

Henry Adams | died | Feb 11, 1842 | æ 47 || Mary S. | wife of | Henry Adams | died | Jan 23, 1858 | æ 55 |

Deborah | wife of | Joseph Adams | Died July 28, 1857 | Aged 84 |

Joseph Adams | died | July 14, 1856 | aged 89 |

Charles Adams Jr. | Wounded at | Batle of Cold Harbor | June 1, | Died at Washington | June 11, 1864, æ 19 |

Henry William | son of | Charles & Julia M. | Adams | Born Dec 8, 1835 | Died Jan 26, 1889 |

Sarah Elizabeth | died | May 7, 1862 | aged 22 years | Francis Scovil | died June 4, 1862 | aged 7 years | Children of | Charles & Julia M. Adams |

Charles Adams | born | at Litchfield | May 18, 1805 | died | at Ann Arbor, Michigan, | Oct 23, 1883 |

Julia M. Adams | wife of | Charles Adams | Died Sept 13, 1869 | æ 59 |

Zina J. | son of Zina & | Abiah Bradley | died Aug 31, 1833 | aged 20 |

This monument is | erected in memory of Amos Benedict Esq | who died | Feb 25, 1816 | in the 36 year | of his age [

Sacred | to the Memory of | Mr Isaac Bull | who died Oct 7th | AD 1789 | Aged 75 years | a strong Advocate for the | Cause of Virtue and the rising Gener | ation |

Belinda | wife of | Henry Bissell |died | Sept. 3, 1861 | aged 54 |

In | Memory of | Almira Bradley | who died | July 3, 1837 | aged 43 |

Norman B. Barber | of 19th Regt. C. V. | died [ Oct. 12, 1863 | aged 26 | He died in the service of his country |

Minerva C. | daughter of | Loyal B. & | Lucretia Barber | died | Apr. 12, 1846 | æ 10 months & 3 d. |

In | Memory of | Charles Baldwin | who died | Sept 4, 1828| aged 72 years |

In | memory of | Rachel widow of | Late Charles Baldwin | who died | June 17, 1844 | æ 81 |

In | memory of | William M. Baldwin | who departed | this life | Oct 1, 1826 | aged 23 years |

In | memory of | David D. son | of Mr David & Mrs | Polly Buell (?) who died | Sept 19, 1814 (?) aged | 6 years | (*epitaph undecipherable*)

A. In B. | Memory of | Anna A. | daughter of [ James & | Nabbe Baldwin | who died | Jan 6, 1835 | aged 46 years | & 4 mo |

James Baldwin | died | May 24, 1843 | æ 84 | A Revolutionary Soldier |

Nabby | wife of | James Baldwin | died Apr. 6, 1850 | æ 83 |

Charlotte Bidwell | died | Nov 24, 1851 | æ 64 |

Stephen Bidwell | died | Oct 25, 1850 | æ 86 |

In | memory of | Hannah | wife of | Stephen Bidwell | who died | Aug 11, 1837 | Aged 75 years |

In | Memory of | M^r Stephen Bidwell | who died | Sept 12, 1807 | Aged 83 years |

In | Memory of | Mrs Anna wife of | M^r Stephen Bidwell | who died | May 16, 1809 | Aged 86 years |

Frederick Bidwell | died | Oct 30, 1873 | æ 55 |
In | memory of | Rachel | wife of | Isaac Baldwin | who died | Nov 2, 1845 | Aged 40 ye. | There is rest in Heaven |

In | memory of Isaac Baldwin | who died June 22, 1882 | Aged 81 | There is rest for the weary. |

In Memory of | Two Sons of Mr Ebenezer | & Mrs Abigail Bolles. | Samuel P. died Sept 18^th | A. D. 1792 Aged 19 months | Joshua died Jan 15^th | A. D. 1799 Aged 17 months |

> Happy the babes who priviledged by fate
> To shorter labors and a lighter weight
> Received but yesterday the gift of breath
> Ordered to morrow to return to death.

Mr. | William Baldwin | Died | Dec 26, 1833 | æ 79 |

In memory of | the following persons | This stone is erected by | the Rev Ashbel Baldwin | of Stratford | Isaac Baldwin Esq. | died Jan 15, 1805 | aged 95 | Mrs. Anna, wife of | Isaac Baldwin Esq. | died April 16, 1790 | aged 67 | Anna aged 12 mos & | Frederic aged 12 da's | children of Isaac & | Anna Baldwin | Capt Horace Baldwin | son of Isaac & Anna Baldwin | died Dec 3, 1822 | aged 57 | Mary daughter of | Horace & Rachel Baldwin | aged 3 years | Charles son of | Horace & Rachel Baldwin | died Feb 22 1824 | aged 38 |

Willie | æ 9 | (*reverse*) | Buell |

Lottie J. | daughter of E. L. & E. S. Buell | died | Oct 2, 1867 | Æ 18 Mo |

E. Lewis Buell | died | Nov 6, 1867 | æ 42 |

In Memory | of Candace | Daughter of Capt Archel ( ?) and Mrs. Mary | Bull who | died May y^e | 7, 1781 in | (*underground*)

Deacon | Peter Buel | Born at Lebanon | May 22, 1710 | Died May 4, 1784 |

Here lies the Body | of M^{rs} Hannah wife | of Deacon Peter | Buell, who Departed | this Life Jan ^y 15^{th} | 1764 in the 42^{nd} | year of her Age |

In Memory of | Dan Son of Deacon | Peter and M^{rs} | Hannah Buell who | Departed ...... (*underground*)

In | Memory of | Mrs. Hannah Baldwin relict of | Mr. David Baldwin | who died | Oct 29, 1784 | aged 72 years |

In | Memory of | Mr. David Baldwin | who died | June 4^{th}, 1778 | aged 64 years |

In Memory of | David Baldwin | Son of M^r David & M^{rs} Hannah Baldwin | who died Nov^r | the 7^{th} A. D. 1760 | in y^e 19^{th} year | of His.... |

Elizabeth Mary | Daughter of | David & | Annabella Burr | died Sept 12, 1813 | Aged 7 mo. | & 5 days |

Emily Catharine | daughter of Josiah & | Delia Barnes | of Buffalo, N. Y. & | Grand-Daughter | of Rev. | Truman Marsh | died July 17, 1837 | aged 5 years | & 4 mo. |

Thomas Bell | died | Mar 15, 1893 | Aged 68 |

Jane | Wife of | Thomas Bell | died March 27, 1861 | Aged 26 |

Lucretia | wife of | William Buell, 2^d | died | May 15, 1851| æ 58 |

William Buell | died June 16, 1874 | æ 80 |

Marina | wife of | Norman Buell | died Feb 1, 1852 | æt 61 |

Norman Buell | died | Nov. 17, 1865 | æt 76 |

Abigail | wife of | Isaac Baldwin | Born May 8, 1813 | Died April 1, 1886 |

Sarah Jane | daughter of | Garry & | Sarah M. | Bissell born | Nov 24, 1833 | Died March | 21, 1834 |

In | Memory of | Capt. Norman Buell | who departed this life | March 25, 1813 | in the 46 year | of his age |

Lyman | son of | Lyman & | Amelia Barber | of Wrentham, Mass. | died | Feb 9, 1843, | aged 2 mo. |

To the memory of | Mr. Peter Buel | who died | Jan 30th, 1797 | in the 58th year | of his age |

In | memory of | Capt. Archelaus Buell | who died | Aug 13, 1811 | aged 75 years |

In | memory of | Mary wife of | Capt. Archelaus Buell | who died April 23, 1822 | in the 82 year | of her age |

In | Memory of | Capt. Phineas Baldwin | who died | July 27, 1817 | in the 70 year | of his age |

In | Memory of | Mary wife of | Capt. Phineas Baldwin | who died | June 21, 1817 | in the 64 year of her age |

In | Memory of | Mr George Baldwin | who died | July 18th 1802. | aged 68 years |

In Memory of | Mr. Jonathan Bull | who died Feb 21-st. | 1809 | Aged 78 years |

In memory of | Mrs Rebecca Bishop | Consort of Mr Calvin | Bishop who died June | the 16, 1808 in the 47th | Year of her Age |

Capt | Daniel Baldwin | died | June 26, 1834 | æ 36 | Mary | his wife died | Dec 27, 1874 | æ 83 || Sarah Jane | daughter of | Daniel & Mary | Baldwin | died | Aug 22, 1836 | æ 11 || Elizabeth Ann | daughter of | Daniel & Mary | Baldwin | died | Mar 11 1840 | æ 18 || Charles H. | son of | Daniel & Mary | Baldwin | died | April 14, 1850 | æ 19 ||

Ursula Bull Buell | Daughter of Charles & Susan Buell | Born July 16, 1809 | Died May 26, 1831 |

> If worth departed e'er deserved a tear
> Oh! gentle stranger stop and drop it hear.

Susan Buell | Wife of | Charles Buell | died | July 9, 1836 | æ 58 |

George D. Buell | died | May 1, 1851 | æ 38 |

Lucretia | wife of | George D. Buell | died | Feb 23, 1886 | æ 80 |

This monument | is to distinguish the grave of | Mary Harvey Buel | Who died July 6th 1896 | aged 18 years |

Sally Bird | relict of | John Bird, Esq | died Aug 4, 1815 | aged 35. |

Horace Baldwin | died | Dec 3, 1821 | Aged 57 | Rachel Baldwin | died | Dec 10, 1852 | Aged 82 |

Samuel E. | Son of Horace & | Lucy | Baldwin | died | June 6, 1842 | æ 10 wk's |

George A. | son of Horace & | Lucy Baldwin | died | Sept. 5, 1826 | aged 1 year |

Caroline A. | daughter of | Alonzo B. & | Martha Ann Bigelow died | Aug 30, 1832 | aged 7 months |

Jane Seymour | daughter of | Doct. Josiah G. Beckwith | & Jane Marsh | his wife | born | June 15, 1833 | died | Jan 23, 1837 |

Lucretia M. Bolles | Wife of | Ebenezer W. Bolles | died Jan 8th 1831 | Aged 29 years | their Daughter | Frances Grace | died March 17, 1829 | aged 16 months |

Mr. | Ebenezer Bolles | died | Aug 29, 1826 | æt 62 |

Abigail | widow of | Ebenezer Bolles | died | Dec 29, 1844 | aged 81 |

Caroline A. | Daughter of | George & | Clarissa Bolles | died | July 7, 1830 |

Sarah A. Baldwin | died | Mar. 8, 1833 | æ 65 |

In | Memory of | Dea John Baldwin | who Departed this life | June 3, 1813, in the 48 year of his Age |

The sweet remembrance of the just
Shall flourish while they sleep in dust.

Charles S. Buell | born | March 12, 1805 | Died June 23, 1881 | Eliza Barber | his wife | Born July 19, 1806 | Died Feb 25, 1885 |

Victorine Bissell Bogert | daughter of | John B. & Elizabeth C. | Bogert | died at Brooklyn | March 23rd 1858 | aged | 3 years & 4 months |

Lucy Ann | daughter of | John & | Catharine Bissell | died | Aug 16, 1822 | æ 11 yrs | Katherine | wife of | Roswell Hoyt & | daughter of | John Bissell | died at Stamford | Sept 27, 1855 | æ 39 | BISSELL || Elizabeth C. | Bissell wife of | John B. Bogert | died May 9, 1872 | æ 54 || Mary E. Bissell | daughter of | John & Catharine | Bissell | born Oct 7, 1819 | died | July 27, 1897 || Samuel M. | Bissell died | at Harrisburg | Texas, Nov 14, 1837 | æ 37 ||

I. H. S. | Here lies the body | of | Mrs. Catharine Bissell | who died March 7, 1837 | Aged 59 Years || John Bissell | died | March 22, 1855. | Aged 80 Years ||

I. H. S. | Here rests the body | of | Passed Midshipman | George Beckwith Bissell | acting master | of the | U. S. Frigate Cumberland | U. S. Navy | died September 10, 1848 | aged 24 years |

Harriet, dau'tr | of Leonard & | Rumina Blakeslee [ died | Sept 2, 1825 | aged 9 mon |

In | memory of | Roxana C. | daughter of S. P. & Roxana P. | Bolles | born May 6, 1826 | died Nov 5, 1846 ]

Fremand | son of Harvy & | Betsey Bulkley | Died Dec 5, 1830 | æ 4 y-rs |

To the | memory of | Frederic A. Beecher | son of Lyman & | Harriet Beecher | born Sept 11, 1818 & | died July 28, 1820 |

To the memory of | Roxana Beecher | who died | Sept 23, 1816 | aged 42 years |

To the | memory of | Mary Beecher | relict of David Beecher | of New-Haven | She was born Nov | 6, 1744 and died June 20, 1818 | aged 73 years |

David Buell | died | Jan 10, 1859 | æ 83 |

In | memory of | Polly Buell | wife of | David Buell | who died | June 6, 1824 | æt 59 |

In memory of | Dan Bradley | who died Sept 13, 1802 | aged 77 years | Mehetabel Bradley | his wife died July 20, 1810 | Aged 64 years |

In | Memory of | Ruth wife of | Elihu Bradley | died | June 2, 1816 | æt 40. |

Silas G. Butler | died | March 25th 1864 | Aged 34 Years |

Julia A. | daughter of | William & | Augustine Butler | died | Feb 26, 1853 | æt 11 |

Marietta Caroline | daughter of | John M. & Caroline Baldwin | Aged 13 Months | 1837 |

Mary | daughter of | Samuel P. & | Roxana P. Bolles | born | May 4, 1842 | died | Nov. 13, 1843 |

Penfield | son of | Samuel P. & | Roxana P. Bolles | Born May 24, 1831 | Died April 12, 1835 |

In | memory of | Asa Barnes | who died | Nov 9, 1848 | Ætt 37 yrs |

Wᵐ Henry | son of | S. M. & | A. E. Bronson | died | June 3, 1848 | æ 2 mo |

Silas N. Bronson | Feb 8, 1812 - Jan 13, 1890 | BRONSON |

Asa Bacon | died | February 5ᵗʰ 1857 | Aged 86 Years | Lucretia Champion | wife of Asa Bacon | Born February 17, 1783 | Died January 19, 1882 || To | the memory of | Epaphroditus Champion Bacon | while traveling in Europe | he died, among strangers | at Seville, in Spain | on the 11th of Jan. A D 1845 | aged 34 years || Major General | Francis Bacon | The last of the three sons of | Asa and Lucretia Bacon | Died September 16, 1849 | aged thirty years | The dutiful Son the kind Husband | the able Senator, sound Lawyer | and eloquent Advocate | lies here ! || To | the memory of | Frederick Asa Bacon | late an officer in the Navy | of the United States | attached to the schooner | Sea Gull | (of the Exploring Expedition) | which foundered off | Cape Horn | on the 1ˢᵗ of May A. D. 1839 | All on board perished | He died | at the age of 26 years | a highly meritorious | and promising young officer |

Elizabeth Sheldon Dutcher | widow of Francis Bacon | wife of | Lewis | Carr | Born May 10, | 1825 | Died | Oct 9 | 1867 |

Anna M. Buell | died | Feb 5, 1893 | æ 81 | Daughter of | Timothy & | Anna Miller |

Julia E. Buell | born | Jan 15, 1822 | died | July 26, 1842 |

Julia | wife of | Elisha L. Buell | died Feb 19, 1868 | æ 74 |

Elisha L. Buell | died | Nov 29, 1866 | æ 74 |

Hannah | Wife of | Henry Baldwin | died | Dec 3, 1876 | æ 76 |

Henry Baldwin | died | July 22, 1845 | æ 61 |

James L. | son of | Henry & | Hannah Baldwin | died | June 22, 1842 | aged 14 years |

Mary M. | wife of | Horace Baldwin, Jr. | Died Dec 9, 1869 | æ 32 |

Daniel Lewis | son of | Rev. D. E. & H. J. | Brown | died ! Jan 27, 1854 | Aged 18 y'rs |

Charles G. Bennett | born | Oct 2, 1782 | died | Oct 2, 1841 |

William Buel M. D. | Born | Nov 24, 1767 | Died Oct 15, 1851 |

Abigail Buel | Born | Feb 8, 1775 | Died March 12, 1858 |

George S. Buel | Died | July 26, 1842 | æ 38 |

Jonathan Buel | Died | Dec 21, 1862 | æ 86 |

Abigail B. Buell | Died | Oct 4, 1867 | æ 90 |

Harriet B. Buell | daughter of | Capt. Charles Buell | born | Feb 23, 1817 | died | Mar 6, 1874 | aged 57 Y'rs |

Capt. Charles Buell | born | Oct 1, 1778 | died | Apr 21, 1851 | Aged 73 y'rs |

Samuel Buel, M. D. | Born Sept 27, 1782 | Died July 10, 1854 | æ 71 |

Minerva Buel | wife of | Samuel Buel M. D. | Born Sept 28, 1793 | Died June 24, 1874 | æ 80 |

Edward C. Buel | Born May 26, 1824 | Died Aug. 25, 1852 | æ 28 |

Samuel D. Buel | Born June 15, 1832 | Died Aug 25, 1851 | æ 19 |

In | memory of | Maria Louisa | Infant Daughter | of Samuel & | Minerva Buel | Died Aug 16, 1831 | æ 9 weeks |

Mary Anna | Bronson | died Nov 30, 1872 | Æ 4 D's |

Julia M. | July 15, 1857 | æ 26 y'rs | Ellen J. | died | June 29, 1857 | æ 4 y'rs 10 mo. | Children of | Frederic I. & | Lois L. Braman |

Lucy Sheldon | widow of | Theron Beach | Died April 7, 1889 | in the 101st year | of her age |

Theron Beach | Born at Goshen | July 9, 1785 | Died at Litchfield | Oct 29, 1864 |

Frederick D. Beeman | born | Jan 1, 1821 | died | Aug 4, 1860 |

Maria Hall | widow of | Frederick D. Beeman | and daughter of | J. W. & M. S. Brisbane | Born June 14, 1831 | Died Jan 17, 1863 |

Mary Susan | widow of | John W. Brisbane | and daughter of | Commodore Alex. Gillon | of Charleston, S. C. | Born July 8, 1793 | Died Nov 21, 1859 |

Susan Gillon | daughter of F. D. & M. H. Beeman | Born Nov 6, 1858 | Died May 8, 1860 |

Seth Preston Beers | Died Sept 9, 1863 | aged 82 | BEERS || sons of | S. P. & B. W. Beers | Horatio Preston | Died Dec 12, 1824 | Aged 14 | Henry Augustine | Died Nov 11, 1834 | aged 12 | George Webster | Died Feb 3, 1862 | aged 46 | Alfred Horatio | Died Jan 5, 1869 | aged 40 || Julia Maria | daughter of | S. P. & B. W. Beers | Born July 20, 1819 | at Litchfield, Conn. | Died Oct 17, 1876 | at Rome, Italy, | where she was buried in | the cemetery of | San Lorenzo || Belinda | wife of Seth P. Beers | & Daughter of | Reuben Webster | Died Jan 4, 1868 | Aged 80 y. |

Alfred H. Beers |

H. R. B. | (*Beers*)

David C. Bulkley | Died Jan 18, 1892 | æ 87 | Mary Ann | wife of | David C. Bulkley | died Aug 28, 1847 | æ 36 |

Harriet A. | wife of David C. Bulkley | Died Dec 26, 1895 | æ 76 | BULKLEY || Lieut. | William S. Bulkley | of Co. A. 12th C. V. | Killed in Battle | near Winchester, Va | Sept. 19, 1864 | æ 32 | Edwin K. Bulkley | Died May 19, 1844 | æ 6 Y'rs | sons of D. D. & M. A. Bulkley ||

Edwin C. | son of Henry & Mary M. | Baldwin | died | June 4, 1874 | æ 22 |

William H. | son of | Henry & | Mary M. Baldwin | died | Feb 2, 1861 | Aged 11 years | & 8 mo. |

Emma R. | daughter of | Henry & Mary | Baldwin | died | Aug 4, 1878 | Aged 20 Y'rs & | 8 M's |

Mary M. | Wife of | Henry Baldwin | died | Feb 5, 1882 | Aged 55 |

Sumner | son of | Simeon S. & | Melissa Batterson | died | Oct 4, 1842 | æ 16 months |

Wilmot A. | son of | Samuel G. & | Elmira Beach | died Oct 2, 1857 | Aged 18 |

Virgil E. Beach | son of | Samuel G. Beach | died | Nov 12, 1867 | æ 28 | his only child | Elizabeth | Sedgwick Beach | died | Oct 2, 1867 | æ 9 Mo |

Samuel G. Beach | died | July 8, 1885 | aged 70 | BEACH ||
Emily J. Beach | died | Dec 24, 1879 | aged 41 || Harriet F.
Beach | died | Sept 26, 1855 | aged 4 months ||

Lydia | wife of | Edward W. Blake | died | Oct 3, 1852 |
æt 32 |

Joseph D. son of | E. W. & Lydia | Blake | died Dec 27,
1848 | aged 6 months |

Horace Baldwin | died | Jan 28, 1878 | æ 80 |

William E. | son of | Horace & | Lucy Baldwin | died | Nov
28, 1850 | Æ 7 y'rs | & mo. |

Sarah L. | daughter of | Horace & | Lucy Baldwin | died |
Feb 5, 1845 | æ 13 y'rs |

Andrew J. son of | Horace & | Lucy Baldwin | died | July
8, 1844 | æ 6 y'rs & 6 mo |

Helen E. | wife of | Wm. N. Buell | died | Aug 7, 1855 |
Æt 40. |

In | memory of | William N. Buell | who died | Mar 23,
1851 | Æt 43 y'rs |

William N. | son of | William N. & | Hellen E. Buell | died |
Sept 2, 1844 | Æt 9 Mo's |

Louisa Ann | daughter of | Ruel & | Mary Bradley | died |
June 2, 1844 | æ 21 y'rs 4 mo |

Harriet | daughter of | Ruel & | Mary Bradley | died | Nov.
19, 1828 | Æ 11 years |

Ruel Bradley | died | June 18, 1848 | æt 62 y'rs |

William C. Buell | died Aug 13, 1887 | æ 40 Y'rs | BUELL ||

Henrietta | daughter of | William R. | & Dotha L. Buell |
died | May 25, 1858 | æ 24 |

William R. Buell | died | Feb 20, 1875 | æ 68 | His wife |
Dotha L. | died | Jan 11, 1878 | æ 67 |

Samuel G. Braman | born | Apr 17, 1801 | died | June 5,
1871 |

Mary N. Palmer | wife of | Samuel G. Braman | Born Nov.
1, 1809 | Died Sept 23, 1887 |

Webster Belden | born in Litchfield | June 18, 1853 | died in Buffalo, N. Y. | October 19, 1880 || Col. Charles O. Belden | born | May 2, 1827 | died | November 22, 1870 | BELDEN | Georgia | daughter of | Charles O. & | Harriet B. Belden | born September 30, 1855 | died September 15, 1859 |

Dorothy (*Belden*)

Elmer E. Baldwin | Mar 15, 1861 | Feb 23, 1895 |

Willis J. Beach M. D. | born | Feb 9, 1844 | died | Nov. 5, 1892 |

Julia E. Kilbourn | wife of | W^m H. Braman | Aug. 9, 1843-Apr. 28, 1892 | BRAMAN || William H. Braman, Jr. | Sept 29, 1880-May 1, 1895 ||

Charles | July 13 | 1791 | December 31 | 1871 | (*Bishop*)

Mary | January 7 | 1797 | November 17 | 1884 | (*Bishop*)

J. G. B. | July 20, 1829 | September 8, | 1892 | (*Bishop*)

Annie | October 1, | 1867 | July 25, | 1885 | (*Bishop*)

Baby | June 11, | 1872 | July 24, | 1872 | (*Bishop*)

Charles F. Baldwin | born | July 20, 1819 | died | January 12, 1854 | Hannah M. Baldwin | born | December 24, 1824 | died | August 17, 1894 | BALDWIN ||

Charles F. Baldwin | son of C. F. & H. M. | Baldwin | born | August 17, 1854 | died | June 14, 1883 |

Henry W. Buel | Born April 7, 1820 | Died Jan 30, 1893 | BUEL || Children of | Henry W. and Mary A. Buel | Mary A. | born Dec 31, 1864 | Died Aug 17, 1865 || Catharine K. Laidlaw | wife of | Henry W. Buel | Born June 9, 1827 | Died Aug 26, 1882 | Mary A. Laidlaw | wife of | Henry W. Buel | Born May 11, 1822 | Died Dec 31, 1864 |

Julia J. | wife of | George Carter | died | July 27, 1875 | æ 83 |

Charles Carter | Co. F 29 Regt. Conn Vols. | died | Jan 6, 1889 |

Mary N. | wife of Augustus Cook | Died | Dec 28. 1854 | Æ 55 |

Esther Murray | wife of | Orlando Crane | born | May 8, 1797 | died | Nov 17, 1876 |

Orlando Crane | died | Jan 30, 1866 | Aged 63 |

Philo Chase | died Mar. 2 1866 | Æ 76 |

Anna | wife of | Philo Chase | died | March 21, 1843 | aged 46 years | The marble monument may | return thy memory but can | never speak thy worth |

Lydia consort to Mr | John Collins died Sept 26th A D 1790 In | the 52 year of her age | (*Epitaph unreadable*)

This stone is Erected | In Memory of | Mr John Collens wh | Died February 25th 1792 | in the 52d year of his | Age | This mortal must put | on Immortality |

In | Memory of | Thomas Coe | who departed this life | Febr 23rd A. D. 1810 | in the 83rd year | of his age |

In | Memory | Mrs Mary relict of | Mr Thomas Coe | who died | Sept 10, 1812 | Aged 85 |

In Memory of | Mr. James Cranston | Who Died August | ye 10th 1771 in ye | 59th year of his age |

Mary (*relict of ?*) | James Cranston & Mr Joshua Garritt who died | Jan 23d A. D. 1798 | in the 81st year | of her age | *Footstone:* | Mrs. Mary Garritt |

In memory of | Mr. Buzi (?) Cranston | Who Died Septbr ye 2nd | 1772 in ye 22nd Year of | his age |

In Memory of | Mr James Cranston | Who Died Decembr | ye 20th, 1783 in ye 29th Year of | his Age |

Mrs. | Avis Cranston | wife of | Elon Cranston | died April 30, 1828 | æ 65 |

Elon Cranston | died | May 27, 1837 | aged 77 years |

To the Memory of | Joseph Platt Cooke, M. D. | Born Feb. 9, 1808 | Died Jan 15, 1835 |

Zebulun Colver | Age 90 |

Eleanor Culver | Age 82 |

E. C. | Ebenezer Clark | died | Nov 5, 1848 | Æ 80 |

In Memory of | Elizabeth, wife of | Ebenezer Clark | who died jan 4th 1802 | Aged 27 years |

Mr | Ebenezer Clark | died March 26, 1820 | in his 23, year |

The Bodies of | Peggy | and | Harriot W. Collier | lie here | Peggy died Dec 1, 1794 | Harriot Aug 26, 1794 |

Elizabeth | Wife of | William Clark | Died Oct 3, 1875 | æ 52 |

In | memory of | Lieut. Thomas Catlin | who died | Dec 9, 1829 | in the 93 year | of his age |

In Memory | of | Mrs. Avis Catlin | wife of | Mr. Thomas Catlin | who died | June 24th 1807 | aged 62 |

To the memory of | Elizabeth daughter of | the Rev. Judah Champion | born Sept 1, 1759 | died Sept. 28, 1817 |

Elizabeth Champion | relict of Rev. Judah Champion | died | Oct 30, 1823, in the 87, year | of her age | Irene Champion | their daughter | died April 30, 1834 | in the 62. year | of her age |

In | Memory of the | Rev. Judah Champion | who died | Oct 8th A. D. 1810 | in the 82d year of his age | and in the 57th year | of his Ministry. |

Elon Crampton,* Jr. | Died | May 30, 1837 | æ 47 |

Caleb Croswell | died | Sept 23, 1803 | Aged 27 |

Alexander Cameron | born in Rossshire | Scotland | Feb. 29, 1864 | died | May 21, 1898 |

Anna E | daughter of | Levi & | Lucretia E. Curtiss | died | Mar. 15, 1869 | æ 5 yrs & 3 mo |

Jessie M. | daughter of | Levi & Lucretia E. | Curtiss | died | Oct 1, 1865 | æ 4 y'rs 6 mo | & 22 d's |

Eveline | Daughter of Clark | & Ruth Carrington | Died | Aug 26, 1824 | æt 12. |

Azuba Carrington | relict of | Jonathan Carrington | died | Jan 11, 1835 | aged 85 |

Nabby | Wife of | Jonathan Carrington | Died May 28, 1857 | æ 56 |

Jona. Carrington | Died | Sept 2, 1859 | æ 75 |

Hannah | wife of | Martin Corcoran | died | Aug 12, 1888 | æ 59 |

---

*Is not this a mistake of the stonecutter's, possibly, for *Cranston?*

Jerusha | the wife of | doctor Abel Catlin | died Oct 22, 1805 | aged 41 |

Abel Catlin, M. D. | Born March 16, 1770 | Died Jan 13, 1856 |

In Memory of |
Capt. Thomas | Catlin Jr. | who died | Nov 29, 1827, | Aged 63 yrs |

|| Mary wife of | Capt Thomas Catlin | who died | Oct 22, 1827. | aged 63 y'rs |

Eleanora S. | died | May 3, 1837 | æ 3 y's & 21 d's | Emma A. | died | April 30, 1837 | æ 8 mo's & | 4 d's | Children of | Cyrus & | Emeline A. Catlin |

Jane | wife of | James H. Cooke | & daughter of | Jonathan Buel | died | Dec 11, 1846 | æ 34 | Also an infant buried by her side |

J. H. Cooke | died | Nov. 2, 1859 | æ 49 |

B. C. | Betsey daughter of | Roger & Elizabeth Cook | died June 8th 1808 | æt 16 |

In memory of | Mrs Elizabeth Cook | Consort of Roger Cook | who died June 11th 1807 | aged 31 years |

Grove Catlin | born Dec 1, 1755 | died Sept 29, 1829 | aged 73 years | 10 months |

Silas E. Chiney | died | Sept 2, 1821 | aged 44 years |

M. C. | In memory of | Mary, daughter of | William & | Sally Chittenden | who departed this life | Dec 25, 1820 | aged 8 years & 8 mon's |

Mr. | Stephen Clarke | Died | Sept 18, 1828 | æt 53 ]

Mrs. Roxana Clarke | relict of | Mr. Stephen Clarke | died | Jan 19, 1837 | aged 73 |

Edward G. | son of | Seth & | Caroline Catlin | Born Dec 6, 1831 | Died Jan 21, 1833 |

Caroline A. | daughter of | Seth & | Caroline Catlin | born June 1 ( ?) 1828 | died May 4, 1837 |

Seth Catlin | died | Nov 18, 1841 | æ 37 |

Caroline G. Catlin | wife of Seth Catlin | died | July 13, 1883 | Aged 78 |

Guy Catlin | died Feb 11, 1861 | Aged 42 |

Achsah Catlin | died | June 4, 1841 | æ 24 |

Mrs Levi Catlin | died Sept 24, 1868 | æ 90 |

Levi Catlin | died | Oct 16, 1841 | æ 69 |

In memory of | Susan C. | wife of | George Cook | who died |
Dec. 14, 1837 | in the 35 year of her age |

George Cook | died | Feb 28, 1883 | Aged 82 |

Sarah Woodruff | wife of | George Cook | died Sept 4, 1894 |
Aged 91 |

In | memory of | Mary E. Cook | who died | June 3, 1837 |
aged 24 years |

Thomas B. Cook | died Oct 6, 1838 | æ 15 yrs | & 9 mo |

Eliza Cook | died | Jan 1, 1877 | æ 85 |

Virgilius G. Cook | died | Sept 17, 1841 | æ 27 |

Eliza M. | Wife of | Arthur D. Catlin | Died Feb 13, 1859 |
æ 29 |

Isabelle S. | daughter of | Leonard | & Ann D. | Carring-
ton | died | Sept 12, 1851 | æ 1 y'r & 2 mo. |

David M. Candee | of the 2 Ct. H. A. | Died in the Ander-
sonville Prison | Oct 31, 1864 | Aged 33 | His remains could
not be recovered | Charlie | son of D. M. & Helen Candee |
Died at Litchfield Aug 21, 1864 | Aged 6 mo. | 4 d's |

Edward O. Crossman | born | Sept 2, 1847 | died | July 1,
1886 |

Ellen Jane | Daughter of | Wm H. & Mary Ann | Cross-
man | Died Feb. 10, 1856 | æ 13 |

Mary Ann Wentworth | wife of | Wm H. Crossman | died |
Sept 24, 1872 | æ 58 |

William H. Crossman | born | Oct 18, 1814 | died | July 4,
1884 |

George Crutch | Born in | Woodstock, Oxfordshire | Eng-
land | Feb 5, 1834 | died | Aug 31, 1896 |

Mary | Wife of | Aaron Crutch | died Feb 10, 1880 | æ 36 |

M. L. C. (*Crutch?*)

In memory of | Captain | George M. Colvocoresses | U. S. Navy | Born at Scio, Grecian Archipelago | Departed this life June 3, 1872 | Aged 50 Years || COLVOCORESSES || Eliza T. Halsey | wife of | Capt G. M. Colvocoresses | Born at Newark, N. J. | Oct 15, 1827 | Died at Norrich, Vt., | Aug. 23, 1862 ||

Edith B. | daughter of | George P. & | Minnie D. | Colvocoresses | born Aug 7, 1876, | died July 3, 1877 |

Henry R. Coit | born at Plainfield, Ct. | Oct 5, 1820 | died at Litchfield Ct. | Mch 31, 1887 | COIT |

Silas E. Cheney 1777-1821 | his wife | Mary Young | died March 11, 1874 | Charlotte M. Cheney | 1810-1886 | Silas E Cheney Jr. | 1820-1894 | CHENEY || Mary Ida | 1864-1864 |

Charles Daniels | Aug. 8, 1828 | Mar. 14, 1872 |

Charles F. Daniels | Jan 9, 1849 | Aug. 3, 1903 |

In Memory of Capt | Michael Dickinson | Who Died July ye | 25 1784 in ye | 44th year of his Age |

> Here from Earthly
> Joyes I am fled unto
> Ye Mansions of ye Dead
> Prepare Reader for
> thou must Like me be
> Buried in the            Dust.

In Memory of | Abigail | wife of Mr Daniel Lord | and former consort of Capt | Michael Dickinson who died | Dec 22, 1817 æ 74 |

Briget | wife of | James O. Day | died | May 28, 1845 | Aged 29 |

Lucretia Deming | born | August 13th 1804 | died | April 29th, 1887 |

Mary Deming | daughter of | Julius & Dorothy | Deming | Born Oct 16, 1798 | died April 18, 1847 | aged 48 years |

Dorothy Deming | daughter of | Julius & Dorothy | Deming | born Dec 29, 1784 | died Oct 24, 1835 | aged 50 years |

Julius Deming | born April 16, 1755 | died January 23, 1838 | aged 82 |

Dorothy Deming | wife of | Julius Deming | born Oct 29, 1759 | died Dec 4, 1830 | aged 71 years |

Erected to the memory | of | Julius Deming, Jun. | who was born July 28, 1782 | and died at New-Haven August 8, 1799 | Aged 17 Years 11 Days |

Charles Deming | born | December 23rd 1789 | died | April 26th 1852 |

William Deming | Born Mar. 1, 1792 Died May 2, 1865 | Charlotte T. Bull | Wife of William Deming | Born May 30, 1807 Died June 16, 1886 | DEMING || Adelaide Louisa | Born Feb 14, 1831 Died Dec 26, 1851 | Emma Dorathea | Born June 2, 1835 Died June 17, 1885 | Daughters of William and Charlotte T. Deming ||

Stephen Deming | Born Dec 19, 1780 | Died June 29, 1867 | Sarah Buel Deming | Born June 7, 1784 | Died Mar 31, 1860 |

In | Memory of Buel H. Deming | son of | Stephen & Sarah Deming | Born July 15, 1805 | Died May 1, 1826 | while a member of the Law- | School in Litchfield |

Erected | to the memory of | Frances B. Deming | daughter of Stephen & | Sarah Deming | who died | of a consumption | Oct 6, 1828 | aged 14, years & | 8 months |

In | memory of | Col Henry B. | son of | Stephen & | Sarah Deming | born Feb 24, 1812 | died July 4, 1837 | æ 25 y's. 4 mo. | & 10 d's |

Here | Rest the remains | of | John Sanford Dart | Son of | Isaac Motte & | Arabella A. Dart | of Charleston S. C. | who died at this place | on he 9 of Apr. 1823 | æ 22 y'rs & 5 mo's || Although | It was the fate of this youth to die, | Remote from the home of his friends | and among those who were | Comparatively, strangers | Yet he received, in his last hours | The kindest offices of friendship & | Humanity: | In commemoration | Of which, and of her maternal | Affections, his bereaved & surviving | Parent has caused this humble | MEMORIAL | To be erected |

Minerva | wife of | Samuel Delliber | died | Feb 17, 1842 | æ 53 |

Louisa Deming | born May 8, 1822 | died Dec 27, 1892 || DEMING || Frederick Deming | Born Sept 9, 1873 | died July 15, 1892 |

William Deming | born | March 16, 1833 | died | September 20, 1891 |

In | Memory of | Charles W. | son of | Nehemiah C. & | Cynthia Ann Edwards | who died | Aug. 5, 1848 | æ 23 |

In | Memory of | Cynthia Ann | wife of | Nehemiah C. Edwards | & daughter of Louden & | Mary Ann Webster | who died | Mar 24, 1844 | æ 39 |

Nehemiah C. Edwards | died | Mar 31, 1854 | æ 52 |

David R. Ensign | 1841—1893 |

........ine wife of | Harry Fitch | Died March 12 | 1817, æ 41 | Abigail Fleming (?) Died Nov 1, | 1816 | æt 13 |

Cornelia A. Winship | wife of | Walter Filley died | Mar 21, 1857 | æ 31 |

Grace C | only child of | Walter & Cornelia | Filley | died | Dec 24, 1860 | æ 3 yrs, 10 mo | & 11 d's |

Julia C. | wife of Asa J. French | died | Dec 9, 1846 | Aged 31 |

Charles Freeman | died | Oct 16, 1859 | æ 41 years |

Cato Freeman | died | July 27, 1840, aged 78 |

Royal A. Ford | 1818—1887 | Marina Buell | his wife | 1818—1890 |

Walter | Son of Guerdon | & Polly Filley | Died | April 6, 1825 | aged 3 years | & 7 months |

In| memory of | Hannah Huntington | wife of | Rev. Frederick Freeman | daughter of Frederick & Betsey | Wolcott | Born Jan 14, 1803 | Died Feb 26, 1838 (?) | Hannah | Infant daughter of | Frederick & Hannah H. Freeman | Born Dec 1838 | Died June 1839 |

Sarah P. Fish | daughter of | Lodovick & | Susan Fish | died | May 2, 1830 | aged 18 years | Samuel | her brother | died | Sept 17, 1821 | aged 13 years |

> Early and sudden their lamented fate,
> Soon and surprising the destroyer came.

Betsey A. | wife of | Nelson H. Ford | died Oct. 18, 1851 | æt 42 |

Albert N. | son of | Nelson H. | and | Betsey A. Ford | died| June 9, 1849 | æt 15 |

Guerdon Filley | died | Oct. 24, 1866, | æ 72 |

Polly | wife of | Guerdon Filley | died | June 1, 1876 | æ 79 |

Samuel | son of Rev. | Samuel Fuller, Jr. | Rector of St. Michael's Church | in this village | and Charlotte Kingman | his wife, born | Dec 15, 1832 | died | Feb 6, 1837 |

Kenneth | Aged 1 year | & 8 mo's | (*Fisher*)

Lilian A. | daughter of | Charles C. & | Harriet E. | Fisher | died Aug. 2, 1873 | æ 12 y'rs & 3 Mos |

Sergt. | Charles C. Fisher | Co. I. 13, Regt. | Conn Vols. | died | Dec 28, 1888 |

Lieut George W. Fish | Co F 3, Ohio | Vol. Infantry | Died at Muscatine, Iowa | May 3, 1866 | Aged 28 | Interred here May 13 |

Temperance Ford | died | Feb 12, 1873 | æ 70 |

Heman Ford | died | Aug. 18, 1872 | æ 74 |

Phebe Ford | died | Sept 4, 1859 | æ 99 yr. & 5 mo |

Daniel Ford | died | Sept 17, 1838 | æ 84 |

Arthur Butler | eldest son of | William John and Mary Ann| Fitz Gerald |

Huldah, daughter | of Joshua and E- | zabiah Garrit who | departed this life | february ye 5 th 1793 | she was 8 mo | nths and twenty days o!d. |

Daniel Garritt | died | July 28, 1849 | æ 75 |

Huldah | wife of | Daniel Garritt | died | April 23, 1857 | æ 81 |

In | Memory of Abba daughter of | David & | Huldah Garritt| who died | May 25, 1823 | in her 19 year |

In | Memory of | Anna, daughter of | David & Huldah Garritt | who died | July 9, 1820 | in her 21st year |

In | Memory of | Roxana wife of | Joshua Garritt | & daughter of | Joseph & | Abigail Foote | who died | June 19, 1824 | æ 18 |

In memory of | Joshua F. Garritt | who died | Aug. 30th 1824 | aged 4 months |

Mary Ann | wife of | Daniel Garritt Jr. | & daughter of | Lemuel & Nancy Smith | died Aug 8, 1844 | aged 28 |

Daniel Garritt, Jr. | died | Aug 27, 1846 | Aged 31 |

Harriet L. Grant | born | September 9, 1814 | died | January 3, 1892 |

David M. Grant | born | August 11, 1812 | died | Sept 6, 1885 |

Paulina E. | wife of | David M. Grant | died June 27, 1873 | aged 49 years |

Caroline B. | wife of David M. Grant | died | Nov. 7, 1865 | aged 34 years & 3 mo's |

Charles W. Grant | born | April 28, 1810 | died | January 17, 1881 |

H. J. S. | Jacobus Gould L. L. D. | Hujus Reipublicae | Curiae Supremae | Olim | Judidicus | Obiit | Die | undecimo Maii | Anno Domini | MDCCCXXXVIII | Ætatis suae LXVIII | Filii posuerunt |

Julia | Daughter of James Gould | Born Nov 7, 1809 | Died Feb 24, 1872 |

Henry Guy Gould | son of James Gould | Died at Litchfield June 25, 1875 | æt 74 |

Sally McCurdy | widow of | James Gould | Born Feb'y 14, 1783 | died May 20, 1847 |

Edward Sherman Gould | son of James & | Sally McCurdy Gould | Born May 11, 1805 | Died Feb 21, 1885 |

Mary Susan | daughter of | James & | Sally McC. Gould | was born March | 5, 1824 & | died | in the evening of the same date. |

In Memory of | John W. Gould | son of | James & Sally Mc C. Gould | who died Oct 1, 1838. | in the 24 year of his age. | At sea, on board the Brig Tweed | in Lat. 40° 41′ So. Long. | 35° 50′ W, On his passage | from Rio de Janeiro to the United States. |

Mrs. Mary Gould | relict of William Gould Esq | of Branford | died on the 15, day of | Sept 1816 | in the 79 year of her age. |

In Memory of | James Reeve Gould | son of James & Sally McCurdy Gould | who died at Augusta, Ga | Oct 11, 1830 | Closing a useful, exemplary | & blameless life | by a peaceful but much | lamented death | in the humble & joyful hope of | Glory & Honor & Immortality | æ 27 |

EAST CEMETERY—I. JUDGE GOULDS

Sacred to | the memory of | Ruth Goodwin | wife of Russel Goodwin | who died | June 30, 1831, | aged 64 years |

In | Memory of | widow Lucretia Guernsey | who deceased on the | 23ᵈ day of March 1809 | aged 67 years |

> Here rests secure from wordly cares,
> One whose life furnished signal examples
> of Industry charity and unassuming piety
> Reader imitate her virtues
> And your reward will be like hers.

Hannah | wife of Ambrose Grant | died | July 3, 1832 | æ 87 |

In | Memory of | Mʳ Ambrose Grant | who died | Dec 7, 1816 | æ 69 |

Hannah Mc Neil | Relict of | Charles Grant | Born July 8ᵗʰ 1785 | Died Sept 2ⁿᵈ 1871 |

In | Memory of | Mʳ Charles Grant | who died | March 10, 1821 | aged 38 years | 10 mon. & 15 da. |

Mrs. | Naomi | Gillet | wife of Asa Gillet | died Jan. 30, 1828 | Aged 57 |

Elizabeth L. Gates | died | July 9, 1886 | æ 57 |

Aaron C. Gilbert | died | Nov 30, 1842 | æ 69 |

Betsey | wife of Aaron C. Gilbert | died | Oct 3, 1840 | æ 60|

Moses Gilbert | died | Apr 2, 1870 | æ 93 |

Patty | wife of | Moses Gilbert | died | Dec 12, 1862 | Aged 77 |

Wᵐ W. Gernon | died | Feb 27, 1859 | æ 27 |

Albert | Son of | Rev Hiram A & | Mary H. Graves | Died Aug. 1847 | æ 14 Mo's |

Ann P. Gillon | relict of | Com. Alexander | Gillon | of Charleston, S. C. | died May 13, 1844 | aged 75 years |

Henry B. Graves | April 4, 1823,—Aug 10, 1891|GRAVES| Lucy | Gerard |

Charlotte Wessel's | Daughter of | Howard E. & Grace M. | Gates | Died Nov. 3, 1885 | Aged 2 y'rs |

Chloe Haywood | Died | Mar. 13, 1866 | æ 70 | The faithful servant of | Rev. Truman & Clarissa | Marsh |

In | memory of | M^r Benjamin Hart | who died | Jan 30, 1831 | æt 78 |

In | memory of | Martha | wife of | Isaac Hart | who died | Apr 8, 1839 | Aged 52 years |

In | memory of | Isaac Hart | who died | Mar. 6, 1834 | aged 47 years |

In | memory of | Hannah Hart | wife of | Benjamin Hart | who died | April 20, 1833 | aged 79 years |

Hannah Law | wife of | Andrew Hawley | died | March 15 | 1885 | Aged 73 y'rs |

Amelia O. Perkins | wife of | A W. Healy | died | August 9, 1870 |aged 32 | William Edwin | Their infant son |

Sally | Relict of | John Hubbard | Died Aug 17, 1862 | æ. 90. |

To | the memory of | Gen'l John Hubbard | Died | May 5, 1837, æ 86 y'rs |

In | Memory of | Mr. William Hosford | who died | Feb. 5, 1802 | æt 63 |

Lewellyn F. | Son of | Elijah W. & Mary A. | Hewitt | Died Oct 7, 1853 | æ 19 |

> Look, youth and view this silent tomb,
> Nor think this life a lasting home,
> Improve your time and God adore.
> You soon like me will be no more.

Abby Maria Hand | daughter of | Stephen P. & | Julia J. Hand | died Feb 11, 1829 | æ 19 years, 9 mo's | & 8 days |

In memory of | Uriel Holmes Jun'r|who died July 4^th 1818 | aged 22 years | A member of the Theological | Seminary, Andover |

Henry Holmes M. D. | born | Feb 14, 1795 | died | July 31, 1870 |

To the Memory of | Esther Holmes | Wife of | Uriel Holmes Jr | Daughter of | Aaron Austin Esq^r | and M^rs Esther Austin | Born May 6^th 1772 | Died August 30^th 1802 |

To the Memory of | Caroline Holmes | Daughter of | Uriel Holmes Jr | and Esther Holmes | Born May 12^th 1796 | Died May 28, 1802 |

Hon. Uriel Holmes | Died at Canton | May 18, 1827 | æt 62 |

In | Memory of | M^r John Hosford | who died | Feb 8, 1812 | æt 72 |

Thomas Coe Hart | died | Dec 28, 1839 | æ 33 |

In |memory of | Rhoda | wife of | Worham Harvey | who died | Oct 2, 1833 | aged 26 years |

Wolcott | son of Worham & | Rhoda Harvey | died | Oct 25, 1828 | æt 8 mo's |

Lucy Maria | daughter of Harvy (?) | and Lucy Hatch | died Nov 18, 1814 | aged 15 months | An Infant son | died Nov 2, 1816 |

To the memory of | Mary Ward Hubbard | who died | Sept 11, 1813 | aged 28 years | (*In Beecher lot*)

Caroline Louisa Head (?) | Aged 4 yrs 4 mos | Died Oct^r 9^th 1828 |

In | memory of | Henry D. | son of | Jacob & | Lucetta Hubbard | who died | Aug 18, 1831 | aged 9 years | & 7 months |

Mary D. | daughter of | Jacob & Lucy | Hubbard | died | Nov 11, 1818 | aged 3 months | & 24 days |

In | Memory of | Polly wife of | Jacob Hubbard | who died | Jan 11, 1815 | Aged 24 years |

Joseph Hubbard | died | Nov 27, 1822 | æt 54 yrs | Also | Lydia wife of | Joseph Hubbard | died | Nov 22, 1848 | æt 80 years |

Julia A. Hand | died | May 27, 1855 | æ 68 |

Candace | wife of | Canfield Hayden | Died Apr 14, 1869 | Aged 71 |

Gideon H. Hollister | 1817-1881 | Mary S. Brisbane | his wife | ———— | Robert Treate, 1856-1866 | John Brisbane | ———— | sons of | Gideon H. and Mary S. Hollister |

Abbot Brisbane | son of | G. H. & M. S. | Hollister | Born Age 5, 1850 | Died June 24, 1859 |

Gertrude | daughter of | G. H. & M. S. | Hollister | died Sept 13, 1849 | aged 16. mo's |

Lieut | Geo. Benjamin | Son of Elisha & | Elizabeth Hempstead | Born at Bath, N. Y. | Jan 19, 1838 | Wounded June 22, | Died at City Point Hospital | June 29, 1864 |

Caroline Elizabeth | Daughter of | Elisha & Elizabeth | Hempstead | Died July 30, 1861 | æ 18 y'rs 1 mo & 4 dys |

Elisha Hempstead | Died | Mar 12, 1855 | æ 59 |

Elizabeth L. | Wife of | Elisha Hempstead | Died | June 10, 1877 | æ 75 |

Lydia Hotchkiss | died | Jan 4, 1860 | æ 85 y'rs |

Mary Hotchkiss | died | Sept 9, 1851 | æt 75 y'rs |

Augustus P. Hinman | died | Jan 12, 1854 | æ 57 |

Harriet M. | wife of | A. P. Hinman | died | Sept. 24, 1852 | æt 55 |

Cornelia B. | daughter of | A. P. & H. M. | Hinman | died | Oct 22, 1846 | aged 15 |

Mary D. | daughter of | Augustus P. & | Harriet M. Hinman | died | Sept 16, 1840 | aged 6 years |

Elias Hull | born | April 15, 1782 | died Jan 21, 1862 |

Seney | wife of | Elias Hull | born Jan 15, 1783 | died May 5, 1849 |

Chauncey M. Hooker | born | Dec 3, 1816 | died | Jan 16, 1872 |

Caroline M. | Wife of | C. M. Hooker | Died | July 1, 1852 | æ 23 |

Francis M. Hale | died | Aug 4, 1896 | æ 74 | Lydia A. | his wife | Died Feb 22, 1872 | æ 48 |

Mary Elizabeth | daughter of | Jennie E. & Isaac H. | Hutchinson | Jan 9, 1878 | Sept 8, 1878 || HUTCHINSON || (*See Wheeler*)

Caroline | daughter of Martin & Barbary | Iffland | died | Oct 11, 1864 | æ 10 mos |

Bertha E. | daughter of | Hubert S. & | Ellen A. Ives | born | Nov 21, 1866 |died | June 8, 1880 |

Hubert L. Ives | died | Feb 11, 1868 | æ 34 |

Meriman C. | Son of | Eliza Jackson | died | Dec 8 1833 | aged 9 months |

Sarah S. Johnson | died Nov 22, 1867 | Aged 26 |

In | Memory of | Eben Judson | who died | Sept. 17, 1864 |
æ 77 |

In | memory of | Polly | wife of | Eben Judson | who died |
Feb 8, 1873 | æ 87 |

Elijah Judson | departed this life | Feb 4, 1826 | aged 79
years |

Abigail Judson | wife of | Elijah Judson | died Jan 21, 1819 |
aged 64 years |

Helen Maria | daughter of | Hiram & | Harriet Jackson |
died | Jan 25, 1837 | æ 8 y'rs |

Hiram Jackson | died | Jan 3, 1866 | Aged 70 |

Maria Jones | daughter of | Eaton & | Mary Jones | died |
Nov 24, 1847 | æ 52 |

Mary | wife of | Capt. Eaton Jones | died | Sept 22, 1841 |
æ 71 |

In | memory of | Capt Eaton Jones | who died | Jan 5, 1838 |
aged 76 |

Julia Henrietta | daughter of | Rev Isaac Jones | died | Nov
14, 1851 | aged 46 |

Tabitha | wife of the | Rev. Isaac Jones | born at Wood-
bridge | May 18, 1787 | died at Litchfield | Oct 9, 1852 | æ 65 |

Rev | Isaac Jones | born at New Haven | Feb 18, 1775 |
died at Litchfield | March 17, 1850 | æ 75 |

Eva Freelon | daughter of | G. M. & Eliza F. | Colvoco-
resses | wife of | George Eaton Jones | Born at Norwich, Vt. |
Died at Litchfield, Conn. | Nov. 18, 1875 | æ 22 Y'rs. & 4 Mos |

Mary | daughter of | John M. & | Mary Kienley | died Apr
13, 1863 | æ 1 yr. 5 mo. 12 Ds |

Harriot Kirby | Daughter of | Ephraim Kirby, Esq | & Mrs.
Ruth Kirby | was born | the 20 of March | A D 1788 | and
died | the 25th of Aug. A. D. 1789 | aged 17 months and 5 days |

Ruth Kirby | daughter of | Reynold Marvin | Esquire | and
wife of the | Hon. Ephraim Kirby | Ob. Oct. 17, A. D. 1817, |
æt 57 years | 9 months | and 27 days |

Harriette W. | wife of | E. Barstow Kellogg | and daughter
of Reuben M & Eliza R. | Woodruff | born | Aug 6, 1843. |
died | Oct 17, 1889 |

Charles Catlin | only child of | Truman C. & Ellen | Kilbourn | Died Sept 12, 1866 | æ 10 M'os |

Aurelia | wife of | Frederick Koehler | died | Apr. 22, 1886| Aged 33 |

Levi Lepian | Died Feb 5, 1867 | æ 67 | His wife | Maria | Died Oct 24, 1840 | æ 34 |

Henry | son or | Levi & Maria Lepeon | Died | Oct 23, 1834 |

Morris | son of | Levi & | Maria Lepian | died | Oct 7, 1839| aged 10 mo's |

In Memory of Mrs | Hannah late Consort | of Mr. Daniel Lord | who Departed this | life the Sixteenth | Day of December AD | 1785 in the 42ᵈ year | of her age |

Oh Ruin (Vain?) is Grief when Life
Extent and Fled the Sluggish
Mass Returns not from the
Dead, not Sorrow Tears
Nor Mourning can Retrieve
The Clay Cold Victim
From the Opening Grave.

In Memory of | Patty Daughter of Daniel | and Hannah Lord | who died Nov. | yᵉ 1, 1778 in the | 5 year of her age |

In Memory of | Daniel Lord | who died | June 9, 1828, æt 84. |

In Memory of | Huldah Daughter | to Mr. Daniel and | Mrs Abigail Lord | who Died May 29, | A D 1789 in the 28 (?) 2ᵈ (?) | Year of her age |

Belinda | Daughter of | Capt. Phineas | & Mrs. Polly Lord | died Aug. 11, 1822 | æt 14 |

Benedict A. Law | died Jan 31, 1856 | aged 80. |

In | Memory of | Thankful | wife of | Benedict A. Law | who died | Nov 25, 1829 | aged 51 years |

Here | Lies the Body of | Elizabeth | the Daughter of Mr Gershom & | Mrs Mary Lewis | who died Augst | the 19th 1767 In the | 21st year of her Age |

Here (lies) (?) the.... of Mr Gershom Lewis | who died October | the..th A. D. 1766 | in the 62ᵈ year of h.. Age |

In Memory of | Mrs Mary relict | ........ | ........86th | .... of her Age | (Footstone): | Mary Lewis |

Sacred | to the Memory | of Ozias Lewis | who died | March 8th 1812 | Aged 62 | Who loved thee living; and laments thee dead | Pays this last tribute to thy gentle shade |

Lucy | relict of | Ozias Lewis | born | Nov 18, 1752 died | April 19, 1840 |

Eli Todd Lewis | Son of | Daniel W. Lewis & | Elizabeth his wife | died Aug. 16th 1798 Aged 4 years | It is sown a natural body | It is raised a spiritual body | Suffer little children | to come unto me and forbid them not for of such is |the Kingdom of God |

Dudley Saltonstall Lewis | Son of Daniel W. Lewis & | Elizabeth his wife, | died Dec 25, 1793, | Aged 16 months |

Mary J. | wife of | George Leach | Died June 6, 1862 | æ 43 |

In | Memory of | Gilbert R. | son of James | R. & Charlotte| Livingston | æ 17 mo-s |

In |memory of | Luke Lewis | who was born | March 25, 1769 | died Dec 6, 1839 |

Mary H. Lewis | wife of | Luke Lewis | born | Mar. 17, 1772 | died | Dec 3, 1856 | Aged 84 |                    ffl

Amelia Catherine | daughter of Luke & | Mary H. Lewis | born Oct 27 1799 | died March 24, 1820 |

Jane Roxana | daughter of Luke & | Mary H. Lewis | born Jan 14, 1806 | died Jan 10, 1830 |

Mary Ann Lewis | born | Feb 1, 1797 | died | June 7, 1884 |

Mary W. Lord | died | Aug 29th 1864, | Aged 62 years |

LEWIS

Ozias Lewis|died|Dec 23, 1860 | aged 83 years | ‖ Mary Jones | his wife | Died ‖ Aug 31, 1850|Aged 74 years|

Lucy Bigelow | daughter of | Ozias & | Mary Lewis | born Dec 18, 1804 | died Mar 14, 1883 |

Jennette Lynde | born Mar. 6, 1813 | died Oct 12, 1819 | Julia | born Jan 19. 1817 | died Nov 16, 1819 | Children of | Ozias & | Mary Lewis |

Charles Sidney | son of | Ozias Jr. & | Mary Lewis | died | June 18, 1804 | aged 18 mo |

Albert | A. P. L. | (*Lewis*)

George Sidney | son of | Dr. Algernon S. & | Cornelia M. Lewis | died | Dec 17, 1838 | aged 5 yrs 2 mo | & 10 d's |

Algernon Sidney Lewis, M. D. | born | Dec 10, 1807 | Entered into rest | Oct 3, 1870 | Cornelia M. Lewis | born | April 21, 1809 | Entered into rest | Apr 19, 1890 |

Willis Law | died | Feb. 26, 1860 | æ 40 y'rs & 3 mo. |

Susan B. | wife of | Willis Law | died | July 21, 1877 |Aged 57 |

He'en | Louisa | daughter of | Willis & | Susan M. Law | died | July 8, 1857 | Aged 10 |

William Lim | born | in Bolsover, Eng. | Apr 16, 1816 | died at Litchfield | Apr. 27, 1875.

Phineas Lord | died Oct 10, 1842 | aged 66 | Mary Candee | his wife | ——— | LORD || Daniel | son of Phineas & Mary | Lord | died Aug 21, 1866 | aged 66 || Belinda | daughter of | Phineas & Mary Lord |died Aug 11, 1822 | aged 14 | Mary | daughter of | Phineas & Mary Lord | ——|| David C. | son of Phineas & Mary | Lord | died Dec 15, 1840 | aged 37 |

William Wisner Lockwood | born Sept 16th, 1893 | died Sept 20th 1895 |

Beneath this Tomb | there lies intered | the Body of | Mrs. Sarah consort | of Capt. Archibald | McNeile, who departed | this life March the 21st | A. D. 1785 in the 72nd | Year of her Age | (*epitaph undecipherable*).

Here lies Inter^d the Body of | Capt. Archibald McNeil who | Departed this life Jen. 8th | 1789 in the 81st year of his | Age . |

Sweet soul we leave thee
to thy rest
Enjoy thy Jesus & thy
God
Till we from Bands of
clay releaset
spring out and climb the
shining road.

This monument is erec- | ted in memory of Jem- | ima Mc- Neile Cons | ort to Archibald | McNei'e who depart | ed this life Dec. 24, 1798 | in the 58th year of her age | Blessed are the dead which die in | the Lord |

In | Memory of | Capt. Archibald McNeill | who died | Jan 31, 1813 | Aged 76 years |

Eliza McNeil | Daughter of John | & Polly McNeil died | May 15, 1831 | æ 24 |

> Slow waves the willow o'er the stone
> That marks where sleeps a friend most dear
> Oft have I sought the spot alone
> To shed at ease the friendly tear.

| Erected by Aaron B. Caul | J. L. Church, Fecit |

In memory of | John McNeil| who died | Feb 26, 1854 | æt 80 |

Polly wife of | John McNeile | Died | May 6, 1860 | æ 81 |

Samuel McNeil | died | Aug 27, 1863 | æ 82 | Lavinnia | his wife died | Dec 24, 1874 | æ 92 |

In | Memory of | Capt Isaac McNeil | who died | Oct 31, 1821 | in the 74 year | of his age |

To the | memory of | Lewis J. McNeil | who departed this | life Oct 19, 1829 æ 20 |

> How soon we part; and one by one
> Like leaves and flowers the group is gone.
> One gentle spirit seeks the tomb,
> His brow yet fresh with childhood's bloom.

Juliette | daughter of | Samuel & | Levinia McNeil | died Oc 5 1821 | æt 1 year | & 7 months |

> Happy infant early blest
> Rest in peaceful slumbers, rest.

Char'es L. | son of | Samuel & | Lavina McNeil | born Dec 8, 1825 | died June 26, 1830 |

Roxana C. Morse | wife of | Harmon C. Morse | died | Feb 22, 1885 | aged 69 years |

Sidney N. Morse | died | Nov 8, 1879 | Aged 25 years | Only Son of Harmon C. Morse |

In Memory of | M^rs Elizabeth | the wife of M^r | Amos Moss | who died | April the 15^th ( ?) 1767 in the . . ^th | . . ar of her . . . . |

In | memory | of | Joshua Mason | who died | Nov 17, 1813 | Aged 77 years |

In | memory of Anne Mason | wife of | Joshua Mason | who died | June 4, 1814 | aged 78 years |

Charlotte | daughter of | Aaron & Rhoda Moss | died | Aug. 16, 1832 | aged 14 months |

In | memory of | Mehetable | widow of | John Morse | who died | June 22, 1840 | aged 87 |

In | Memory of | Mr John Moss (*Morse*) | who died |Aug 17, 1820 | aged 69 years |

Mathew Morse | died | Sept 29, 1852 | aged 48 |

Minerva | wife of | Matthew Morse | died | Oct 13, 1852 | aged 50 |

In | memory of | Eliza wife of | Matthew Morse | who died May 9, 1838, | Aged 31 years |

Amos Moss | died April 23, 1851 | æt 78 | Caleb A. Moss | his son | died | at New Orleans | Dec. 5, 1837 | æ 25 |

Betsey P. | wife of | Amos Moss | died | Aug 13, 1850 | æ 53. |

Sarah H. Murray | born | March 9, 1799 | died | July 13, 1879 |

Holmes O. Morse | died June 5, 1898 | MORSE |

Philo Moss | died | Dec. 9, 1841 | æ 72 |

Isla E. | daughter of | Albert L. & | Lizzie R. Morse | died | Sept 7, 1873 | Aged 1 mo. |

In Memory of | Mrs Elizabeth | McNeile wife of | Capt Adam | McNeile who De | parted this Life | May the 15th | A. D. 1756 | Aged 37 years |

In memory of | Alexander | Son of Mr. Alex. | & Mrs Deborah Mc Neile who | died March ye 7th | 1756 two (?) Months | and 4 days Old |

In Memoory of | Mr. John Marsh | Who Died Jan | ye 23rd 1781, in ye | 32d Year of his Age |

> Oh Cruel deth to Fill
> this Narrow place
> in younder house
> Left A Grate Emty
> place.

In Memory of | Ozias Marsh | y<sup>e</sup> Son of Corn'l | Ebene<sup>r</sup> Marsh | who Died Sept<sup>r</sup> y<sup>e</sup> 15<sup>th</sup> 1760 In | the 18<sup>th</sup> year of | His Age |

Here lies Interd | The Body of Colo'l | Ebenezer Marsh, Es. | Who departed this | Life April the 18<sup>th</sup> | A D 1773 in the 72<sup>nd</sup> | year of his Age |

In Memory of | M<sup>rs</sup> Deborah | Marsh Relict of | Co<sup>l</sup> Ebe<sup>r</sup> Marsh | who Died July | y<sup>e</sup> 30<sup>th</sup> 1784 in | y<sup>e</sup> 77 Year of | her Age | The sweet Remem | brance of the Inst | When Dying .... | Sleeps in dust |

To the | Memory | of | Rhoda Marsh | wife of Ebenezer Marsh | who departed this life Nov 9<sup>th</sup>, 1798 | in the 58<sup>th</sup> year of her age |

The Monument of | M<sup>rs</sup> Lucy Marsh, Consort to | Ebenezer Marsh who died | on the 14<sup>th</sup> day of February AD 1772 | in the 32<sup>d</sup> Year of her age | Ah! dear departed shade, hover once more | around this dreary Tomb: | receive our last adieu! | While the bare remembrance of Thee | in kindred Souls shall ever move | the tributary Tear : | Indulge thy Sons, Oh! fondest Parent | with tearful Eyes & aching Hearts | to raise this Monument | Sacred | to a Mother's Memory |

Sacred | to the | Memory | of | Ebenezer Marsh | who departed this Life | Oct<sup>r</sup> 30, 1807 | in the 69<sup>th</sup> year | of his age |

MARSH

Julia D. Hempstead his | Riverius Marsh | Aug. 19, wife | July 30, 1840, | 1837 | Feb. 18, 1902. |

Ann Elizabeth | Daughter of Charles & | Matilda D. Mc- Neil | died Sept 8, 1855 | æt 12 years |

> Rest, dear departed victim to the flame.
> Thy pains are ended, and thy mortal frame
> Beneath the sod is sleeping with the dead.
> But when th' Archangel's silver trump shall sound
> We trust that thou will rise with glory crowned
> By Christ, our living and all comprising Head.

Matilda D. | wife of | Charles Mc Neil | died | Aug 31, 1860 | æ 39 yrs |

Ferebe Tracy | wife of | John Mc Neil | died Jan 6, 1865 | aged 47 ! John Mc Neil | died | Aug 24, 1894 | aged 78 | Samantha Pratt | wife of | John Mc Neil | died Jan 31, 1890 | aged 60. | McNEIL || Melissa Tracy | mother of Ferebe Tracy | died Aug 9, 1870 | aged 74. |

Rev. | Truman Marsh | Late Rector of the first | Episcopal Society in Litchfield | Died Mar. 27, 1851 | æ 84 | Clarissa | His wife | and Daughter of Maj. Moses Seymour | Died Sept. 2, 1865 | æ 93 | They rest from their labors and | their works do follow them.

In Memory of | Truman Marsh | Infant Child to Rev[d] | Truman Marsh & | Clarissa Marsh | who died the 11th of | March, 1800 aged 9 | months |

In | Memory of | Delia Marsh | Daughter of Rev[d] Truman | Marsh & Clarissa Marsh | who died July 31st 1807 | aged two years & seven | months. |

Benj. Moore | Born Dec 28, 1786 | Died Mar 1870 | æ 84 | His wife | Polly | born 1790 | Died July 1863 | æ 73 |

William W. Moss. | died | Sept 28, 1843 | æ 31

S. M. | In | Memory of | Sally, wife of | John Moss | who died | Oct 15, 1830 | aged 46 |

Betsey Fenn | wife of | John Moss | died | Mar 4, 1847 | aged 65 |

John Moss | died | Mar 14, 1856 | æ 72 |

Dea. Levi Morse | died at Harlingen, N. J. | Jan 30, 1841 | æt 65 | Thalia | wife of Dea. Levi Morse | died Jan 16, 1854 | æt 78 |

In Memory of | John W. S. Marsh | Son of Ormond | & Ann Marsh died | Feb. 11, 1815, aged | 10 Months. |

Mrs. Ruth Marvin | Wife of | Reynold Marvin Esq. | and daughter of | Paul Welch, Esq. | was born Dec. 20th, 1739 | and died May 12, 1793 | Aged 53 years |

In | Memory of | Roswell Mc Neile | who died Sept 1. 1813 | Aged 66 | Also wife | Elizabeth Mc Neile | died March | 20, 1791 aged 44 |

Deborah Mc Neil | died Dec 16, 1808 | aged 82 | Rhoda Marsh | died Feb. 4, 1822 | aged 71 |

Deborah | wife of | Alexander Mc Neil | æ 82 |

Here rests the body of | Alexander Mc Neil | originally of Antrim | County in Ireland | died April 16, 1795 | aged 72 (?)

In | memory of | Mabel wife of | Isaac Mc Neil | afterwards wife of | Joel Bostwick | died April 28, 1864 | aged 72 |

Emery son of | Isaac & | Mabel Mc Neil | died | May 7, 1832 | aged 18 |

In | memory of | Isaac Mc. Neil | who died | Mar 21, 1832 | aged 51 |

Roswell Mc Neil | died | Feb 3, 1846 | aged 68 |

Olive Mc Neile | wife of | Roswell Mc Neile | died May 28, 1829 | æ 50 |

Truman Mc Neil | Died July 12, 1831 | æ 43 | Emeline E. Died Dec | 13, 1830 æ 4 y-rs | & 8 mos | Jared Died July 31, | 1831 æ 4 mo's | Children of Truman | & Elmina Mc Neil |

Elizabeth | wife of | Ebenezer Marsh | died | Feb 25, 1845 | Aged 78 |

In | memory of | Ebenezer Marsh | who died | April 25, 1827 | æt 63 |

Polly Marsh | Wife of | Samuel Marsh | died Oct 20, 1835 | Aged 32 years |

Lucy | daughter of | Ebenezer & | Elizabeth Marsh | died | Apr 1, 1838 | æ 35 years |

Henry Marsh | died | Oct 25, 1863 | æ 71 |

Susan | wife of | Benj. Mory | Born Apr 3, 1812 | Died Dec 19, 1870 |

Charles Marsh | died | April 1, 1822 | Aged 50 | Charlotte Marsh | died | Aug 14, 1857 | Aged 83 |

Lucretia | daughter of | John A. & | Esther Merriman | died | Jan 14, 1829 | æ 11 mo-s |

Reuben Merriman | died | Sept 22, 1866 | æ 83 | Melia Byington | Wife of | Reuben Merriman | died June 23, 1856 | æ 69 |

Reuben B. Merriman | died | & was buried at Fort Donelson | Feb 22, 1862 | Aged 48 | Mary A. Merriman | died | May 25, 1863 | Aged 40 |

Edward Payson | son of | Rev. J. B. Martyn | of Edgarton, Mass. | Died Nov 6, 1829 | Aged 19 weeks |

In | Memory of | Zerviah R. Miner | daughter of | Phineas Miner | who died | Feb. 3, 1839 | aged 28 |

Henry B. Miner | son of | Phineas Miner | died July 12, 1835 | aged 32 years |

In | Memory of | Hon. Phineas Miner | who died | Sept 16, 1839 | aged 60 |

Sarah Miner | Died Sept 10, 1860 | æ 74 |

Parmelia Miner | Died Nov 14, 1869 | æ 78 |

Timothy Miller | died | June 10, 1840 | Aged 54 | Anne his wife | died June 14, 1863 | Aged 80 |

Timothy E. Miller | died | Dec 17, 1884 | æ 69 |

Martha B. | wife of | Timothy E. Miller | died | April 2, 1877 | æ 65 |

An Infant | daughter of | Hiram & Mary | Merriman | died | Apr 29, 1854 | æt 3 d's |

Flora A. | wife of John Mc Mahon | & daughter of | Canfield & Candace | Hayden | died Jan 15, 1861 | aged 38 |

Olive C. | daughter of | John & Flora A. Mc Mahon | died | Dec 25, 1860 | Aged 19 |

Sarah L. | wife of | F. D. Mc Neil | born Feb. 28, 1828 | died Apr 27, 1880 |

Sarah | Daughter of | Frederick D. & | Sarah L. McNeil | born June 21, 1869 | died Aug 23, 1870 |

Frederick W. | son of | Frederick D. and | Sarah L McNeil | born Dec 26, 1856 | died Sept 2, 1866 |

Margaret Marsh | wife of | Capt George Marsh | died | Sept 2, 1841 | aged 75 |

Elizabeth Chipman | wife of | Samuel J. Marsh | Born Apr 28, 1823 | Died Dec 16, 1884 |

Georgeeanna | daughter of | Samuel & | Elizabeth Marsh | died | Aug 21, 1854 | æt 4 y'rs |

Samuel Marsh | died | July 10, 1861 | aged 66 |

Mary E. | Only child of | Samuel & | Julia L. Mc Neil | died | Feb 21, 1856 | æ 3 y'rs |

Elisha Mason | Born April 5, 1759 | Died June 1, 1858 | æ 99 |

Lucretia | Wife of | Elisha Mason | died Feb. 11, 1853 | æ 87 |

David Burr | Son of | Benjamin W. & | Susan F. Mason | Died | Aug 30, 1850 | Aged 7 Years |

Robert Goodwin | son of | George W. & Julia E. | Mason ||
Died Jan 2, 1865 | æ 4 y'rs & 3 mo |

Benjamin W. Mason | died | Jan. 16, 1888 | Aged 82 |

Susan Ford | wife of | Benj. W. Mason | died Oct 20, 1869 |
Aged 61 |

George Hempstead | Died Dec 7, 1881 | aged 9 Y'rs 4 Mo's |
& 5 D's || Charles Riverius | Died Jan 1, 1873 | Aged 4 Y'rs 4
Mo's | & 15 D's | Children of Riverius & Julia D. Marsh |

Thomas Mason | Co E 8th Regt C. V. | Killed at Bat. Antie-
tam | Sept 17, 1862 | Aged 41 | Mary A. Williams | his wife |
Born Sept 8, 1825 | Died Dec 13, 1893 |

Fanny Morse |

In | memory of | Orra wife of | Moses Morse | who died |
Sept. 29, 1834, aged 46 years |

Moses Morse | died | May 24, 1848 | Aged 66 years |

Asahel Hall Morse | Born Mar 21, 1823 | Died Jan 31,
1892 || Children of Asahel H. & || Lucindia R. Morse: | Lu-
cretia J. Died | Nov 22, 1871, æ 21 | Mary E. Died | Sept 21,
1849, æ 2 Mos | An Infant, died | June 13, 1856 ||

Harley Morse | Died Dec 21, 1870 | aged 78 | Susan | wife
of | Harley Morse | Died Aug. 1, 1845 | Aged 49 | MORSE ||
Harriet | wife of | Harley Morse | died | Apr 28, 1889 | Aged
87 || Caroline E. | Died Aug. 17, 1844 | Aged 23 | Lucretia
H. | Died May 1, 1844 | Aged 10 | Edwin K. | Died | May 2,
1844 | Aged 4 | Children of | H. & S. Morse |

Henry P. | son of | Richard & Mary | Mc Manus | died |
Oct 27, 1860 | æ 11 y'rs | & 11 ds |

William S. | son of | Richard & Mary | Mc Manus | died |
Nov. 5, 1860 | æt 8 y'rs |

Benjamin A. McCall | 1806-1895 | Caroline Culver; His
Wife | 1801-1848 | Cornelia Bidwell, His Wife | 1800-1868 |
Mary P. Hall, His Wife | 1817-1895 | Levi | Son of Benjamin
A. and Caroline Mc Call | 1829-1846 | McCALL |

Lieut. Thomas H. McKinley | 29th C. V. | born in Chester
Co. Pa. | Oct. 17, 1844 | died at | Chesapeake Hospital | For-
tress Monroe | Jan. 3, 1865 | of wounds | received in the bat-
tle | of Chaffin's Farm | Sept 29, 1864 | Erected by | his
brother officers | McKINLEY |

Emily R. | Daughter of | John McKinley | of Philadelphia | Died | July 1, 1864 | æ 27 y'rs & 9 mo's |

Allan Mc Lean | 1837-1882 | Pastor First Congregational Church | Litchfield | 1875-1882 |

Edward Tompkins Mc Laughlin | Professor of | Rhetoric and Belles Letters | in | Yale University | Born May 28, 1860 | Died July 25, 1893 | "Think clear, feel deep ; | bear fruit well." |

I know that my Redeemer liveth | Rev. D. D. T. Mc-Laughlin | 1812-1895 | Children | Lawrence Brownell | 1862-1863 | Buried in Sharon | Prof. Edward Tompkins | 1860-1893 |] McLAUGHLIN. |

Harmon | son of | Smith & | Mary A. Nickerson | died | Nov. 28, 1851 | æt 22 |

Samuel Erastus | son of Miles & | Lois Norton | died Jan 16, 1811, | æt 2 |

Mrs Luna Norton | wife of Birdsey Norton | Died at Tor-ringford | May 14, 1831 | in the 45th year of her age |

In Memory of | Betsey S. Daughter | of Birdsey & Luna | Norton who died | March 30, 1812, | æ 22 months |

Mary E. | Daughter of | Wm & Susan | Norton | died | April 19, 1861 | Aged 14 |

William Norton | born | March 25, 1811 | died May 25, 1895 | NORTON |

Clarissa M. | daughter of | Ambrose & Clarissa | Norton | born July 23, 1819 | died Sept. 8, 1851 |

Ambrose Norton | died | May 24, 1867 | æ 85 |

In | memory of | Clarissa | wife of | Ambrose Norton | who died | Aug 30, 1851 | aged 69 years |

Wm T. Noyes | born | Nov. 8, 1848 | Died Jan 28, 1850 | Mary T. Noyes | Born. Jan. 31, 1852 | Died Dec 21, 1856 |

Julia F. Tallmadge | widow of | William Curtis Noyes | Born July 5, 1818, | Died March 11, 1899 |

Amelia C. Ogden | died | Jan 15, 1866 | aged 87 |

Emely | daughter of | Can-field & | Candace Hayden | & wife of | John O'Neill | died | Sept 3, 1856 æ 39 |

Emma H. | daughter of | John & | Emely O'Neill | died | Jan 15, 1866 | æ 10 y's & 8 mo. |

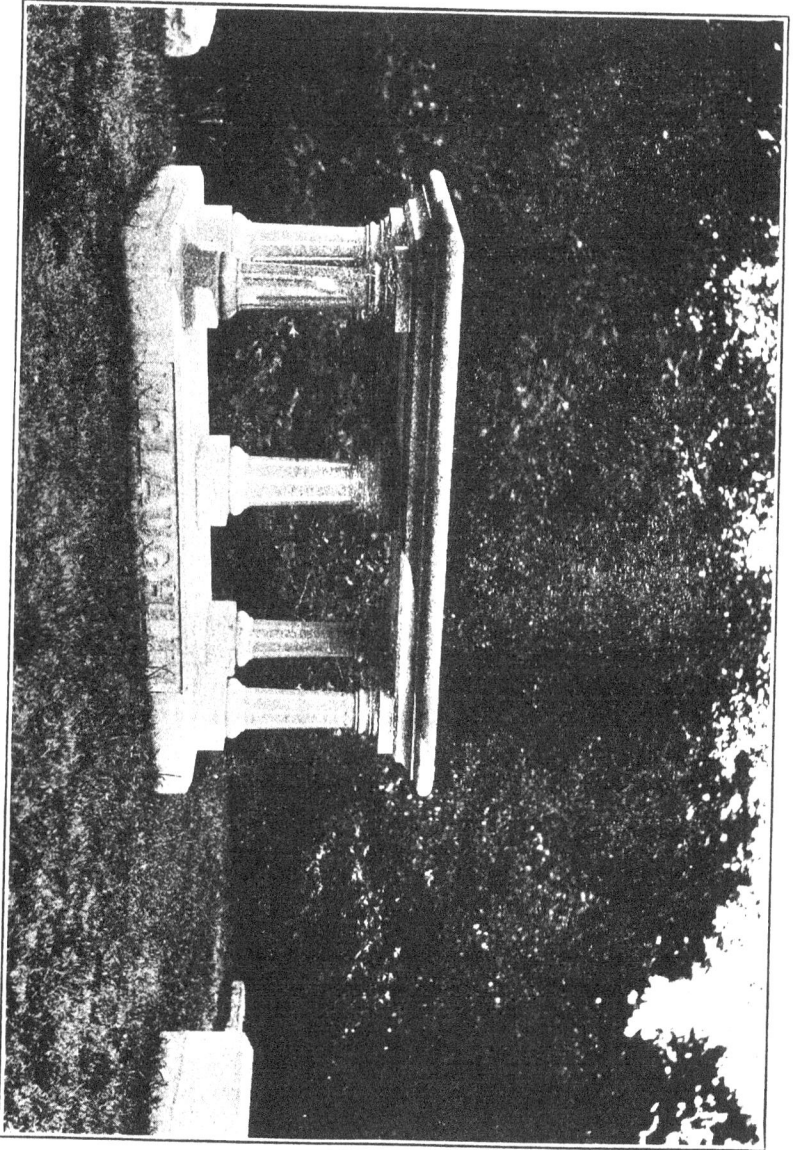

McLAUGHLIN MONUMENT—EAST CEMETERY

Col. William Odell | died | June 7, 1861 | Aged 73 |

Lucena | wife of | Col. W<sup>m</sup>. O'Dell | died | Sept 22, 1846 | aged 56 years |

Henry Palmer | died | Aug 10, 1869 | aged 85 |

Experiance | wife of | Henry Palmer | died | Oct 16, 1881 | aged 77 |

Willis Pond | died | Apr 21, 1865 | æ 77 |

In memory of | Elizabeth | daughter of | Willis & Hannah | Pond who died | Sept 9, 1818 æt | 1 year & 7 months |

In | memory of | Emely | daughter of | Josiah & | Eliza Parks | who died | March 9, 1836 | Aged 14 years |

Harriet | widow of | Henry Perkins | died June 11, 1875 | aged 65 years |

Henry Perkins | died | Oct. 5, 1871 | aged 64 years |

Francis H. Pratt | died March 3, 1879 | æt 74 |

Emeline Moss | wife of Francis H. Pratt | died | March 8, 1863 | æt 51. |

In | memory of | a son of Josiah | & Eliza Parks | who died | May 30, 1824, | aged 5 months | & 10 days |

Mary Ann | daughter of | Elijah M. & Harriet Peck | died Nov 3 | 1821, æ 3 y-rs | & 7 mo's. | Adaline & Angeline | Twins |

Harriet | wife of | Elijah M. Peck | died | Nov 21, 1879 | æ 83. |

Elijah M. Peck | died | July 17, 1872 | æ 78 |

Chauncey Peck | born Aug 25, 1789 | died | Feb 18, 1867 |

Minerva Peck | born | April 21, 1790 | died | March 8, 1870 |

Stephen | Son of Chauncey | & Minerva Peck | Died Aug 2, 1820 | æ 7 mo & 24. |

Harriet L. | daughter of | Chauncey & | Minerva Peck | died Sept 18, 1829 | aged 15 years | "weep not for me" |

In | Memory of | Mrs Mary Peck | who died March 12, 1815 | aged 89 years |

This stone is Erect<sup>ed</sup> | In Memory of M<sup>r</sup> | Benjamin Peck
who | Departed this life Decem<sup>ber</sup> | the 4<sup>th</sup> 1788 in the 67<sup>th</sup> |
year of his age |

> Ye living men as you shall tread
> to vew the mansions of the dead
> Remember this as you pass by
> As you are now so once was I
> As I am now so you must be
> Prepare for death and follow me.

James | son of Eliada | & Abigail Peck | who died | March
21, 1812 | in the 2 year of | his age. |

M<sup>rs</sup> Abigail Peck | wife of | M<sup>r</sup> Eliada Peck | died | Aug
19, 1825 | æ 42 |

> If worth departed e'er diserved a tear
> Oh! gentle stranger pay the tribute here.

In | Memory of | Mrs Sally Peck | the *amiable* consort of |
Mr. Eliada Peck | who departed this life | Nov 29<sup>th</sup>, A. D.
1799 | In the 24<sup>th</sup> year | of her age |

Benjamin | died Nov 18, 1829 | æ 3 years | George died Jan
9, 1821 | æ 6 months sons of | Eliada & Abigail Peck |

In | memory of | Benjamin B. Peck | son of | Eliada & Sally
Peck | who was drowned | July 23, 1816 | aged 17 years |

Fanny J. Peck | wife of Eliada Peck | Died Jan 18, 1866 |
æ 78 |

Eliada Peck | died | July 18, 1849 | Aged 80 |

In | Memory of Mr. | Edward Phelps | who died March
26<sup>th</sup> | A. D. 1797 In the 70<sup>th</sup> | year of his Age |

In memory of | Cap<sup>t</sup> Edward | Phelps who | Departed this
Life May the | 3<sup>d</sup> AD 1790 | in the 93<sup>rd</sup> | year of his Āge |

In Memory of | M<sup>rs</sup> Deborah wife | of Cap<sup>t</sup> Edward |
Phelps She died | Jn<sup>ry</sup> the 18<sup>th</sup> AD | 1771 in the 72<sup>d</sup> | year of
her Age |

In Memory | of Ozies son | of M<sup>r</sup> Edward | And M<sup>rs</sup> Han-
nah | Phelps he died | Apr the 28<sup>th</sup> A D | 1776 in the 11 | year
of his age |

Edwin F. Perkins | Co A. 2<sup>nd</sup> Conn | Heavy Artillery | Died
in Alexandria Va. | Aug 16, 1864. | Aged 29 |

Frances E. Pitcairn | Born July 29, 1847 | Died | April 20, 1872 |

In | memory of | James Prescott | who died | May 22, 1845 | aged 72 |

In | memory of | Henry T. Prescott | who died [ Jan 22, 1829 | aged 16 |

Martha Prescott | Born | at Whitesboro, N. Y. 1807 | Died at Litchfield | Sept 23, 1883 |

Frederick Prescott | died | Sept 1, 1847 | æ 43 |

Lines Parmalee | died Feb 24, 1875 | Aged 77 | also | His wife Irene | died Dec. 9, 1875 | aged 77. Married Nov. 1820 |

George Lyman | son of | Lyman B. & | Caroline H. Prindle| Died Sept 5, 1864 | Aged 14 Y'rs | 5 Mo. & 5 D's. |

In | Memory of | Abigail Perkins | who died June 13, 1820 | aged 38 years | wife of | Harvey Perkins |

Harvey Perkins | died Mar. 11, 1856 | æ 75 | Harriet Amelia | his daughter | æ 4 yrs | & 4 mo. |

Lieut John Phelps | died | Mar 29, 1863 | æ 79 | Abby Phelps | first wife | Died .. 18.. | æ .. | Sarah A. Phelps | second wife | Died Dec 20, 1881 | æ 92 y'rs 1 Mo | & 20 D's |

In | memory of | Capt. John Phelps | who died | June 25, 1833 | aged 77 years |

In | Memory of | Sarah | Wife of | Capt. John Phelps | who died May 8, 1844 | æ 83 | Erected by her Daughter Sarah |

David Pierpont | died | Feb 16, 1826 | æ 62 | his wife | Sarah died | Feb 14, 1853 | æ 84 |

Edward Pierpont | died | Aug 9, 1871 | Aged 79 | His wife| Olive | died | Oct 25, 1866 | Aged 77 |

Charles H. Pierpont | June 17, 1830-May 27, 1896 | PIER-PONT |

Rev. David L. Parmelee | born | Nov 11, 1795 | died | June 29 1865 |

Sally | wife of | Rev David L. Parmelee | born | Nov. 5, 1795 | died April 1, 1874 |

Mrs Lucy Parmelee | Born Nov 24 | 1773 | Died July 15, 1854 |

In | Memory of | David Parmelee Esq | who departed this life | May 29, 1811 | in the 45 year | of his age |

Celeste Parmelee | died | April 15, 1868 | aged 59 years | Caroline Parmelee | born | April 15, 1803 | died December 20, 1886 |

John E. | died | Dec 19, 1838 | aged 15 | Mary | died | Sept 10, 1836 | aged 2 mo | Children of | Lodovick & | Mary Pendleton |

Lovovick | Pendleton | died | July 29, 1849 | æ 56 Y'rs. |

Mary | wife of | Lodovick Pendleton | died at Sheffield, Mass. | Oct 11, 1865 | æ 76 |

Henry Phelps | born | Sept 16, 1800 | died Nov 22, 1868 |

Louisa C. Lewis | wife of | Henry Phelps | born | Nov 7, 1802 | died | Nov 22, 1889 |

Peter Perkins | died | July 4, 1870 | æt 81 |

Sally | wife of | Peter Perkins | died | March 19, 1868 | æt 77. |

Jane P. Picket 1827-1886 | PICKETT || Carrie Pickett | 1853-1885 ||

Elizabeth | daughter of Charles L. & ⌈ Lucy A. Perkins | died | Oct. 5, 1849 | æt 11 mo's | & 5 days |

Charles J. Perkins | born | February 16, 1843 | died March 8, 1868 |

Julia A. Perkins | wife of | Charles L. Perkins | died | Mach 13, 1843 | æ 22 |

Charles L. Perkins | died Feb. 18, 1874 | æt 56 |

Helen Peck | Born July 26, 1802. | Died May 27, 1822 |

Edward Phelps | died | Oct 3, 1859 | aged 77 |

Lavina | wife of | Edward Phelps | died | May 20. 1858 | aged 76 |

Lucy Maria | Daughter of | Edward & Lavina | Phelps died | Sept 10. 1825 | æt 5 y'rs |

Edward Phelps | died | Sept 15, 1872 | æt 63 |

Eliza Marsh | wife of | Edward Phelps | died | Mar 30, 1873 | æt 66 |

In | memory of | Benjamin Phelps | who died | Sept 23, 1841 | aged 72 years |

Lydia | wife of | Benjamin Phelps | died | May 6, 1859 | æ 87 |

Sacred to | to the Memory of | Mrs. Ana Persons | who died | Jan. 19, 1813 | Aged 76 years |

In memory of | Clarissa consort of | Charles Perkins, Esq | & 2nd daugher of Julius Deming, Esq | born Dec 21, 1795 | & died Aug 6, 1837 || Charles Perkins Esq: | born in Norwich, Ct. | June 21, 1792 | died in London, Eng. | Nov 18, 1856 | His remains were brought | here for interment||In memory of Julius Deming | first son of Charles & | Clarissa Perkins | born July 30 | & died Aug 16, 1819:| Of Cha's Wm Their 2nd | son born Nov 13, 1820 | & died Jan 23, 1837 | of Lucretia Champion|Their 2nd daughter | born July 20, 1826 | & died Aug 26, 1827 | Of Clarissa Their | 3rd daughter: born | & died May 8, 1828 | Of Edward Their | 4th son born May 27 & died May 30, 1837 || Abby Perkins | daughter of the late | Andrew Perkins | of Norwich, Ct | born May 3, 1795 | died Feb 6, 1875 |

My Redeemer liveth | Amelia Lewis | widow of Elijah Peck | Sept 10, 1810 | June 20, 1893 |

Jennette Lynde | wife of | Frederick Phelps | & daughter of | Ozias & Mary Lewis | died May 12, 1844 | aged 23 | Jennette Lewis | daughter of | Frederick & | Jennette L. Phelps | died Oct 14, 1844 | aged 5 months |

Charles J. Peck | died | Oct 1, 1885 | Aged 64 Y'rs |

Julia A. | wife of | Charles J. Peck | died | Dec 19, 1890 | Aged 65 yrs |

Lydia Jane | Daughter of | Charles J. & Julia A. | Peck | Died Feb 17, 1865 | æ 16 Y'rs |

Charlie E. Peck | son of | Charles J. & Julia A. Peck | Died Nov. 1st, 1889 | aged 33 y'rs & | 8 Mo. |

Cora E. | died Feb 11, 1853 | æ 6 y'rs | Alice E. | died March 3, 1853 | æ 3 yrs & 6 mo's | Children of | George R. & Elizabeth | Prescott |

M. Elizabeth | daughter of | John & Martha L. | Phelps | died | June 4, 1859 | Aged 12 |

Col. John Phelps | died | July 18, 1881 | Aged 73 |

Martha L. | wife of Col John Phelps | Born Feb 3, 1819 |
Died Apr 5, 1896 | Aged 77 Y'rs |

Perry |

David Palmer | died | Mar 5, 1854 | æ 79 |

Sally | wife of | David Palmer | died | Mar. 31, 1849 | æ 75 |

Emma G. Parks | died | Aug. 22, 1871 | æ 30 |

Elsie || Willard | and | Howard | Peck |

William Guy Peck | Born Oct 16, 1820 | Died Feb 7, 1892 |
For 35 years a Professor in | Columbia College |

Wm. L. Ransom | Mar. 28, 1822. |—| Mary H. his wife |
Jan 24, 1820, | Sept. 28, 1894 | RANSOM |

Devillane | born Jan 18 | died Mar. 5, 1844 | Sarah E. | born
Apr 17, 1845 | died Feb 18, 1846 | children of | ........ |
(*In same lot with following*)

To the memory of | Samuel D. Rowe | died | March 8, 1890 |
Aged 73 y'rs & 8 mo. |

Gilbert B. | son of | Solomon and | Adeline S. Rowe | Died |
Oct 27, 1859 | æ 12 yrs |

Caroline L. | daughter of | Solomon & | Adaline S. Rowe |
died | Sept 6, 1847 | æ 2 y'rs & 7 mo. |

Elizabeth M. | daughter of Solomon & | Adaline Rowe |
died | Mar. 18, 1848 | aged 1 year |

Ruth B. | died Dec 6, 1833 | æt 7 yrs | Mary A. | died | July
25, 1838 | æt 25 d's | Orlen L. | died | Aug 31, 1830 | æt 1
year | Intered in the family | yard of John Wait | of Winstead |
Children of Loomis & | Rachel Rowley |

In Memory of Oliv | Daughter of Mr Jonathan | & Mrs.
Millesent Rossetter | Who Died November | 22d 1780 in the
15 year of her Age |

In Memory of | Mr Jonathan Rossitar who | Departed This
Life NoV. the 7th | 1770 in the 33rd | Year of his Age |

Tapping Burr Reeve | a member of the | senior class Yale
College : | died Aug 28, 1829 | Aged 20 years & 12 days | The
only child of the late | Aaron B. Reeve Esq | and the last de-
scendant | of the late eminently | learned and pious Chief
Justice Reeve |

Elizabeth Reeve | Aged 60 | Dec 13, 1842 |

EAST CEMETERY—JUDGE REEVES

The Honourable | Tapping Reeve, L. L. D. | late chief Justice of the State | died Dec 13, 1823 | in the 80, | year of his age. |

Sally Reeve |

In | Memory of | Sarah Phelps | wife of | John C. Riley | Died May 12, 1870 | æ 83 |

Anna Rowland | relict of | Andrew Rowland | died Feb 18, 1819 | aged 39 |

Harriet Newell | daughter of Daniel | & Mabel Roberts | died | Oct 19, 1827 | æt 12 years | & 8 months |

Maria | wife of | Almon P. Roberts | died | Dec 18, 1843 | aged 46 |

Almon P. Roberts | died | April 15, 1832 | Aged 34 |

In | Memory of | Daniel Roberts | who died | Mar 26, 1841 | æt 68 y'rs | Also | Mabel, his wife | died | Mar 20, 1848 | æt 70 y'rs |

Emeline F. Trall | wife of | Fred'k Remer | died | June 7, 1865 | æ 27 |

Nathaniel Rochester | child | 1849 |

John L. | son of | John W. & Mary E. | Ruwet | died | May 7, 1873 | æ 2 Y'rs & 6 Mo |

Cornelius M. Ray | Born 8, Nov. 1834 | Died 9, June, 1868 || RAY ||

Eunice | wife of | Zacheus Sanford | died | May 25, 1844 | aged 90. |

In Memory|of|James son of Mr | James & Anna | Stone ( ?) who departed | this life March yᵉ |.....AD 1780 in the |....|

Patty | wife of | Jesse Stevens | died | Dec 11, 1862 | aged 79 |

Alma Stevens | died | March 7, 1858 | æ 55 |

In | Memory of | Amy Stevens | who died | Dec 31, 1837 | aged 60 |

In | Memory of | Jesse Stevens | who died | July 23, 1823. | aged 39 |

In Memory of | Esther Stevens | died | Jan 4, 1834 | æ 65 |

Lavinia | wife of | Thomas Stevens | died | June 1, 1848 | æ 85 |

In memory of | Thomas Stevens | died | Feb 14, 1834 | æ 91 |

Thomas B. Stevens | died | Sept 22, 1869 | æ 54 |

Henry B. Stevens | Son of | Thomas B. & | Emily E. Stevens | Died Oct 6, 1865 | æ 7 m. 6 d's |

Homer Sharp | died | Jan 10, 1880 | æ 74 years & 6 m's | Gone but not forgotten |

Nabby C. | wife of Homer Sharp | died | Feb 23, 1888 | æ 82 years |

Thomas L. Saltonstall | Born at Philadelphia | Nov 30, 1805 | Died at | Litchfield Sept. 6, 1884 | aged 79 y'rs |

Mrs Abigail | Saltonstall | died | July 18, 1825 | æt 49 |

Edward E. Saltonstall | was lost | off Cape Horn | Oct 22, 1834 | aged 17 |

John Edward Sedgwick | 1st. Lieut, Co. K. 2nd Conn. Heavy Art. | 1838-1899 | SEDGWICK |

Theodore S. Sedgwick | 1837-1898 | Lucy Farnsworth | his wife | 1837-1902 | Bessie C. Sedgwick | 1874-1896 | SEDG-WICK |

Mary J. | wife of | Edson Staples | died Apr 28, 1869 | æ 28. |

Albert Washington | son of | William & | Emeline Scovill | Died Jan 8 | 1837 æt 1 year | & 8 mo-s |

Augustus | son of | William & Emeline Scovill | died | June 18, 1837 | aged 2 years | 1 month & | 12 days | Twin brother | of Augusta. |

In | memory of | Huldah | wife of Amos Sanford | who died | July 26, 1853 | æ 60 |

D. S. | In | Memory of | Mr. Daniel Starr | who died | March 23ᵈ | 1809 | aged 50 years |

In memory of | Sarah Shethar | Consort of | Samuel Shethar | who died | Nov 26, 1810 | Aged 82 years |

Timothy Son of | Gen'l Timothy & | Mrs. Susannah | Skinner, was born | August the 18ᵗʰ A D 1771 | & died Novʳ the 3ʳᵈ A D | 1790 in the 19ᵗʰ year of | his Age | This monument is erected | in memory of a beloved son |

In memory of | Mrs. Abigail Skinner | Consort of | Mr. Peter Buel | & | Gen Tim° Skinner | She died May 16, AD 1806 | æ 60 years & 5 days |

This stone is erected by | Fannie J. Sherman | to the sacred memory | of her dear parents |
Peter Sherman | was born | || Elizabeh | his wife was born | April 24, 1758 | and died | || Oct 11, 1765 | and died | Nov 29, 1821 | || August 18, 1821 |
Proud of thy birth, we boast th' auspicous year
Struck with thy fall we shed a general tear
With humble grief inscribe our artless stone
And from thy matchless honor date our own.

In | memory of | Peter Sherman | who was drowned | Aug 14, 1825 | aged 29 |

Mary King | Twin Daughter of | Rev. W^m & Harriet R. | Southgate | Died May 8, 1863 | æ 16 Mos |

Henry W. Stevens | died | Feb 25, 1850|æ 39|STEVENS|| Mrs | Jane W. Stevens | died Dec. 11, 1862 | æ 46 || Henry W. | son of Henry W. & | Jane Stevens | died Sept 12, 1850 | æ 5 weeks ||

Moses Seymour | Jr. Esq. | died | May 8, 1826 | aged 52 |

Mrs | Mabel Seymour | daughter of | Hon Josiah Strong | of Addison Vt. | & wife of | Moses Seymour Jr. | died Dec 10, 1839 | aged 57 |

Moses Seymour, Jr, Esq. | died May 8, 1826 | aged 52 | Mabel his wife | died Dec 10, 1839, | aged 57 | SEYMOUR || Henry Seymour | died at Painesville, O. | Nov 25, 1857 | aged 49 | Epaphro Seymour | died in California | Oct 23, 1850 | aged 38 || Delia Storrs Seymour | died Dec 25, 1887 | aged 81 || George Seymour M. D. | died Jan 29, 1861 | aged 44 | Jane Seymour Beckwith | died Aug 13, 1858 | aged 57 |

Amelia Selima | wife of David C. Sanford | & daughter of | Ozias Seymour, Esq. | died at Norwalk | July 15, 1833 | aged 24 years | An infant daughter of | David C. & | Amelia S. Sanford | died July 26, 1833 | aged 11 days |

Margaret Louisa Craney | wife of | William Elihu Sanford| April 6, 1818-November 5, 1902 | SANFORD |

Ozias Seymour | Born July 8, 1776 | Died June 3, 1851 || Selima Storrs | wife of | Ozias Seymour | Died Nov 2, 1814 | Aged 28 years ||

Maria | wife of | Rollin Sanford | & daughter of | Ozias Seymour Esq | died | Apr 5, 1836 | æ 24 | an infant | son of Rollin & | Maria Sanford | died Dec 22, 1835 | age 1 day. |

This monument | is erected | to the memory of | Maj. Moses Seymour | who died Sept 17, 1826 | in his 85, year | He held the office of town clerk | 37 successive years & discharged | the duties of various other public offices || This monument | is also erected | to the memory of | Mrs. Mary | wife of | Maj. Moses Seymour | she died July 17, 1826 | aged 74 years | By their benevolence, integrity & | intelligence they secured the ardent attachment of a large circle of | friends, relatives & descendants & | by their christian graces they furnished | strong grounds of confidence that they | have entered into a blessed immortality. |

In | Memory of | Samuel Sheldon, Jr. | Member of Yale College | who departed this life | on the 28th day of | Feb. AD. 1802 | in the 18th year | of his age |

Samuel Sheldon | 60 years | a resident of | Litchfield | Died in Troy | Jan 2, 1842 | æ 91 | Elizabeth Baldwin | His Wife | Born in L'd | Died in Troy Sept 10, 1840 | æ 89 || Elisha Sheldon M. D. | Son of | Sam'l S. | Born in L'd | Died in Troy | Dec 14, 1832 | æ 50 | Ann Beach | wife of | Doct. Sheldon | Died in New Haven | Jan 22, 1844 | æ 60 || Erected | in Memory of the | departed worth | of a family | whose name is lineally | extinct | by |Mrs. H. E. Peck | Nov. 1846 |

Sally Smith | died | May || George W. Smith | died Feb 12, 1864 | aged 79 | || 10, 1866 | aged 68 |

Horace Smith | died | Feb 25, 1874 | æ 84 |

Sally | wife of | Horace Smith | died | Jan 30, 1861 | æ 70 |

Russell Smith | died | July 30, 1844 | aged 28 |

In | memory of | Caroline | daughter of | Horace & | Sarah Smith | who died | Oct 25, 1843 | æ 19 |

Charles H. | Son of | Horace & | Sarah Smith | died | March 3, 1831 | æ 9 y'rs | An infant died | June 24, 1832 | æ 13 days |

Eunice Elizabeth | Daughter of | Horace & Sarah | Smith | died Nov 14, 1835 | aged 22 years |

Lorinda L. | wife of | Russel Smith | died | Feb. 9, 1843 | æ 28 years | Also | Charles | only child of | Russel & | Lorinda L. Smith | died | April 9, 1843 | æ 4 mo's |

Deborah | wife of | Capt Eli Smith | died | Nov 6, 1843 | Aged 84 |

In | Memory of | Capt Eli Smith | who died | March 29, 1824 |

James H. Smith | born July 11, 1819 | died .... | Sarah A. Munger | beloved wife | of James H. Smith | born Oct 5<sup>th</sup> 1822 | died July 3<sup>rd</sup> 1891 | aged 68 Y. 8 M. 28 Days |

Mrs. | Abima Sweet | died Oct 2, 1826 | aged 53 years 2 mo | & 23 days |

Howard L. | son of | Leonard & | Lucinda | Stone | died | June 1, 1884 | Aged | 12 Y'rs |

The Angels whisper come | Sarah || Daughter of | Leonard & | Lucinda M. | Stone | died | May 13, 1875 | æ 7 Y'rs |

Frank | æ 1 Y'r 7 M's | died | Apr 14, 1867 || Son of Leonard & | Sarah Stone |

Sarah | wife of | Leonard Stone | died | Mar 21, 1866 | Aged 38 |

In memory of | Cap<sup>t</sup> John Smith | who died Feb<sup>y</sup> 15<sup>th</sup>, 1807 | in the 69<sup>th</sup> year | of his age |

Catharine Maria|daughter of | Truman and | Maria Smith | born Feb 24, 1833 | died Aug 17, 1834 |

George Webster | son of | Truman & | Maria Smith | born May 4, 1837 | died Jan 13, 1840. |

This stone is erected | by widow Ruth Smith | to mark the place where | are deposited the remains of | her husband Maj. Gen. David Smith | born Dec 20. 1747 | died Oct 16, 1814 || In memory of | David Smith Jr | Merchant, son of David & Ruth Smith | who died at Neworleans. Oct 29, 1825 | æ 49 || M<sup>rs</sup> Ruth Smith | relict of | Maj. Gen. David Smith | died at Batavia, N. Y. | Nov 8, 1831 | in the 82 year of her age || In memory of | Col. Aaron Smith Son of Gen. David & | Ruth Smith who died | Sept 29, 1834 | æ 63 | George Smith | Son of Col Aaron & | Amanda Smith | Who Died in New-yo- | rk April 20, 1822 | æ 27 |

Amanda Smith | died | Nov 19, 1839 | aged 66 years |

Electa Amelia | daughter of | Ephraim & | Eliza Sherman | died May 27, 1822 | 4 months. |

William E. | son of | Ephraim & | Eliza Sherman | died | Jan. 13, 1833 | aged 7 years |

> I came here young
> You soon must come.

M$^r$ | W$^m$ E. Simpson | died | Nov 27, 1825 | æ 38 |

Mary A. Stevens | died | April 17, 1867 | æ 29 |

Betsey A. | Scofield | died | Dec 17, 1839 | aged 24 years. |

Catharine L. | Daughter of | Theodore R. & | Mary A. Sedgwick | died | Dec 11, 1860 | Aged 20 Y'rs | & 5 M'os |

Mary Ann Stoddard | wife of | T. R. Sedgwick | Born Dec 19, 1818 | Died April 3, 1877 |

Theodore R. Sedgwick | born | July 1, 1812 | Died Dec 22, 1877 |

To the memory of | Huldah wife of | Doct. Daniel Sheldon | died Oct 5, 1817 | aged 57 |

In | Memory of | Daniel Sheldon M. D. | Born Oct 19, 1750 | Died April 10, 1840 |

Lillian | Isadora | daughter of | John R. & | Lucretia M. Stanton | died | Aug 31, 1864 | Aged 8 mo | & 6 days |

Emeline A. | wife of | Thomas B. Stevens | & daughter of | Christopher & Orinda Wheeler | died Oct 7, 1859 æt 39 Y's |

Nellie E. Sprague | died | Dec 20, 1865 | Aged 21 |

Josiah Stone | Died Feb. 1, 1858 | æ 78 |

Catharine | wife of | Josiah Stone | died | Oct 12, 1843 | aged 62 |

Gideon S. | Son of Josiah | & Catherine Stone | Died, | Oct 26, 1834 | æ 17 yrs |

Catherine L. | Daughter of | John B. & Susannah Stone | Died | April 2, 1836 | æ 12 mo-s |

J. B. Stone | died | Aug 13, 1846 |

In | memory of | Isaac Stevens | who died | May 12, 1851 | æt 58 y'rs |

In | memory of | Hannah S. Platt | wife of Isaac Stevens | who died | Apr 13, 1871 | æt 78 y'rs |

Mary Allen | Daughter of | William Scott | Died Sept. 29, 1859 | æ 31 |

Margaret Dryden | Daughter of | James & Elizabeth Scott | Died Apr. 11, 1866 | æ 67 |

Mary Ann | daughter of | James & Elizabeth | Scott | Died Jan 25, 1871 | Aged 76 Yrs |

Joseph Slack | Born in Wingfield | Derbyshire, England | Apr 22, 1824 | Died in Litchfield | Feb 20, 1897 | Emily Law | His wife | Born in Litchfield | Jan. 27, 1817 | —— | SLACK || Daniel J. Slack | Son of Joseph & | Emily L. Slack | Born Feb 15, 1858 | Died in New York | Nov. 15, 1884 |

Sarah Emily | daughter of | Joseph & | Emily Slack | died | Mar. 21, 1861 | Æ 19 Mo. & 20 D's |

Origen Storrs Seymour | born | at Litchfield | February 9, 1804 | died at Litchfield | August 12, 1881 | Also his wife | Lucy M. Woodruff | born 1 July 1807 | died 20 October 1894 | Maria Seymour | daughter of | Origen S. & Lucy M. | Seymour | born October 27, 1838 | died September 11, 1878 || SEYMOUR | Edward Woodruff Seymour | born | August 30, 1832 | died | October 16, 1892 |

Remus F. Sharp | born | 24 Aug. 1838 | Died 18. Oct 1895 | SHARP ||

SIDDALL | Joseph Siddall | Nov 16, 1838-Feb 17, 1900 | Mary Siddall | his wife | Apr 22, 1843-Jan 24, 1895 |

Died | Mrs | Susan Tracy | widow of | Hon Uriah Tracy | Jan 7, 1843 | aged 84 |

Gilbert Golden | infant son of | Ruth & G. Golden | Tracy | died Aug 21, 1863 | aged 7 mos & 21 days |

Miles Taylor | died | Apr. 18, 1876 | Æ 86 |

Rhoda Taylor | died | Aug 19, 1878 | Æt 82 |

Lydia Taylor | Æ 77 | "Bury me by the side of little Mary" | (*See Mary Kienley*)

Olive Taylor | died | Feb 29, 1852 | Æ 87 |

In | memory of | Elisha Taylor | who died | Oct. 30, 1843 | aged 83 years |

Lydia | wife of | Elisha Taylor | died | July 28, 1837 | Æ 82 y's |

Phila Taylor | died | Mar 30, 1850 | æ 50 |

Charlotte | daughter of | Phineas & Sidna Taylor | died Apr. 17, 1852 | Æ 18 |

Phineas Taylor | died | Feb 20, 1861, æ 66 |

Harriet | daughter of | Phineas & Sidna | Taylor | Died Sept 29, 1865 | Aged 19 |

In Memory of | Mrs Rhoda wife | of Capt Zebulon | Taylor who died | Sept the 9, 1777 | in the 32ᵈ year | of her age |

Enos son of | Enos & Phebe | Tompkins | died | Aug 16, 1851 | Æt 4 m's | & 16 d's |

> Here lies my babe that I did love
> Departed from me like a dove
> The babe which I did once adore
> Is gone and cannot come no more.

John R. Tompkins | 8ᵗʰ Regt. C. V. | Died at | Washington Va | Sept 5, 1862 | Æ 18. | Enos S. Tompkins | 1ˢᵗ Conn. | Cavalry | Killed by | lightning at | Sperryville Va. | July 16. 1862 | Æ 44. | Phebe L. Curtis | died | July 28, 1892 | Aged 74. |

Mary Jane | Died Apr 26, 1869, | Æ 28 | Another tie is broken | another child is dead | Julia Elizabeth | Died Nov 9, 1872 | Æ 23 | Children of Enos & Phebe Tompkins | This stone was erected by their mother. |

Isaac Trumbull | Died Nov. 3, 1902 | Aged 40 Yrs. |

Rachel M. | daughter of | Thomas & | Sally S. | Trowbridge | died | Mch 6, 1820 | Æ. 2 mo 11 d's |

Phebe Wyckoff | wife of Zechariah Thompson | died | Dec 20, 1868 | Æ 76 |

Wᵐ H. Thompson | died Sept 5, 1864 | Æ 78 |

Anna Thompson |

Zachariah Thompson | died Oct 14ᵗʰ 1816 | Æt 67 |

To | the memory of | Sarah, relict of | Zachariah Thompson | born June 10. 1746 | died | Jan 16 1831 |

Henry W. | son of | Henry & Jenette Tyrrel | died | Aug 13, 1839 aged 1½ years |

William H. Turner | born | November 1, 1811 | died | March 7, 1885 |

Billy Turner | died | May 26, 1842 | æ 68 | Philena | His wife died | Dec 12, 1861 | æ 82 |

In | Memory of | Mrs. Mehetabel Thacher | who died | Sept 6, 1807 | æ 63 |

Mary wife of | George Treadway | Died | June 16, 1828 | æ 28 |

Jula C. | wife of | Frederick M. Thrall | Died July 30, 1877 | Aged 26 |

Myron J. Thrall | died | July 27, 1871 | æ 40 |

Mary L. | wife of | Myron J. Thrall | Died Mar 2, 1886 | Æ 54. |

Luke Trall | died | Mar. 20, 1840 | Æ 40 |

Harriet A. Wife of | Luke Trall | died May 24, 1875 | Æ 74 | (*Note: These two stones are in the same lot with the three preceding.*)

Maria Tallmadge | Relict of | The Hon. B. Tallmadge, | Born February 19th 1776 | Died September 18th 1838 |

Honble Benjamin Tallmadge | Born Feby 25, 1754 | Died March 7, 1835 |

In Memory | of | Mrs Mary Tallmadge | The Wife of | Benjamin Tallmadge, Esq: | who was born March 6th 1764 | and died June 3d 1805 |

Mabel | widow of | Hezekiah Thompson | died | Jan 13, 1854 | Æt 63 |

In | Memory of | Hezekiah Thompson | Who died | June 13, 1838 | aged 61 years |

James Trowbridge | Died June 8, 1841 | æ 47 | Lucy Parmelee | his widow | Died Feb 12, 1875 | æ 78 |

Hiram Taylor | died | Oct 8, 1852 | Aged 52 Y'rs |

Malinda | Wife of Hiram Taylor | Died Sept 15, 1862 | Aged 62. |

Susie || Infant | daughter of | Julius & | Sarah J. Treadway | Born Nov. 11, 1871 | Died Nov 14, 1871 |

Egbert W. Tompkins | born in Litchfield April 7, 1829 | Died at Bridgeport | April 4, 1866 |

Addison K. Taylor | Mar. 7, 1836 | ——— | Laura L. Andrews | Oct 27, 1839 | May 20, 1895 |

Arthur Floyd | Tallmadge | only son of | Frederick S. & | Julia L. | Tallmadge | Born Feb 19, 1858|Died June 28, 1874 |

Julia Louisa | wife of | Frederick S. Tallmadge | born | July 27, 1828 | died Dec. 13, 1894 |

Frederick A. | Tallmadge | Born Aug 29, 1792 | Died Sept 17, 1869 |

Eliza H. | wife of | F. A. Tallmadge | Born Aug 19, 1793 | Died Dec 1, 1878 |

William F. Tallmadge | born | Nov 14, 1820 | died | August 21, 1893 |

George Wm Thompson | Nov. 19, 1816-Oct 22, 1891 | Harriet Roberts his wife | Nov 23, 1816-Feb 24, 1892 | THOMPSON || Sarah E. Thompson | Oct 29, 1817-Nov 26, 1885 | Anna P. Thompson | Aug. 13, 1814-April 11, 1894 || Mary E. Thompson | Apr 1, 1849-Sept 5, 1894 |

John Arene | son of John A. and Emily N. Vanderpoel | Born Jan 4, 1866 | Died January 28, 1901 |

VAN WINKLE | 1883 |

Martha P. Webster | died | July 7, 1849 | Aged 24. |

In Memory of | Timothy & Sarah | Webster | Timothy | died April | 30, | Sarah | died Oct | 27, 1814 | 1803 | in the 79 year of his | | in the 89 | year of her | age | age |

In Memory of | Mr. Richard Wallace | who departed this life | the 30 day of Aug 1794 | aged 38 years | In Him | The State lost a useful & respectab'e Citizen : | his acquaintance | a man worthy of their Friendship ; | his domestic connections | an affectionate Husband & tender Parent | In testimony of esteem | his surviving Relatives have erected this Monument. |

In Memory of Mrs | Elizabeth wife of Capt Richard | Wallace who Died | the 14th of August | 1785 in the 62d (?) | year of her age | (*epitaph undecipherable*).

Mary | widow of | Richard Wallace | died | Feb 18, 1835 | aged 75 |

Emily F. | wife of | Egbert L. Warner | died | June 28, 1859 | Æ 19 |

Ralph W. | son of David & | Sally Winship | was drowned at | Hartford | Aug 31, 1835 | aged 14 years |

Sarah Winship | daughter of | David & Sally Winship | died July 2, 1828 | Æ 10 y'rs |

David Winship | son of | David & | Sally Winship | died | July 18, 1843 | aged 23 years | & 6 mo |

Andrew A. Winship | son of David & | Sally Winship died | Sept 2, 1830 | Æ 18 yrs |

Capt | Benjamin Webster | 1795, 1881 | Rachel Baldwin | his wife 1794, 1886 |

Mrs Sally | wife of | M^r Benjamin Webster | died | June 5 1818 | Æ 49 |

In | memory of | Benjamin Webster | who died ] Mar 2, 1842, Æ 73 |

In Memory of | Mr Benjamin | Webster Who [ Died Oct^r y^e 29 | 1782 in y^e 46 | year of his Age |

Mrs. Elizabeth | widow of the late | Dea. Benjamin Webster | one of the first settlers | of this town in 1720 | died July 17, 1775 | aged 69 years | For the memory of numerous and pious descendants | this monument is erected in | 1839 by her grandson | Solomon Marsh. |

In | Memory of | Honour | wife of | Stephen Webster | who died | March 30, 1813 | Aged 75 years |

In | memory of | Stephen Webster | who died | Nov 28, 1823 | aged 85 |

| Resting | Hattie E. | wife of | Edwin H. | Wentworth | died | Sept 22, 1878 | Æ 30 years & 9 m's. |

Dan. son of | Laudon & Mary | Ann Webster | died June 13, | 1829 Æ 1 yr. |

A morning flower in early bloom
Cut down in a night to fill the tomb.

Bennet T. Warner | died | Nov 17, 1859 | Æ 29 |

In memory of | John Stoughton Wolcott | Born 28 Aug. 1787 Died 4 Feb 1789 | Oliver Wolcott | Born 27 May 1790. Died 17 July 1791 | Oliver Stoughton Wolcott | Born 18 Jan 1800, Died 23 May 1832 | John Stoughton Wolcott M. D. | Born 4 Dec 1802 Died 22 Nov. 1843 | Sons of Oliver and Elizabeth S. Wolcott. | And of Oliver Wolcott, M. D. | son of Oliver S. Wolcott & Jane His wife | Born 14 Sept 1823, Died 22 May 1856 |

In memory of | Oliver Wolcott | Secretary of the Treasury of the United States | and Governor of Connecticut | Born 4 Jan. 1760 Died 1 June 1833 | and of Elizabeth Stoughton, his wife | Born 27 Oct 1776, Died 25 Sept 1805 | This monument was erected by their daughter | Laura Wolcott Gibbs. |

To the Memory | of | Oliver Wolcott late Governor | of | the State of Connecticut | who was born Dec$^r$ 1$^{st}$ 1726 | & who died Dec 1$^{st}$ 1797 | Also of | Laura Wolcott | who was born Jan 1$^{st}$ 173? | & who died Apr 19$^{th}$ 1794 |

In | memory of | Mrs. Sally W. Wolcott | wife of | the Hon. Frederick Wolcott | born Aug 7, 1785 | Died Sept 14, 1842 |

To | The memory of | Hon. Frederick Wolcott | Born November 2, 1767 | Died May 28, 1837 |

To the Memory of | Mrs. Betsey Wolcott | wife of | Frederick Wolcott, Esq$^r$ | and daughter of | Joshua Huntington, Esq$^r$ | and | Mrs. Hannah Huntington | of Norwich | Born November 8$^{th}$ A. D. 1774 | Died Apr. 2$^{nd}$ A. D. 1812. |

Henry Griswold Wolcott | Born | in Litchfield Conn$^t$ | November 24$^{th}$ 1820 | died | in New-York | May 8$^{th}$ 1852 |

Mary E. | wife of | Charles M. Wolcott | and daughter of | Samuel G. Goodrich | born at Hartford Oct 26. 1818 | died at Philadelphia Dec 13, 1845. | Frederick | son of Charles M. & Mary E. Wolcott | born Dec 23, 1844 | died March 25. 1846. |

In memory of | Chauncey Goodrich | Wolcott | son of | Frederick & Sally W. | Wolcott | Born March 15, 1819 | Died Oct 28, 1820 |

Truman Marsh | infant son of | George B. & Maria | Webster, of Buffalo | N. York who died | August 10, 1826 | Aged 10 months |

Eliza | wife of | Orlando Wadhams | died Oct 13, 1833 | aged 31 years |

Stiles D. | son of | Stiles D. & | Mary Wheeler | died Jan. 31 | 1835, æ 2 years | The cause of his | death was by | falling into a | cittle of hot water. |

Stiles D. Wheeler | Died Dec 25, 1876 | Age 67 years | Mary Moore, his wife, | Died July 16, 1872 | age 62 | their daughter, | Adele Moore | Died November 11, 1875 | Age 30 years |

Eunice A. | adopted daughter of | William & | Eunice Wheeler | Died | Oct 22, 1854 | Æt 17 |

EAST CEMETERY—WOLCOTT LOT

In | Memory of Mr | Lawrence Wessells | who died May 8th | 1798 In the 68th year of his Age |

In | memory of | Abigail Wessells | who died | Jan 16 1822 | aged 82. |

Julia wife of | Hosea Webster | born Dec 23, 1797 | died Dec 19, 1823 |

Moses Wheeler | Died Nov 19, 1868 | Æ 97 Y'rs & 4 Mo | Hannah | Died Apr 24, 1804 | Æ 29 | Anna | Died Apr 4, 1824, | Æ 48. | Wives of Moses Wheeler |

Mary | daughter of | Moses & Anna | Wheeler died | Feb 29, 1828 | Æ 18 |

In | Memory of | Two Children of | Daniel & Mary Wooster |
Harriet | died Aug | 13, 1818. | aged 4 years | Corredon | died Sept. | 7, 1818 | aged 1 year | & 6 months |

In | memory of | Wm Wheeler | who died | Mar 2, 1846 | aged 63 years | Also Serephina | wife of Wm Wheeler | died | Aug 3, 1850 | aged 65 years |

Maria L. Wadhams | born Sept 19, 1797 | died Feb 19, 1879|

Walker Wilmot | died | Dec 3, 1835 | Aged 64 |

Polly Wilmot | died | Apr 12, 1866 | Aged 84 |

Caroline S. Ward | died | July 10, 1875 | Æt 44 |

Frances Adeline | daughter of | Amos & Amanda M. | Wadsworth | died | Sept 29, 1831 | aged 4 years | & 5 months |

> Approving guides caressed thee
> Where'er thy footsteps rov'd.
> The ear that heard thee blessed thee,
> The eye that saw thee loved.

Amos Wadsworth | died | Oct 1, 1850 | Æ 62. |

Julia J. | daugher of | Cornelius L. | & Elizabeth | L. Wetmore | died | April 2, 1837 | Æ 2 y's |

Delia E. | daughter of | Cornelius L. | & Elizabeth | L. Wetmore | died | May 2, 1837 | Æ 7 y's |

Denman Woodruff | died | Jan 21, 1873 | Æ 81 |

Naomi | wife of | Denman Woodruff | died | Aug 8, 1874 | æ 63 |

Mary-Ann Smith | daughter | of | Tomlinson & | Electa Wells | died | July 1, 1840 | aged 8 mo's | & 8 da's |

Susannah-Augusta | daughter of | Tomlinson & | Electa Wells | died | March 31, 1834 | aged 5 years | & 5 months |

Electa Smith | wife of | Tomlinson Wells | died | Jan 1, 1854 | Aged 52 | .

Tomlinson Wells | died | April 12, 1886 | Aged 93 Y'rs |

In | Memory of Philip Wells | who died Dec 23, 1818 | aged 65 |

In | memory of | Elizabeth Wells | wife of Philip Wells | who died | Nov. 27, 1848 | aged 91 |

In | Memory of | Hannah | Wife of | John Williams | who died | Aug 21, 1816 | Æ 29 |

Cornelia | daughter of | James C. & | Sally Wadsworth | died Dec 17, 1828 | Æ 7 yrs |

Gen. Morris Woodruff || Died May 17, 1840 || Born Sept 3, 1777 ||

Candace | Wife of | Gen. Morris Woodruff | & Daughter of | Lewis Catlin, Esq: | Born Apr 2, 1786 | Died July 22, 1871 |

Reuben M. Woodruff, M. D. | born | May 8, 1811, | died | April 29, 1849 |

Eliza R. Wadhams | Widow of | Geo. D. Wadhams | Formerly Wife of | Reuben M. Woodruff, M. D. | born | Jan 13, 1821 | died | Oct 7, 1895 |

Henrietta E. | Daughter | of | Dr. Reuben M. & Eliza R. | Woodruff | Born July 1, 1846 | Died Nov 25, 1862 |

Robert Watts | killed at the battle of Cold Harbor | Va June 1, 1864 | Aged 25 |

Mary J. Watts | died | Sept 30, 1869 | Aged 53 Years |

Mary Jane | Daughter of | Adam & Nancy | Watts | died | July 6, 1862 | Æ 1 Yr. 7 Mo. | & 2 D's |

Charles L. Webb | died | Feb 13, 1870 | Aged 89 |

Catharine | wife of | Charles L. Webb | died | Feb 2, 1861 | Aged 76 |

Mrs. | Abigail Wessells | died | Sept 29, 1846 | aged 78 |

D. W. | In | memory of | David Wessells | who died | Jan 15, 1836 | aged 72 years |

George B. Wessells | died | May 15, 1850 | Æ 75 |

Nabby | wife of | George B. Wessells | died | Dec 30, 1850 | Æ 80 |

Eunice B. | wife of Wᵐ H. Wheeler | died | Dec 25, 1890 | Aged 84 |

William Wheeler | died | Oct 3, 1865 | Aged 60 |

John Nelson | son of | Rev. Horatio N. & | Melissa M. Weed | died | Apr 13, 1855 | Æt 1 week. |

Benjamin N. | son of | William M. & | Jane Webster | died| Sept 12,·1860 | Aged 1 year | & 8 d's |

Jason Whiting | died | Jan. 24, 1879 | Æ 82 Y'rs | 8 M's | & 5 D's | his wife | Sarah G. Whiting | died | Jan 25, 1878 | Æ 69 Y'rs 9 M'o | & 9 D's |

Mary Mercy | Wheelock | died | Jan 4, 1872 | Æ 4 Mo's & 18 d's |

Reuben Webster | died | Aug 2, 1833 | aged 76 || Annie Webster | wife of | R. Webster | died | Nov 24, 1841 | aged 77 || (*see Margaret Marsh*) ||

David M. Wheeler | son of | Christopher & | Orinda Wheeler | Died Feb 3, 1879 | Æ 51 Y'rs & 1 Mo |

William C. | son of | Christopher & | Orinda Wheeler | died Sept 11, 1848 | Æt 27 y'rs |

Christopher Wheeler | died | Jan 24, 1858 | æ 70 | WHEELER || Orinda | wife of | Christopher Wheeler | died | Aug 27, 1858 | Æ 67 |

In | memory of | Mary A. Wetmore | who died | April 18, 1857 | aged 48 years |

John Wetmore Jr. | died | Mar 23, 1852 | aged 37 years | & 10 mo |

Anna | wife of John Wetmore | died | Dec 5, 1863 | Æt 87 |

John Wetmore | died Oct 26, 1847 | Aged 80 |

Anna M. | daughter of | Edward & | Adaline | Wetmore | died | Feb 28, 1856 | Æt 6 yrs |

Emeline | daughter of | Edward & | Adaline [ Wetmore | died | Mar 7, 1856 | Æt 4 yrs |

Hosea Webster | born in Litchfield | December 14, 1789 | died in Brooklyn, N. Y. | June 1, 1883 || Maria Buel | wife of | Hosea Webster | born | January 21, 1796 | died | August 24, 1852 |

Lydia Eliza | daughter of | James & | Mary Ann Williams | died | Dec 14, 1842 | aged 19 |

Lavinia A. Hos- | John A. Woodruff | | Nicy M. Hopkins | ford | 1st wife | | 1797-1880 | | 2nd wife | 1807-1802-1861 | | | 1888 | WOODRUFF || Walter W. | 1832-1851 | Harriet L. | 1834-1837 |

William Woodin | died | Aug 31, 1866 | Æ 67 |

John F. Williamson | Died | Dec 7, 1887 | Æ 67 | WIL-LIAMSON |

George Catlin Woodruff | born | at Litchfield | December 1, 1805, | died | at Litchfield | November 2, 1885 | Henrietta Sophronia Seymour | born | at Litchfield | October 25, 1806 | died at Litchfield | June 22, 1892 | WOODRUFF || Henrietta Selina | daughter of | George C. & Henrietta S. Woodruff | born April 11, 1831 | died July 30, 1834 |

John P. White | born | Oct 8, 1808 | died | June 2, 1889 |

Elizabeth Canfield | wife of | John P. White | born | Aug. 1, 1816 | died | Apr 24, 1897 |

Charles D. Wheeler | Nov. 18, 1817 | Dec 28, 1895 || (*see Hutchinson*)

Prof. Robert M. Weiss | Born in Wirtemberg | Germany | Sept 29, 1857 | Died in Litchfield | Conn | Sept 13, 1891 | Organist of St. Michael's Church |

James G. Wadsworth | died | May 22, 1876 | Æ 91 Y'rs & 9 Mos | Sally C. Wadsworth | died | March 6, 1869 | Æ 75 Yrs. & 6 Mos. | WADSWORTH || Henry W. Wessells | Bvt. Brig. Gen. U. S. A. | Born at Litchfield, Ct. | February 20, 1809 | Died at Dover, Del. |. January 12, 1889 | Caroline E. Wadsworth | wife of |: Gen. H. W. Wessells | Died July 18, 1895 | Aged 57 || Cornelia Wadsworth | died | Dec 17, 1828 | Aged 7 years |

W | Asaph S. Wright jr. | Apr. 12, 1863-Jan 17, 1901 | WRIGHT |

ADDITIONAL INSCRIPTIONS.

BALDWIN | Theodore Eli Baldwin | Born in New York
Mar. 22, 1828 | Died Jan. 25, 1899 | Elizabeth Bushnell | his
wife | Born Aug 29, 1831 | Died Sept 24, 1897 |

Eveline E. Beach | 1854-1903 | Horatio Benton | born |
August 24<sup>th</sup>, 1811, | died May 7<sup>th</sup>, 1895. | Juliaett Weed | wife
of | Horatio Benton | born | March 3<sup>d</sup>, 1813 | died | December
23<sup>d</sup>, 1901 |

## KILBOURN.

Dwight C. Kilbourn..........................1837
Sarah M. Hopkins, his wife...................1842

William P. Kilbourn..........................1811   1894
Caroline A. Canfield, his wife................1813   1894

*Norman Kilborn ............................1789   1886
*Lucy Peck, his wife.........................1790   1870

*Jacob Kilborn .............................1767   1859
*Lucy Bradley, his wife......................1767   1850

---

*Buried at Bantam.

# BANTAM

On Church Hill, east of the village of Bantam, lies the newest of the Litchfield burying grounds. At a town meeting on the twentieth of November, 1805, a petition of fifty-eight citizens "residing in the western and Southwestern Part of said Litchfield" was offered, desiring forty dollars wherewith to purchase a piece of ground near the new church for a burying yard. This was granted, and by a deed on page sixty of the twenty second volume of Litchfield Land Records, the land was sold to the selectmen of Litchfield by the historic Colonel Benjamin Tallmadge.

In 1865, the selectmen added to the yard a little more than half an acre on the west, and a strip about two rods wide on the southern side, in area a quarter of an acre. A wall was erected in 1899 along the road front of the yard, built of split stone from Mine Hill. In doing this the selectmen added somewhat to the grounds by encroaching upon the highway.

# INSCRIPTIONS.

Mary Ann | wife of | James B. Ames | died | July 26, 1861 | Aged 21 |

Almon B. Bradley | Private in Co A 2^nd Ct | Heavv Artil-iery, killed in | battle at Cold Harbor, Va | June 2, 1864 | Æ 21 |

Alice F. | Daughter of | Henry L. & Huldah A. | Bissell | and adopted daughter of | Harriett E. Prindle | Died Dec 12, 1864 | Aged 15 |

Daniel Bishop | died | Dec 15, 1865 | Æ 76 | Charlotte, his wife | died | Oct 9, 1873 | Æ 74 |

> We laid them down to sleep
> But not with hope forlorn
> We laid them but to ripen them
> Till the resurrection morn.

Charlotte A. Bissell | wife of | Leonard C. Bissell | died | April 26, 1849 | Æt 27 |

Clarrissa Bradley | born | Nov 27, 1807 | died Dec 15, 1879 | Cornelia Bradley | born | Sept. 18, 1805 | died July 2, 1898 |

Henry W. Birge | died | Sept 26, 1875 | Aged 57 |

Charles H. | son of | Henry W. & | Abigail M. Birge | died | Aug 19, 1863 | æ 9 yrs 7 mo | & 10 d's |

Amelia Wilson | wife of | Frederick Bradley | died | Apr 4, 1861 | Aged 23 |

Maria E. | daughter of | H. W. & A. M. Birge | died Apr 20, 1854 | Æ 5 Months |

Harvey P. | son of | Henry W. & | Abigail M. Birge | died | Sept 29, 1862 | Æ 5 mo. |

William Benedict | died | Feb 1, 1847 | Æ 22 |

In | Memory of | Lorenzo Bradley | who died | Nov 10, 1848 | aged 37 years |

Frederick M. | son of | Daniel & | Sophrona Bradley | died | July 17, 1849 | Æ 11 mo. |

An infant | son of | Orrin & | Clarinda Brown | died | May 11, 1841 | aged 12 days |

In | Memory of | Clarinda wife of | Orrin Brown | who died | May 22, 1847 | Æt 30 years |

James | son of | Nathaniel & | Anna Bissell | Died | Dec 20, 1831 | Æ 4 mo |

Roene Bunnell | wife of | Ephraim K. Bunnell | died Sept 30, 1827 | Æ 29 |

Julius Bissell | son of Herman | & Anna Bissell | died | Sept 17, 1826 | Æ 13 months & 13 days |

Mrs. Molly | Wife of | Mr Silvanus Bishop | Died | Nov 14, 1831 | Æ 89 |

Mr. | Silvanus Bishop | died | Dec 24, 1828 | Æ 92 |

Sacred | to the memory of | Mr James Burgess | of Washington who died | June 2, 1815 | in the 71 year | of his age |

In | Memory of | Samuel Beard | who died Nov 12, 1812 | in the 80 year of | his age |

Sacred | to the memory of | Orlando Benton, Esq. | who departed this life | July 18, 1813 | Ætat. 23 |

Dotha | daughter of | Solon & | Juliana Bishop | died | Feb 14, 1838 | aged 15 years |

In | memory of | Juliana | wife of | Solon Bishop | who died | Aug 26, 1831 | aged 41 years |

In | Memory of | Leaming Bradley | who died | Dec 20, 1820 | aged 86 |

In | Memory of | Anna wife of | Leaming Bradley | who died | Oct 11, 1819 | aged 86 |

Sacred | to | the Memory of | Doct. | Comfort Bradley | who died | 21st Aug 1820 | aged 54 years |

Mrs. | Sally Bradley | relict of | Comfort Bradley | died Aug 5, 1830 | aged 63 |

In | Memory of | Joseph Bradley | who died | June 23, 1831 | æ 61 |

Lucy | relict of | Joseph Bradley | died | Apr 19, 1860 | Æ 88 |

Charles | son of Erastus & | Sally Bradley | died | Oct 27, 1840 | aged 17 years |

Frederick | son of | Erastus & | Sally Bradley | died | Sept 5, 1832 | Æ 5 y'rs |

Lucius son of | Lorenzo & | Amy M. Bradley | died | Sept 15, 1832 | aged 8 mo | Also Mary Ann | their daughter | died | Feb 18, 1837 | aged 3 years | & 3 mo. |

Minerva D. | wife of | Heman Beach | & twin daughter of | Henry R. & | Jerusha Goslee | died | Jan 29, 1853 | aged 24 years |

In | memory of | Miss Maria Braman | who died | May 18, 1829 | Æt 29 |

William Braman | died | Nov 25, 1839 | aged 42 |

Aaron Bradley | died | Oct 24, 1843 | Aged 81 | Lois, wife of | Aaron Bradley | died | Jan 4, 1844 | Aged 75 |

In | Memory of | Leaming Bradley | who died July 16, 1819 | aged 29 years |

In | Memory of | Mary wife of | Luman Bishop who died June 14, 1843 aged 33 years |

In | Memory of | Julia | wife of Osander Bishop | who died | May 30, 1843 | aged 31 years |

Fannett A. | wife of | George D. Beeman | died | Mar 28, 1880 | Aged 32 |

Francis J. Bachman | died | Nov 9, 1880 | Aged 12 years |

Edward S. | son of | Samuel C. & | Amy A. Bunnell | died | July 31, 1865 | Aged 18 Y'rs |

Amie E. | daughter of | Samuel C. & | Amy A. Bunnell | Died Mar 4. 1874 | Aged 2 Yrs | & 8 Mo's |

Erastus Bradley | died | Feb 10, 1872 | aged 81 | Sally Bradley | his wife | died Oct 15, 1874 | aged 82 |

Hiram Bradley | Co A, 2, Regt | H'vy Art'y C. V. | died | Sept 24, 1877 |

Lucelia S. | wife of | Uri P. Bartholomew | died | July 5, 1859 | Æ 24 |

Allie E. | Daughter of | Lewis & Clara | Bissell | Died | July 23, 1882 | Aged 6 Yrs 4 Mo's |

Anna M. | daughter of | Frederick & Maria | Bissell | of Emporia, Kansas | 1861-1889 |

Frankie | son of | Enos & Permelia | A. Benedict | died | July 18, 1876 | Æ 13 Mo |

Freddie L. | son of | Enos & Permelia | Benedict | died | Aug 10, 1870 | Æ 1 y'r 8 mo's & 24 days |

Benjamin Bissell | died | April 6, 1849 | Æ 62 |

Lizzie | daughter of | Benjamin & Betsey A. Bissell | died | Mar 6, 1874 | Aged 8 Y'rs |

Nathaniel Bissell | died | June 15, 1872 | Æ 85 | his wife | Anna Bissell | died Aug 24, 1848 | Æ 59 | BISSELL | Sally Marsh | wife of | Nathaniel Bissell | died | Mar 22, 1890 | Æ 87 || Philip Bissell | 1843-1879 | George D. Bissell | 1875-1893 || Henry B. Bissell | Clarissa W. | his wife | died March 3, 1892 | Aged 73 ||

Hellen | daughter of | F. & M. A. | Bissell | Aged 7 Weeks |

Ellen | Aged 2 years | (*Bissell lot*)

Amelia | Aged 4 Years | (*Bissell lot*)

Lucy Churchill | died | June 27, 1860 | Aged 81 |

Russell Curtiss | died | Nov 6, 1891 | Æ 57 | Sarg. Com. A 19 Reg C. V. | Mary E. | his wife | Died Feb. 20, 1859 | Æ 23 |

George Clemons | died | Oct 26, 1850 | Æ 21 |

Mahala | wife of Abel H. Clemons | died | Mar 4, 1857 | Æ 54 |

Abel H. Clemons | died | March 9, 1861 | aged 58 |

Wm Ira | son of | Levi M & | Frances E. Coe | died | Mar 20, 1859 | Æ 2 ys. |

William B. | son of | Ira & Almena Coe | died | Jan 23, 1849 | Æ 24 |

In | Memory of | Ann Curtis | wife of | Martin Curtis | who died | Sept 1, 1840 | aged 76 Years |

BANTAM CEMETERY

Photo by U. P. Bartholomew

In | Memory of | Hannah relict of | William Cable | who died | Jan 16, 1839 | aged 74 years |

Mary L. | daughter of Samuel & Julia Can- | field died May 20, 1827 aged | 3 years & 7 mo |

William C. | infant son of | William & | Marie T. Coe | died | June 23, 1832 | aged 3 days |

Francis H. | only child of | William & | Maria T. Coe | died | Oct 16, 1850 | Æ 16 |

William Coe | died Aug 26, 1874 | aged 72 | Maria T. Coe | his wife | died Feb 3, 1865 | aged 59 |

In | memory of | Abel Clemens | who died | Dec 14, 1843 | aged 80 |

In | memory of | Mahetable | wife of | Abel Clemons | who died | Sept 3, 1839 | aged 76 years |

Anna E. Clemons | died | April 29, 1878 | Aged 73 | Julia Clemons | wife of | Wm Stoddard | Died June 22, 1864 | Aged 63 |

William H. Cable | A Vet. Soldier | of Co. E. 8, Regt Ct. Vol. | Died | Sept 29, 1865 | Aged 21 Years |

Willie C. | son of Harry & Mary A. | Clemons | died | May 13, 1869 | Æ 6 y'rs. & 4 d's |

Harry Clemons | 1831-1887 | Mary A. Chapman | his wife | 1832-1900 | CLEMONS || Willie C. Clemons | 1863-1869 | Katie Clemons | 1866 || George W. Clemons | 1861— - Fannie E. Hull | his wife | 1860— |

Lauren Chapman | died | Dec 18, 1883 | Aged 79 | Sarah | his wife died | Apr 4, 1878 | Aged 79 |

(ARKHIPPOS McCALL)
Thomas M. Coe | died | Nov 22, 1883 | Æ 68 | COE || Tamma M. | wife of Thomas M. Coe | Died Apr 27, 1854 | Æ 27 |

Edith C. | daughter of | Wm B. & Sarah J. | Crane | Died Oct 23, 1877 | Aged 10 y'rs 9 M's | & 7 D's |

Freddie B. | son of | William B. & | Sarah J. Crane | Died | April 16, 1875 | Æ 2 Y'rs | 1 Mo. | & 7 D's |

Mrs. | Betsey Day | Wife of | John Day | Died | Jan 25, 1844 | aged 42 |

In | memory of | John D. Day. | died | Dec 10, 1852 | Æ 90 |

In | memory of | Samuel Denison | who died | May 4, 1830 | aged 63 |

In memory of | Susanna Dudley | who died | Jan 1, 1840 | aged 40 |

In Memory of | Mrs. Ruth Dudley | Consort of Mr. Charles | Dudley who Died | August 27th 1808 | Aged 42 Years |

In | memory of | Charles Dudley | who died | March 2, 1836 | aged 69 years |

Rhoda | wife of | Charles Dudley | died | July 7, 1850 | aged 78 years |

Charles A. Dudley | Born March 21, 1812 | Died Aug 10, 1865 |

Louisa Maria | wife of | Charles A. Dudley | Born Mar 12, 1820 | Died Apr 24, 1879 |

Salome Howe | wife of | Samuel H. Dudley | died | Dec 22, 1872 | Æ 67 |

Ira A. Emmons | July 20, 1838 | — | Angeline E. | Kilborn | his wife | Aug 28, 1846 | July 5, 1895 | EMMONS || Ithel Emmons | their son | July 1, 1877 | Dec 26, 1881 |

Eunice L. | daughter of | William | & Mary Fisher | died June 10, 1818 | aged 4 years |

Charles C. | son of Wm & | Mary Fisher | died Aug 25, 1822 |

Amy W. | wife of | John W. Fish | died | Aug 10, 1852 | Æ 40 |

John W. Fish | died | May 10, 1852 | Æ 36 |

Hugh S. | son of | Henry R. & | Jerusha Goslee | Died at Lynchburgh, Va. | July 10, 1862 | Æ 20 | A Member of Co. E, 5 Regt C. V. | Died while a prisoner being taken at the battle of Fort Royal May 30, 1862 | Bravely fighting for his country | He sacrificed his life in her defence |

Henry R. Goslee | died | Sept 12, 1867 | Æ 67 |

Jerusha | wife of | Henry R. Goslee | died | Oct 9, 1858 | Æ 54 |

George I. Gilbert | Co B. 66, Regt. | N. Y. Vols. | died | Nov 1, 1894 | (*The right name is Kilbourn.*)

Mary Ida | wife of | Frank A. Glover | daughter of | C. H. & B. Babcock | died Oct 5, 1880 | Æ 24 |

William | son of | David G. & | Leva Goodwin | died | Nov 1, 1840 |

Marshall | son of | Chapman & | Sally Griswold | died | Jan 29, 1851 | Æ 10 Y'rs |

Chapman Griswold | died Oct 4, 1859 | Æ 65 |

Capt. | Mideon Griswold | Died | Nov 31, 1829 | Æ 66 | Mrs Annis | Wife of | Capt Mideon Griswold | Died | May 10, 1834 | Æ 76 |

Midian Griswold Jr. | died | March 11, 1823 | in the 22 year | of his age |

In | Memory of | Flora | wife of | Morgan Griswold | who died | Sept 27, 1830 | aged 31 years | 7 mo. & 7 days |

Mrs Lydia Goslee | wife of | Solomon Goslee | died | June 21, 1828, Æ 66 |

Jerusha | twin daughter of | Henry R. & | Jerusha Goslee | died | July 18, 1835 | aged 4 wks |

Mr. | Solomon Goslee | Died | Nov 29, 1834 | Æ 72 |

Charles F. | son of | Chester C. & | Caroline Goslee | died | Nov 8, 1839 | aged 18 years |

Samuel B. | son of | Chester C. & | Caroline Goslee | died | Mar. 29, 1845 | aged 16 years |

Mary L. | twin | daughter of | Henry R. & Jerusha Goslee | died | Nov 13, 1849 | Æ 20 |

Willie B. || son of | Myron R. & | Catharine Goslee | died | Aug 26, 1861 | Æ 5 Yr's & 8 Mo |

Catharine | wife of Myron R. Goslee | died | Apr 11, 1865 | Aged 36. |

Myron R. Goslee | died | Aug 19, 1863 | Aged 45 |

Chester C. Goslee | died | Apr 5, 1871 | Aged 73 |

Caroline Braman | Wife of | Chester C. Goslee | Died Mar. 10, 1878 | Aged 75 |

Dwight Griswold | born May 24, 1845 | — | Jennie O. Jackson | his wife | born Feb 29, 1852 | died Sept 13, 1884 | GRISWOLD |

Baby Inez | born | Oct 31, 1881 | died | June 27, 1883 | (*Probably Griswold*).

Cora L. | wife of | Frederick A. Goodman | died | May 7, 1887 | Æ 17 Y'rs & 5 Mo | Henry J. died June 4, 1887 | Aged 3 mo. son of | F. A. & C. L. Goodman |

Sarah Sanger | Wife of | Lewis Hotchkiss | died | Feb. 6, 1876 | Æ 57 |

Elizabeth K. | daughter of | Lewis & Maria Hotchkiss | died | Sept 25, 1859 | Æ 21 |

Maria | wife of | Lewis Hotchkiss | died | Feb 28, 1859 | Æ 48 |

Jason Hallock | died | Sept. 12, 1865 | Æ 43 |

In | memory of | Hobert | only son of | Jason & Polly | Hal'ock | who died | May 22, 1849 | Æ 3 y'rs |

Hubert | son of | Jason & | Polly Hallock | died | Aug 29, 1853 | Æ 1 ye & 10 m |

Mary Louisa | daughter of | Jarvis & | Harriet M. Hallock | died | March 9, 1852 | aged 2 mo. & 9 d's |

In | memory of | Zephaniah Hull | Who died | March 22, 1841 | Aged 77 yr-s |

Rachel | wife of | Zephaniah Hull | died | Mar 13, 1853 | Æ 78 |

Jay Hallock | died | Oct. 29, 1873 | Æ 16 y'rs | Jason A. | died Mar 19, 1867 | Æ 15 mo | sons of | Albert B. & Cynthia A. | Hallock |

Curtis Hallock | died | Nov 18, 1864 | Æ 63 |

Amanda | wife of | Curtiss Hallock | died | Feb 5, 1845 | aged 44 |

Infant | son of | Albert B. & | Cynthia Hallock | died Feb 23, 1855 | Æ | 1 day |

Alice Jane | Daughter of | L. D. & | C. J. Hosford | died | June 4, 1858 | Æ 10 Mo |

Caroline M. | wife of | Dudley Hosford | Died | Feb 18, 1860 | Æ 58 |

Dudley Hosford | Born Aug 23, 1799 | Died July 9, 1865 | Aged 66 |

Erected | by | James Hore | as a tribute of love to | his affectionate wife | Mary Jane | daughter of | Lorenzo & | Anthe Wheeler | died | Feb 3, 1854 | Æ 20 |

In memory of | Sally Hull | who died | May 6, 1849 | aged 46 years |

Horatio | Son of Guy & Sally Hand | died Nov 29, 1811 | aged 6 years |

In | Memory of | Sally Hand | wife of Guy Hand | who died | April 30, 1811, Aged 28 |

In | Memory of | Guy Hand | who died Sep$^t$ 10, A D, 1813 in the 31 | Year of his age |

Hiram Hand | died | April 6, 1868 | Aged 77 | Mary Ann | his wife | died | Jan 26, 1835 | Aged 45 | HAND |

Marilla | Wife of | Elisha Horton | Died | Nov 6, 1860 | Æ 69 |

In | memory of | Elisha Horton | who died | Nov 30, 1837 | aged 80 years |

Hannah Horton | wife of | Elisha Horton | died July 6, 1824 | aged 53 |

In Memory of | Hannah Hoyt | Daughter of Levi | and Hannah Hoyt | who died sept 24 | 1811, in the furst | year of hur age |

In | Memory of | Mrs Hannah Hoyt | Wife to Mr. Levi Hoyt | Who died Sept 5$^{th}$ | A. D. 1811 in the 26$^{th}$ | Year of her Age |

John M. Haager | died | May 19, 1879 | aged 60 yrs |

In | memory of | Sally Hoyt | who died | Sept 13, 1838 | in the 75 year | of her age |

Almira | wife of | Lewis G. Humiston | died | July 28, 1856 | Æ 11 |

In | memory of | Harmon Putnam | son of Roseville & | Lorina Hart | who died | June 30, 1833 | aged 7 years | & 4 mo |

Mary A. | Wadsworth Hannahs | Died | Oct 1, 1859 | Aged 64 |

Harriet M. | Wife of | Jarvis Hallock | Died Dec 9, 1870 | Æ 46 | Edwin L. son of | Jarvis & Harriet Hallock | Died Nov 9, 1865 | Æ 16 |

Lottie E. | daughter of | George W. & Annie E. Hard | died | Jan 20, 1875 | Æ 7 Mo. & | 12 D's |

Estella | daughter of | George W. & | Annie E. Hard | died | Sept 24, 1884 | Æ 2 Mo's & 19 D's |

Annie E. | wife of | George W. Hard | died | Oct 18, 1884 | Aged 35 |

Louisa J. | Daughter of | George M. & | Elizabeth Hard | died | July 16, 1865 | aged 4 y'rs |

Adam Herdlein | died | Nov 21, 1888 | Aged 75 | Mary | his wife | — | Herdlein |

In | memory of | Benjamin Johnson | who died | May 12, 1848 | aged 54 years |

Sacred | to the memory of | Benjamin Johnson | who departed this life | Jan 7, 1829 | in the 70 year of | his age |

In | memory of | Lucretia | wife of | Benjamin Johnson | who died | March 28, 1832 | aged 66 years |

Caroline F. | daughter of | Horace & | Harriet Johnson | died | Mar 29, 1849 |

In | Memory of | Lambert Johnson | who died | Nov 29, 1842 | aged 78 years |

In | memory of | Tilda wife of | Lambert Johnson | who died | Dec 27, 1815 | aged 51 years |

Armenia | died | Sept 23, 1888 | Æ 5 Mo's 9 D's | Mildred A. | died | Aug 11, 1890 | Æ 9 Mo's 3 d's | Children of Joseph S. & | Carrie L. Jones |

Annie C. | daughter of | Henry L. & | Helen L. Kenney | died | April 9, 1859 | Æ 1 year 1 mo | & 7 d's |

Leonard H. | Son of | Henry L. & Helen L. | Kenney | died | May 20, 1863 | Aged 9 Mo. & 10 D's |

Frank L | Son of | Henry L. & Helen L. | Kenney | Died Jan 29, 1864 | Aged 3 Y'rs 5 Mo | & 16 D's |

Helen L. | wife of | Henry L. Kenney | died | Aug 14, 1874 | Aged 43 |

Frances | wife of | Henry L. Kenney | died | Mar 6, 1888 | Aged 36 |

Leonard Kenney | died | Aug 20, 1875 | Aged 78 | Louisa B. Kenney | died | July 28, 1880 | Aged 78 |

In | Memory of | Joseph Kenney | who died | Jan 6, 1852 | in the 25 year | of his age |

Homer Kilbourn | died | Oct 29, 1858 | Æ 40 |

Henry Kilbourn | died | June 14, 1859 | Æ 46 |

Hobart Kilborn | died | Jan 4, 1857 | Æt 31 |

Jeremiah Kilborn | died | Dec 1, 1850 | Æt 29 |

Riley P. || son of | Rollin F. & | Louisa M. Kilborn | died | July 6, 1865 | aged 1 year | 9 m. & 5 d's |

Freeman J. || son of Rollin F. & | Louisa M. Kilborn | died | July 11, 1865 | aged 12 y'rs | 5 mos & 10 d's |

Rollin F. Kilborn | died | Nov. 12, 1883 | Aged 65 |

Harriet | wife of | Hiram G. Kilborn | died Feb 23, 1850 | Æt 32 |

Hiram G. Kilborn | died | Mar 9, 1887 | Aged 72 Yrs |

Catharine | wife of | Putnam Kilbourn | died | Dec 28, 1863 | aged 71 years |

Putnam Kilborn | died | Feb 27, 1863 | Æ 72. |

Dea. Truman Kilbourn | died | Mar 16, 1882 | Aged 87 |

Emeline Coe | wife of | Truman Kilbourn | died | May 2, 1863 | Æ 62 |

Charles J. Kilbourn. M. D. | died | Jan 21, 1853 | Æ 32 |

Elizabeth D. | only | daughter of | Truman & | Emeline Kilbourn | died | July 18, 1841 | Aged 5 years | & 11 mo |

Sarah Ann | daughter of | Murray & | Abigail Kenney | died | Aug 23, 1848 | Æ 11 w'ks & 3 d's |

Charles Russell | son of Murray & | Abigail Kenney | died March 6, 1841 | aged 7 mo & 14 d's |

Murray Kenney | died | Aug 7, 1848 | Æt 35 |

In | Memory of | Mrs Hannah Keeler | the wife of | Mr. Daniel Keeler | who died | Feb 10th 1817 | Aged 29 years |

William R. Keeler | 1823-1886 | Elizabeth M. Throop | his wife | 1823 —— |

Martha O. | daughter of | Wm & Elizabeth | Keeler | Died Sept 21, 1878 | Æ 17 |

Julia E. | daugher of | Wᵐ & Elizabeth | Keeler | Died Aug 29, 1870 | Æ 20 |

Martha M. | daughter of | Daniel & Eliza | Keeler | died | May 4, 1853 | Æ 22 |

In | memory of | Eliza wife of | Daniel Keeler | who died | Jan. 11, 1850 | Aged 58 |

Mrs | Kaziah Keeler | wife of | Mr. Joseph Keeler | died Aug 13ᵗʰ, 1824 | Æt 80 |

Mr. | Joseph Keeler | died Feb 8ᵗʰ 1825 | Æt 79 |

In | Memory of | Daniel Keeler | who died | July 21, 1854 | Æ 69 |

Samuel Kilbourn | died | July 24, 1851 | Æ 38 |

In memory of | Mr. David Kilborn | who died Sept 17, 1815 | aged 73 years | Also of | Mrs Diadana wife of | Mr. David Kilborn | who died July 3, 1817 | aged 69 years |

In | Memory of | Mr. Jesse Kilborn | who died | April 2, 1813 | in the 70 year | of his age |

Lucretia | daughter of | Jeremiah & | Anne Kilborn | died | April 27, 1859 | aged 73 years |

In | Memory of | Anna wife of | Jeremiah Kilborn | who died | Feb 27, 1849 | aged 77 |

Sacred | to the memory of | Jeremiah Kilborn | who died Feb 21, 1821 | in the 59 year | of his age |

Charles P. | son of Putnam & | Catharine Kilborn | died Apr 27, 1831 | aged 2 years & | 3 months |

Mr. | Noah Kilborn | Died | Aug 23, 1827 | Æt 40 |

Levi Kilborn | Born April 15, 1773 | Died April 13, 1850 |

Anna B. | wife of | Levi Kilborn | Born Nov 30, 1773 | Died Sept 22, 1861 |

Maria Kilborn | Born Jan 28, 1800 | Died April 21, 1867 |

Whitman Kilborn | died | June 18, 1843 | aged 71 years |

Thalia O. | wife of | Whitman Kilbourn | died | May 8, 1865 | Æ 88 y'rs & 6 mo |

Laura A. | Wife of | Wᵐ H. Knickerbocker | Died Aug 11, 1867 | Æ 20 |

Laura L. | Daughter of | Wᵐ & Emma Knickerbocker | died May 6, 1874 | Aged 1 Ye 1 Mo | & 18 D's |

Merritt | son of | Chas. L. & Phebe D. | Keeler | died Sept 1, 1882 |Aged 11 Months |

Father | Eliada Kilbourn ‖ Mother | Mary Ann Dudley | 1809-1883 | ‖ 1809-1887 | | KILBOURN |

Sherman C. Keeler | Born | July 8, 1810 | Died Jan 22, 1880| Laura E. Beebe | his wife | Born July 30, 1808 | Died Feb 15, 1889 | KEELER | Fanny I. | daughter of | A. G. & June Keeler | Beach | Born Jan 10, 1870 | Died July 29, 1871 |

Maria | daughter of | Truman & Phebe | Leavenworth | died | Mar 19, 1852 | Æ 35 |

Almira | daughter of | Truman & Phebe | Leavenworth | died | Mar 3, 1852 | Æ 41 |

Selleck O. Landon | died Oct 13, 1858 | Æ 51 |

Gertrude L. | daughter of | Alvah N. & Jerusha A. | Landon | died Aug 14, 1864 | aged 3 yrs 2 mo | & 21 d's |

Alvah N. Landon | died | June 9, 1865 | Aged 29 Y'rs | 7 Mo. & 15 d's |

Mary | died | July 22, 1848. | Æ 5 Yrs | Juliaette | died | July 25, 1848 | Æ 2 Y'rs | Harriet | died | Aug 6, 1848 | Æ 4 Y'rs | children of Earl K. and | Sally Little. |

Robert E. Lewis | infant son | of | Mr. & Mrs. A. Lewis |

Eveline M. | daughter of | Truman & Phebe | Leavenworth| died | July 18, 1885 | Æt 70 |

Lucretia | wife of | Truman Leavenworth | died | July 29, 1851 | Æt 64 |

Truman Leavenworth | died | Mar 26, 1852 | Æ 66 |

Charles J. | son of | Wᵐ & | Almeda Loveland | died | Aug. 14, 1849 | Æ 18 mo's |

In | memory of | Betsey wife of | Charles Landon | who died | Feb 16, 1846, Æ 61 |

Charles Landon | died | May 20, 1855 | Æt 75 Yrs |

Minerva | wife of | Abner Landon | died | Nov 10, 1874 | Aged 77 |

Abner Landon | died | Feb 26, | 1863 | Æ 67 |

In Memory of | Almeda Landon | Daughter of John Landon | who died | July 10<sup>th</sup> 1810 | in the 16<sup>th</sup> year of her | age |

In | memory of | Theron Landon | Son of John & | Abigail Landon | who died May 10, 1812 | Aged 23 years |

Irene | daughter of | Horace & | Rachel Landon | died Sept 16, 1818 | aged 2 years & | 7 months |

Susannah | wife of | Sherman Landon | died | Oct 29, 1851 | Æ 53 |

Sherman Landon | died June 9, 1855 | Æ 57 |

In | Memory of | Norman Landon M. D. | who died | Oct 24, 1820 | Æ 30 |

In | memory of | Sarah wife of | Remembrance | Landon | who died | Sept 8, 1843 | Æ 79 |

M<sup>r</sup> | Remembrance Landon | Died | Jan 9, 1831 | Æ 71 |

In | Memory of | Widow Eunice Landon | who died the 29<sup>th</sup> of May | 1812 in the 73 year of | her age |

In memory of | Serg<sup>t</sup> John Landon | Who fell in Battle in | Upper Canada the 25 | of July 1814 | in the 37 | year of his Age | And also In memory of | Anne His Wife who | Died May 20, 1814 in | the 35 year of her age |

> His ashes lies in distant land
> Whilst hers doth here remain
> In fighting for his country's cause
> He fell a victim slain.

In | memory of | Lucy Lina | daughter of John | & Anne Landon | born Oct 2, 1812 | died June 15, 1813 |

In Memory of | Elvira daughter | to Jairus and Anna | Ludinton who | died March 23 | 1809 in the 2<sup>d</sup> | year of her age |

LANE | Georgie H. | born Feb 28, 1863 | died Feb 25, 1866 | Lenora M. | born May 1, 1865 | died March 12, 1866 | Edgar H. | born March 12, 1867 | died Jan 19, 1868 | children of | Henry & Jane | Lane || Henry A. | born June 11, 1873 | died Dec 26, 1874 | Thomas A. | born Jan 8, 1879 | died July 30, 1889 | children of | Henry & Jane | Lane |

Calista Landon | died | Nov 12, 1874 | Æ 49 |

Charles J. Landon | died | Apr 14, 1874 | Æ 49 |

Ida J. | daughter of | William & Ellen | Landon | died Apr 28, 1873 | Æ 11 Y'rs & 6 Mo |

Lansford E. | son of | Joseph C. & | Elvira | Lanphier | May 11, 1869 | Æ 2 y'rs 7 mo | & 9 d's |

Harry J. | son of | Joseph C. & | Alvira | Lanphier | died | Sept 7, 1869 | Æ 4 mo. & 23 d's |

Ximenia D. | daughter of | Theron J. & | Ida E. Loveland | died | Mar 22, 1879 | Æ 2 Y'rs & 2 Mo |

Barnard McConnell | died | Apr 3, 1863 | Aged 61 | Abby his wife | died Jan 9, 1864 | Aged 51 |

Mattie || Son of | Frederick & | Mary A. Morse | died | Nov 11, 1859 | Æ 7 Y'rs |

Leavitt Munson | died | Nov 12, 1878 | Aged 84 |

Julia | daughter of | Nathan & | Ortentia Masters | died | Dec 6, 1851 | Æ 1 y'r & 10 mo |

Harriet | daughter of | George & Mary | Merriam | died | Aug 18, 1833 | aged 3 years | & 5 months |

Infant | son of | E. W. & Mary A. Moulthrop | died | Nov 21, 1888 | Æ 3 days |

In memory of | Leonard Moulthrop | was born Sept 22, 1809 | and died Oct 17, 1810 | son of | Abraham Moulthrop |

In | Memory of | Rachel Wife of | Abraham Moulthrop | who died May 30, 1811 | in the 30 year of | her Age |

In | Memory of | Polly wife of | Thomas Moore | who died | Sept 1, 1819 | Aged 19 years |

Ernest Sidney | son of | Sidney D. & | Jerusha A. Moore | died | Apr 7, 1883 | Æ 18 mo's |

Roderick R. | son of Thomas C. & | Welthy Moore ] died | July 12, 1841 | Aged 4 years |

Thomas C. Moore | died | Aug 29, 1877 | Æ 80 |

Wealthy G. | wife of | Thomas C. Moore | died | Sept 6, 1867 | Æ 77 |

Mary | wife of | George Merriman | died | Oct 13, 1884 | Aged 80 |

George Merriman | died | Feb 19, 1894 | Aged 94 Y'rs | & 6 Mo's |

Cora E. Miller | Sept 21, 1858. | Feb 13, 1895 | Arthur W. | Mar 29, 1890 | July 26, 1892 | This stone is erected | to their Memory | by Uncle Jerry |

John Osborn | Died Dec 13, 1876 | Aged 79 | Abigail | his wife | Died Dec 20, 1876 | Aged 74 |

Harriette E. Prindle | died | Jan 8, 1891 | Aged 74 |

Joseph Prindle | died | Nov 13, 1869 | Aged 77 |

Roxana | wife of | Joseph Prindle | died | Nov 22, 1882 | Aged 84 |

John C. Prindle | died | Mar 20, 1895 | Aged 74 |

Samuel Payne | died | Oct 17, 1858 | Æ 76 |

Juliett | wife of | Henry A. Potter | Died Dec 19, 1859 | Æ 26 | Emma J. Potter | Died Dec 25, 1859 | Æ 3 wk's. |

Henry A. Potter | Died | Feb 15, 1896 | Æ 67 |

Orestes Palmer | Born Feb 21, 1821 | Died May 15, 1861 | Also Little Lizzie | Died Aug 29, 1861 | Æ 1 Mo & 25 D's |

John Palmer | died | Nov 1, 1851 | Æt 77 |

Miner Potter | died | Dec 12, 1850 | Æ 64 |

Polly Gray | wife of | Miner Potter | died | Mar 8, 1878 | Æ 81 |

Garry L. | son of | Garry G. & | Mary A. Potter | died | June 24, 1861 | Æt 5 Y'rs, 2 mo. 21 d's |

M. Louisa | daughter of | Garry G. & | Mary A. Potter | died | June 5, 1861 | Æt 8 y'rs 7 mo. 4 d's |

Harriet | wife of | Martin Pratt | died | Feb 17, 1880 | Aged 79 |

Martin Pratt | died | Dec 18, 1850 | Æt 57 |

Mercy Pratt | died | Nov 12, 1849 | Æt 81 |

Frederick P. | son of | Philemon & | Stattina Pond | died | Oct 13, 1854 | Æ 8 yrs & 5 mo |

Sergt. Ferris Pond | Born Nov 11, 1836 | Died Nov 8, 1867 |

Fanny E. | daughter of | Raphel & | Diana Potter | died | Sept 1, 1853 | Æ 13 |

Alpheus R. | son of | Raphel & | Diana Potter | died | Aug 6, 1848 | Æ 5 y'rs & 6 d's |

Sally Ann | daughter of | Solomon & Martha | Parmelee | died | June, 1858 | Æ 30 |

Elias Peck | died | Sept 9, 1851 | Æt 69 |

Eber Peters | died | Oct 14, 1841 | aged 73 |

In | memory of | Catharine | wife of | Eber Peters | who died | July 6, 1836 | aged 72 y'rs |

Christopher C. Palmer | Jan. 1809—Feb. 1895 | his wife | Rebecca Stone | May 1810—Apr 1876 |

Mary R. | wife of H. S. Pratt & | Daughter of | C. C. & Rebecca Palmer | died | June 16, 1853 | Æ 21 y'rs 9 mo | & 8 d's |

Mary Edith | daughter of | Homer S. & | Mary R. Pratt | died | Feb 23, 1851 | aged 2 y'rs | 4 mo. & 13 d's |

Christopher C. Jr. | son of | Christopher C. & | Rebecca Palmer | died | May 7, 1837 | aged 3 years | 2 monhs & | 15 days |

Elijah L. Peck | died | March 24, 1824 | in the 18 year | of his age |

Jaba. W. Peck | died | July 30, 1822 | in the 40 year | of his age. |

In | memory of | Betsey Parmerlee | who died | June 11, 1842 | aged 63 |

In Memory of | Elizabeth Palmalee | Wife of | Amos Palmalee Ju. | who died April 11, 1813 | in the 47 year | of her age |

Emeline | Daughter | of Liscome & | Charlotte | Palmer | Died Ju'y | 29, 1830 Æ | 2 yrs & 6 mo |

In | Memory of | Benjamin Potter | who died | June 18, 1837 | aged 74 |

In | Memory of | Rachael | wife of | Benjamin Potter | who died [ Aug 30, 1850 | aged 84, y'rs |

In | memory of | Albert Potter | who died | Aug 30, 1839 | aged 35 years |

John Porter | died | Sept 16, 1845 | aged 42 years | Also | Rachel his wife | died | July 16, 1846 | aged 44 years |

Prentice Parkhurst | died | March 12, 1850 | Æt 35 |

Edward Parker | died | June 27, 1885 |Aged 90 | Mary Parker | his wife | Died Aug 12, 1885 | Aged 90 |

Frank J. | died | June 27, 1876 | Aged 3 Mo's | Garfield J. ! died July 29, 1883 | Aged 3 Y'rs || Edgar | died | Sept 23, 1883 | Aged 2 W'ks || Florance L. | died | Sept 1, 1875 || Children of | Frank & Leva A. | Parker |

Julia M. Peck | died | Oct 15, 1895 | Æ 70 |

Caroline E. Hanchett | wife of | Lyman B. Prindle | Died Oct 6, 1885 | Aged 56 |

John T. Peters | died | March 3, 1878 | Aged 75 | Lucy Clemons | his wife | Died Feb 21, 1885 | Aged 87 |

Samuel P. Pond | died | April 12, 1873 | Æ 24 Y'rs 7 Mo. & 7 D's |

Betsey A. | wife of | Seth Pond | Died April 24, 1882 | Aged 73 |

Seth Pond | died Nov 7, 1881 | Aged 74 Y'rs |

Verona Richardson | died | Mar 15, 1896 | Aged 81 |

John S. Richardson | Company H. 3rd Regt | of Minnesota Vol | died | July 30, 1862 | Aged 18 Y'rs |

Georgie S. | Died Dec 15, 1859 | Aged 7 Y'rs | Also lies Sister| Loesa M. | Died Jan 5, 1860 | Aged 13 Y'rs | Children of | Henry & Verona | Richardson |

Theodore | son of | Henry & Verona Richardson | died | Aug 8, 1855 | Æ 9 mo |

Jane Ellis | wife of | William Ravenscroft | born in Wales | 1810 | died at Bantam Falls | Sept 6, 1847 | Æt 37 | "Gwyn cn byd y meirw y rhai sydd | yrr marw yn yr arglwydd" Rev. XIV. 13 |

Charles P. | son of Elijah & | Harriet Rouse | died | Mar 20, 1848 | Æ 4 mo & 9 d's |

Elijah Marsh | son of | Elijah & | Harriet Rouse | died | Oct 6, 1845, Æt 4 mo's | & 7 days |

In | Memory of | Mabel Ransom | wife of Nicholas Ransom | who died Sept 29, 1817 | in the 49 year | of her age |

Mrs. | Sarah Russell | wife of | Capt Stephen Russell | died June 25, 1818 | Æ 40 |

In | memory of | Hannah | wife of | Jonathan Russell | who died | Nov 1, 1836 | Æ 82 yrs |

Mr. | Jonathan Russell | died | Aug 21, 1826 | Æ 78 |

Pearl | Daughter of | F. E. & M. E. | Richardson | died | May 23, 1887 | Aged 1 Y'r |

Leman Stone | died | Feb 14, 1869 | Æ 56

Cornelia, | wife of | Leman Stone | died | Dec 7, 1873 | Æ 56 |

Phebe | wife of | Lyman Stone | died | Jan 30, 1896 | Æ 68 |

Lyman || Son of | Lyman & | Phebe Stone | died | Aug 11, 1864 | aged 1 year | & 3 mo |

The Grave of | Willie | son of | Lyman & | Phebe Stone | died | Dec 2, 1854 | aged 3 weeks | & 3 d's |

Lyman Stone | died June 4, 1873 | Æ 50 |

Frederick J. | son of | James L. & | Almira Stone | Died | July 2, 1859 | Æ 15 d's |

Phebe H. | wife of Lucius C. Stone | died | Jan 28, 1865 |Æ 47 |

Mary E. | daughter of | Lucius & Phebe Stone | died | Aug 20, 1858 | Æ 2 ye 6 mo | & 6 d's |

Ra'ph L. | son of | Lucius & | Phebe Stone | died | Apr 23, 1848 | Æ 1 y'r & 10 mo. |

In | memory of | Parmelia | wife of | Apollos Stone | who died | May 16, 1848 | Æ 22 |

In | memory of | Polly Ann | wife of | Philip M. Salisbury | who died | Jan 5, 1838 | aged 17 yrs |

Cornelia A. | wife of | P. W. Smith | died | Apr 7, 1865 | Æ 26 |

Amelia J. | daughter of | Ephraim K. & | Almira J. Stone | died | Sept 16, 1841 | Æ 4 y'rs 8 mo | Also | Robert G. Stone | died July 27, 1848 | Æt 17 mon |

Ephraim K. Stone | died | July 25, 1852 | Æt 46 |

Martin H. Stone | son of | Ephraim K. & | Almira J. Stone | died | Dec 27th 1861 | aged | 20 Y'rs 7 Mo. |

In | Memory of | Amanda wife of | Eli C. Stone | who died | (*below ground*).

Mrs. | Martha B. Stone | wife of | Mr. Edward L. Stone | died Dec 16, 1816 | in the 30 year | of her age |

In | Memory of | Whiting Smith | who died July 21, 1816 | in the 35 year | of his age |

Harman Stoddard | died | Nov 16, 1874 | Aged 78 |

Nancy | wife of | Harman Stoddard | died | June 26, 1853 | Æ 54 |

Anna wife of | Jesse Stoddard | died | Dec 27, 1848 | aged 80 y'rs |

Jesse Stoddard | died | Jan 23, 1846 | Æ 83 |

Hiram | son of Homer | & Nabby C. | Sharp Died | July 24, 1830 | Æ 4 y-rs |

In memory of | David Camp | Stoddard son | of Samuel and | Sarah Stoddard | who died | Nov 13th 1822 | in the 2nd year | of his age |

Thomas Stone | died | Sept 10, 1843 | Æ 88 | Polly Stone | died | July 12, 1842 | Æ 81 |

Albert | son of Leman & | Permelia Stone | died | Aug 22, 1829 | aged 4 months |

Augustus B. | Son of Thomas | & Polly Stone | Died | April 10, 1828 | Æt 20 |

Jarvis | died | April 7, 1837 | aged 10 years | Myron | died | April 15, 1837 | aged 6 years | Children of Leman | & Permelia Stone |

In memory of | Clarissa Fidelia | daughter of Alvah | and Mary Stone | who died Jan 27, | 1821 aged 16 months |

Anne Ames | former wife of | Alvah Stone | died | April 5 1874 | Aged 70 Y'rs & | 9 Months |

In | Memory of Alvah Stone | who died | Feb 17, 1850 | aged 53 years |

George | Son of | Alvah & Lois | Stone Died | Oct 11, 1836 | Æ 17 yrs |

Julia Ann | daughter of | Willis & | Clarissa Stone | died | Oct 22, 1847 | Æ 20 |

Willis Stone | died | Feb 13, 1857 | Æ 58 y'rs |

BANTAM CEMETERY

Photo by U. P. Bartholomew

Clarisse | wife of | Willis Stone | died | April 25, 1864 | Æ 60 |

Fayette W. Smith | died | Sep 19, 1857 | Æ 26 Y'rs |

Whiting P. Smith | died | July 22, 1873 | Æ 60 Y'rs 9 Mo |

Henry Parlee | son of | Whiting P. & | Olive C. Smith | died | Nov 30, 1846 | aged 3 m'os | & 5 days |

Sybil | relict of | Noah Stone | died | Nov 31, 1850 | Æ 78 |

In memory of | Dr. | Noah Stone | who died | Dec 25, 1837 | aged 72 years |

Frederick | son of | Wyllys & | Clarissa Stone | died | June 3, 1826. | Æ 16 mo-s |

Edwin | son of Willis & | Clarissa Stone | Died | Feb 16, 1831 | Aged 8 years |

Jennett | daughter of | Willis & |Clarissa Stone | died Aug. 14, 1833 | aged 18 mo |

In | Memory of | Matilda Bunnell | wife of Isaac Way | & widow of | Harry Stone | who died | Aug 5, 1853 | Aged 46 |

Harry Stone | died | July 21, 1848 | Æ 33 |

Luesa M. | daughter of | Harry & | Matilda Stone | died | April 5, 1844 | Æ 8 mo & 5 d's |

Henry M. Stone | Of Co. G. 19 Regt C. V. | died | at Alexandria | Jan 15, 1863 | Æ 18 |

In Memory of | Doct. Phineas Smith | who departed this life | August 31, 1807 in the | 48 Year of his age |

Let not the dead forgotten lie
Lest you forget that you must die.

In | Memory of | Mrs Deidama | relict of Mr. Beriah Stone | who died | March 4, 1816 | aged 85 years |

In memory of | Irene wife of Thadeus | Stocker who died | Nov 15, 1812 Aged 55 | Years |

Lois | wife of | Alvah Stone | died Feb 8, 1834 | Æ 35 |

Sarah | wife of | Julius Stone 2ᵈ | died | April 15, 1817 | aged 22 |

In memory of | Mary daughter | of Henry & | Rachel Spencer | Who died Aug | 21, 1809 in the | first year of her | age |

In | Memory of | Chesterfield Stoddard | who died Oct the |
30, 1811, Aged 21 |

> Ye young and gay
> tho thoughtless pass meby
> Come view my tomb
> And learn to die.

Hannah C. | wife of | Enos Stoddard | daughter of | Daniel
Keeler | Died Apr 21, 1877 | Aged 58 |

Died | Oct 27, 1830 | William Stone | aged 30 |

Mr. Apollos Stone | Died | Jan 24, 1826 | Æ 46 |

Julius Stone | died | Nov 22, 1842 | Aged 61 years |

Mrs | Sally Stone | wife of Julius Stone | died | June 16,
1825 | Æ 39 |

Susan Jeanette | daughter of | George W. & | Christiana
Stone | died | April 15, 1837 | aged 9 years |

Irene | daughter of | Lewis & | Anna Stone | died | Nov 11,
1825 | Æt 4 |

Maria | daughter of | Mr. Lewis & | Mrs Anna Stone | died
July 16, 1817 | aged 6 years |

Sheldon son of | Lewis & | Anna Stone | died | Oct 28, 1825|
Æt 16 |

Mr. Lewis Stone | died | Dec 4, 1825 | Æt 48 |

Mrs | Anna Stone | relict of | Lewis Stone | died April 11,
1827 | Æ 40 |

Lewis Stone | died | July 4, 1848 | Æ 23 | adopted son of |
Sherman Landon |

Leman Stone | died | April 19, 1869 | Æ 76 |

Permelia | wife of | Leman Stone | Died July 22, 1876 |
Aged 78 |

Mrs Ruth Stone | wife of | Mr Jonah Stone | died April 30,
1814 | in the 63 year | of her age |

In memory of | Jonah Stone | who died Feb 2, 1825 | in the
75 year | of his age |

Coalman G. Stone | Son of | Israel and Abby | Stone Died |
June 22, 1811 | in the first | year of his age |

Ruth Ann | daughter of | Julius & | Sally Stone | died | April 27, 1821 | Æ 3 years |

James Madison Stone | Son of Julius & | Sally Stone | died August 16th | 1811, in the second | year of his age |

In | memory of | Lucretia relict of | Daniel Stoddard | who died | Dec 26, 1833 | aged 72 years |

In | memory of | Daniel Stoddard | who died | Dec 16, 1826 | Æt 66 |

Mrs. Mary | wife of | Mr. Noah Stone | died March 20, 1825 | Æt 80 |

Mr. Noah Stone | died | Dec 16, 1825 | Æ 89 |

Mr. Osee Selkreg | Died | March 26, 1825 | Æt 56 |

In | Memory of | Meriah Selkreg | who died | Dec 28, 1821 | in her 20 yr |

Henry B. | son of | Frank A. & | Anna E. Smith | born Aug 7, 1877 | died May 14, 1891 |

In | memory of | Solomon Stone | who died | March 19, 1835 | Æ 66 |

In | memory of | Rebecca wife of | Solomon Stone | who died | Dec 2, 1829 | aged 57 years |

Frederick Stone | died | Feb 22, 1825 | Æ 22 |

In | memory of | Noah Stone | who died | Nov 6, 1829 | aged 23 | years |

Jennette A. | wife of | Frederick S. Bishop | died | June 26, 1848 | aged 18 years |

Jennette A. | died | Sept 27, 1869 | daughter of | F. S. & J. A. Stoddard | Aged 21 |

Willie | Son of | Clarence E. & | Jessey M. Senior | died Sept 3, 1882 | Æ 1 Y'r & 8 Mo's |

Clarence E. Senior | died | Jan 19, 1897 | Aged 37 Y'rs | SENIOR |

STODDARD || Daniel B. Stoddard | Died Apr. 6, 1868 | Æ 60 | His wife | Maria D. | Died Nov 7, 1881 | Æ 69 | George C. only son of | D. B. & M. D. Stoddard | Died Mar 15, 1851, Æ 18 || Charles M. Kilborne M. D. | Died Aug 13, 1865 | Æ 29 | His wife | Lucretia M. | — |

Ann Tompkins | died | Feb 4, 1880 | Aged 72 Y'rs 8 Mo's |

Lucius Tompkins | died Apr 1, 1853 | Æ 54 |

George Hobert | son of | Lucius & Ann | Tompkins | died | Feb 13, 1845 | aged 4 m. & 15 d's |

Julia E. | daughter of | Lucius & Ann | Tompkins | died | Feb 7, 1859 | Aged 24. |

Joseph Tryon | died | Nov 5, 1846 | Æ 58 |

In | Memory of | Weltha wife of | Thaddeus Todd | Died Dec 29, 1820 | aged 22 years |

Anna | daughter of | Darius & | Anna Turrell | died Nov 9, 1848 | æ 20 |

Louisa M | died July 19, 1849 | Æt 18 | Ellen A. | died | Dec 1, 1853 | Æt 21 | wives of Benjamin Webster |

Alice C | died | Jan 18, 1863 | Æ 9 Weeks & 5 D.s || infant daughter of | Anson C. & Avis A. | Wedge |

Avis A. Bunnell | wife of | Anson C. Wedge | died | July 12, 1887 | Age 44 Years | & 6 Months |

Jane F. | daughter of | Elizur & Maria | Wilson | died | Oct 21, 1853 | Æ 20 |

Anna E. Starr | wife of | Charles Wilson | died | Feb 9, 1861 | Aged 29 |

John Westover | died | Jan 5, 1875 | Æ 77 Years | & 10 Ms |

Lois | wife of | John Westover | died | Sept 25, 1857 | Æ 59 |

Fanny Maria | wife of | Jerome D. Wheeler | died | Nov 14, 1860 | Æ 30 |

George son of | James & | Abigail | Wallace | died | Dec 25, 1830 | Aged 5 weeks |

Sarah Ann | daughter of | James & | Abigail Wallace | died Sept 9, 1829 | Æ 6 mo |

Samuel Hannahs | son of | James & | Abigail Wallace | died | May 24, 1841 | Aged 6 years |

James Wallace | died | Apr 20, 1863 | Aged 67 |

In | Memory of | John Wallace | who died | Mar 18, 1842 | Aged 78 | In | Memory of | Elizabeth | Relict of | John Wallace | who died | Oct 14, 1842 | Aged 86 |

Bennett H. | son of | William S. & | Sarah M. Wheeler | died | Feb 3, 1852 | Æ 5 Mo |

Franklin J. | son of | William S. & | Sarah M. Wheeler | died | June 19, 1852 | Æ 3 y'rs |

Mehetable | Wife of | Joseph Westover | died | Jan 1, 1852 | Æ 79 |

In | memory of | Joseph Westover | who died | Nov 5, 1832 | aged 67 years |

Orra | Wife of | Philander Westover | Died Oct 11, 1851 | Aged 63 |

In memory of | Capt. Philander Westover | who died | Jan 20, 1842 | aged 74 |

Mrs. Huldah | wife of | Capt Philander Westover | died Nov 29th, 1824 | Æt 58 |

In | Memory of | Elizabeth Westover | wife of | Capt Philander Westover | who died | Aug 26, 1822 | in the 52 year of her age |

Truman Westover | died | Nov 6, 1825 | Æt 28 |

Sally Wilmot | wife of | Truman Westover | died | May 27, 1871 | Æ 74 |

Edwin T. | son of Willis & | Hannah Wilmot | died | Sept 3, 1830 | aged 19 years |

In | memory of | Jane Wilmot | who died | Sept 15, 1827 | aged 16 years | daughter of | Willis and | Hannah Wilmot |

In | Memory of | Mr. Willis Wilmot | who died | Feb 12, 1818 | in the 32 year | of his age |

In | memory of | Hannah | relict of | Willis Wilmot | who died | Oct 9, 1831 | aged 46 years |

In | Memory of | Mr. John Wilmot | who died | Jan 8, 1810 | in the 35 year | of his age. |

In | Memory of | Deac. John Wilmot | who died | Sept 5, 1823 | Aged 71 |

Widow | Sarah Wilmot | died Dec 7, 1828 | in the 71 year | of her age |

Polly wife of | Eli Wilmot | died Oct 6, 1826 | in the 51 year | of her age |

Hiram Wilmot | died | August 25, 1825 | in the 23 year | of his age |

Andrew J. | son of Eli & | Sally Wilmot | died Feb 12, 1838 | aged 2 years | & 2 months |

In memory of | Eli Wilmot | Who died | July 8, 1838 | aged 62 |

In | Memory of | Jason Walker | who died | Oct 6, 1823, | aged 40 years |

David B. | son of John & | Lois Westover | Died July 2, | 1832 æ 6 yrs |

Lavina | wife of | David Westover | Died Nov 9, 1871 | aged 80 |

David Westover | died | Oct 16, 1853 | Æt 80 |

Mrs. Rhoda | wife of | Mr. David Westover | died Apr 6, 1826 | Æ 59 |

Samuel E. | son of David & | Lavina | Westover | died Jan 8, 1831 | æ 11 we. |

Henry Wadsworth | Died | Nov 21, 1830 | Æ 49 |

Lucius Wilmot | Born July 11, | 1808, Died | Aug 5, 1875 | Mary Ann Wilmot | Born June 21, 1807 | Died July 20, 1879 | WILMOT || Ellen Louisa | Born April 8 | 1836 Died | Nov 20, 1849 | Edgar Hudson | Born March | 31, Died April 15, 1834 ||

In | Memory of | Caroline | widow of | John Wilmot | who died | Jan 12, 1844 | aged 71 years |

Dr. James K. Wallace | 1825-1888 | Mary A. McKay |— | WALLACE |

Lorenzo Wheeler | died | July 28, 1881 | Aged 72 |

Antha | wife of | Lorenzo Wheeler | died | Oct 14, 1872 | Aged 64 |

Frankie D. | died Sept 27, 1869 | Æ 3 y's 6 mo | Eddie S. | died Apr 11, 1872 | Æ 1 yr 3 mo | Children of | Henry L. & Frances C. | Wheeler |

Jerome D. Wheeler | born Dec 11, 1836 | died — | Fannie M. Simmons | his wife | born Feb 11, 1830 | died Nov 14, 1860 | Hannah E. Simmons | his wife | born May 21, 1840 | died — | WHEELER || Horace L. son of | Jerome D. & Fanny M. | born Sept 1, 1860 | died Aug 16, 1876 |

Linus Westover | born Aug 17, 1804 | died | Nov 25, 1874 | aged 70 |

Sally Thomas | wife of | Linus Westover | born April 16, 1807 | died July 26, 1843 | Aged 36 |

Walter N. | son of | Anson & | Catherine M. | Yale | died | June 25, 1869 | Æ 19 Y'rs |

# NORTHFIELD.

On the sixth of May, 1795, John Humaston, out of the respect and good-will he bore to his fellow residents in the Church Society of Northfield, deeded to the Society half an acre of land lying south of his residence, about half a mile east of the church; reserving to himself, his "heirs and assigns forever the right of feeding s$^d$ Ground." This tract has been added to twice, and a wall of split stone has been built in front of it along the highway.

# INSCRIPTIONS.

Mary Ann | wife of | Charles Allen | died | July 24, 1877 | Æ 39 | ALLEN ||

In | Memory of | Samuel Anthony | who died | Dec 29, 1812 | Aged 28 years |

Miss Elizabeth Atwater | died June 10th 1802 Æ 23 | Miss Mary Atwater | died April 9, 1804 Æ 23 | Daughters of Mr Abel & | Mrs Elizabeth Atwater |

Samuel | son of Mr | Abel & Mrs | Elizabeth Atwater | died March 5th 1795 | Æ 6 weeks |

Mrs Susannah | wife of | Mr Richard N. Atwater | died | Nov 26th 1802 | Aged 40 |

Juliana | daughter of | Mr Richard N. & | Mrs Susannah Atwater | died April 2d 1795 | aged one year & | seven months |

In Memory of | Mrs Eunice consort of | Mr. Cornelius Atwater | who died | Feb 25th, 1803 | In the 28th year | of her age. |

In | Memory of | Almira Daughter of | Dea. Abel & | Mrs Elizabeth Atwater | who died | Apr 27, 1811 | Æ 18 |

Miss | Bethia Atwater | daughter of Dea. Abel | & Mrs. Elizabeth Atwater | and the adopted child of Mr John | & Mrs Bethia Todd | She died | March 1, 1811 | Æt 26 |

Adeline E. | daughter of | Benj. & Martha A. | Blakeslee | Died Nov 7, 1851 | Æ 6 mo's |

Anna E. | daughter of | Benjamin & | Martha A. Blakeslee | died | Oct 29, 1858 | Æ 15 Y'rs | & 7 Mo. | She rests in peace |

To the memory of | Benjamin Blakeslee | died | April 15, 1882 | Aged 62 years |

In | memory of | Wheeler Beecher | who died | July 2, 1838| Æ 84 |

Burr Beecher | died | Nov 11, 1823 | Æ 66 |

In | memory of | Sheldon Bidwell, Jr. | who died | Nov 15,
1852 | Æt 32 |

  For I know thou wilt bring me
  to death, and to the house appoint
  -ed for all living.

Isaac C. Beach | died | April 28, 1875 | Æ 81 | Maria E.
Beecher | wife of Isaac C. Beach | died | May 26, 1877 | Æ
80 | BEACH || Nancy L. | daughter of | Isaac C. & | Maria
E. Beach | died | June 12, 1834 | Æ 18 |

George Bidwell | died | Mar 4, 1845 | aged 46 |

Walter I. | son of | George & | Jenette Bidwell | died | Sept
2, 1856 | Æ 2 y'rs & 6 mo |

  Rest Wally dear, thy parents watch
  With tears thy narrow bed
  A brother's hand will plant sweet flowers
  To blossom o'er thy head.

  ——————

  For 'tis our Heavenly Father's will
  That we be called to mourn
  The treasure which he gave to us
  In sorrow we return.

Sister | Alice E. Boozer | died | Oct 29, 1881 | Æ 25 Y'rs.
3 Mos |

Our Father and Mother | Henry J. Boozer | Died May 22,
1869 | Æ 41 | Mary his wife | Died Feb 5, 1862 | Æ 27 |

Wilfred R. | son of | Henry J. & | Mary M. Boozer | died |
Aug 1, 1856 | Æ 2 y'rs & 11 mo. |

Hannah Beebe | died | Dec 25, 1851 | Æt 68 |

Lizzie J. | daughter of | George F. & Eliza I. | Beers | Died
Mar 23, 1891 | Age 11 Y'rs 7 Mo's |

Allen T. Blakeslee | 1822-1888 | His wives | Lois M. Tib-
bals | 1829-1866 | Lucy A. Beach | 1837-1883 |

Hiram G. Beach | died | Nov 7, 1877 | Æ 64 | Jennette
Beach | his wife | died | Jan 24, 1895 | Æ 81 Y'rs. 6 Mo's |
BEACH || Frederick S. Porter | died | May 6, 1895 | Æ 75
Y'rs 4 Mo's | PORTER ||

Charles W. Blakeslee | died | Mar 10, 1891 | Æ 70 | Sarah
A. | his wife | 1904 | BLAKESLEE || Walter D. B. Davis |
died | Sept 19, 1872 | Æ 24, | Allie H. B. | his wife | died |
March 14, 1877 | Æ 28 |

In | memory of | Clarissa A. Bartholomew | who died | June 27, 1824 | aged 35 |

In memory of | Harriet | Eveline | Daughter of Geo- | rge A. & Harriet | Blakeslee who | died April 3, 1836 | aged 14. | months |

In | memory of | Eli Son of | M^r Charles & | Mrs Elizabeth | Blakeslee, who died | March 30, 1813 | aged 4 years |

In memory of | Doreas | wife of | Jared Baldwin | who died | Feb 20, 1840 | aged 50 |

In memory of | Polly | wife of | Samuel Blakeslee | who died | Aug 22, 1832 | aged 73 years |

In | Memory | of | Samuel Blakeslee | who died | Feb 16, 1831 | aged 74 years |

Doct. Abner Blakeslee | died | Dec 22, 1817 | Æ 87 |

Austin Blakeslee | died | Feb 13, 1827 | Aged 40 |

George P. Blakeslee | died | Jan 8, 1888 | Aged 63 | Co C. 2^nd Regt | Conn Vols H. A. |

Edwin Dwight | Only Child of | George & Rhoda M. | Barnes | Died April 17, 1856 | Æ 3 Y'rs & 9 Mo's |

Miss. | Phebe C. Bassett | died March 9, 1822 | aged 24 years |

Lothrop Bassett | died | Tredell Co. North Carolina | Nov. 4, 1825 | Æt 30 |

Abner Blakeslee | died | April 26, 1854 | Æt 83 y'rs |

Damaris | wife of | Abner Blakeslee | died | Aug 14, 1854 | Æt 75 y'rs |

In | Memory of | Mrs Martha wife of | Mr. Levi Bristoll | who died | Jan 24^th 1805 | aged 31 years |

In | memory of | Chloe | wife of | Levi Bristol | who died | Aug 31, 1837 | aged 66 years |

In | memory of | Thankful | wife of | Zopher Bassett | who died | Aug 22, 1842 | Aged 79 |

Mr. | Zopher Bassett died Jan 4, 1825 | Æ 62 |

Andre Beach | Died at Conquest N. Y. | Oct 6, 1815 | aged 26 | Polly Ann | His Wife | Died Apr 29, 1862 | Aged 68 |

Asa | son of | Asa S. & | Orra E. Blakeslee | died | Aug 27, 1849 | Æ 2 ye. & 21 d. |

Amariah Blakeslee | Died July 10, 1830 | Æ 51 |

Ana | Wife of | Amariah Blakeslee | Died Nov 4, 1861 | Æ 79 |

Curtiss P. Blakeslee | April 1, 1811. | Nov 4, 1880 | Almira C. Smith | his wife | March 4, 1821 | Dec 8, 1894 | Laura M. | their daughter | June 25, 1853 | Feb 9, 1870 |

Albert E. | son of | John & Sarah J. | Barlow | died | Mar. 30, 1872 | Æ 11 Y'rs |

In | Memory of | Mrs. Sarah Barnes | Relict of | Mr Caleb Barnes | who died Nov 20, 1804 | Æ 86 |

In memory of | Levi Bristol | who died | Dec 19, 1841 | Aged 75 |

Howard | son of Dan & | Emily Catlin | died | Oct 15, 1846 | Æ 1 y'r & 2 mo |

Howard | son of Dan & | Emily Catlin | died | Aug 29, 1844 | Æ 7 mo & 16 d's |

Thomas | son of | Dan & | Emily Catlin | died | Sept 16, 1836 | aged 7 mo | & 8 days |

Homer | died | June 8, 1850 | Æ 19, | Wilbur | died at St. Louis, Mo. | July 8, 1849 | Æ 15 | Louis | died | Aug 27, 1852 | Æ 8 Mo | (*In Catlin lot*)

Rubin Cooper | died | Jan 26, 1861 | Æt 33 |

John Churchill | died | Nov 16, 1815, in the | 73 year of his age |

> Now I forbid my carnal hope
> My fond desires recall
> I give my mortal interest up
> And make my God my all.

Hull Churchill | died | Jan 23, 1845 | Aged 58 Y'rs |

In | memory of | Polly Churchill | wife of | Hull Churchill | who died | Feb. 28, 1842 | aged 55 |

> Weep not, her love is round our hearts
> Her holy thoughts to us are given
> Her spirit lingers where we are,
> To win our souls to heaven.

In Memory of | Huldah | wife of Hull Churchill | who died Oct 24, 1818 | in the 28. | year of her age |

William Churchill | died Sept 10, 1828 | in his 48 year | Watch for ye know not what | a day may bring forth. |

John Churchill | Died Jan 14, 1841 | Aged 70 | Ruhama | His Wife | Died Feb. 17, 1864 | Aged 85 |

Mariamne | Thy will Oh God | be done || daughter of | Merritt A. & | Anna A. Clark | died Dec 14, 1861 | Aged 13 years |

Martha | Wife of | Garner B. Curtiss | Died June 16, 1863 | Æ 38 |

Lucy N. | daughter of | William & Keturah | Churchill | died | Nov 21, 1832 |

In | Memory of | an infant Child | of Wᵐ & Keturah Church-ill | who died March | 13, 1825 |

In Memory of | Samuel Bewel | son of Wᵐ & | Keturah Churchill | who died March | 3, 1810 ( ?) Æ 7 m's |

Lie still still sweet
Babe and take thy
Rest
Thy God has called
the home.

Levinna Churchill | daughter of | Garit & Betsey | Church-ill | died | Oct 15, 1818 | Æt | 3 years |

Joseph D. Churchill | Son of Garit & | Betsey Churchill | died Oct 11, 1818 | Æt 4 years |

CATLIN || John Catlin | May 23, 1814 | Aug 26, 1894 | his wife | Laura Humaston | Oct 1, 1813 | 1901 | their daughter | Mary H. | Mar 3, 1844, | Apr 12, 1846 | James P. Catlin |— | his wife, Ada Platts | Apr 22, 1860 | June 10, 1886 |

CAMP |T Bushrod H. | Son of Jabez M. | and Mary H. Camp | June 4, 1835 | Sept 21, 1895 || Jabez M. Camp | June 26, 1811, — June 14, 1890 | Mary Heaton | his Wife | Feb. 12, 1814. — Feb. 8, 1893 | CAMP || Joseph E. | Oct 7, 1839 | May 22, 1840 | Burton H. | June 20, 1841 | Mar. 27, 1842 | Children of | Jabez M. and | Mary H. Camp. |

Corp. **Joseph E. Camp.** | son of Dr. D. B. W. & | F. J. Camp |
killed in battle at Cold Harbor, Va | June 1, 1864 | Æ 22 |

> He sleeps in secret, but his grave
> unknown to man, is marked by God.

**Fannie J. Fox** | wife of | D. B. W. Camp, M. D. | died |
June 3, 1893 | Aged 79 Y'rs | 6 Mo's |

**D. B. W. Camp, M. D.** | (of forty-six years practice) | died |
Sept 1, 1875 | Aged 71 Y'rs | 7 Mo's |

**Phineas G. Cook** | died | Sept 29, 1884 | Age 57 Yrs. | 8
Mos |

**Esther** | wife of | Daniel C. Churchill | died | July 26, 1863 |
Aged 50 |

**Daniel C. Churchill** | died | Sep. 6, 1878 | Aged 65 |

**Lucy Margaret** | wife of | Daniel C. Churchill | died | April
30, 1892 | Aged 60 |

**Louisa A.** | wife of | Ralph G. Camp | died | June 29, 1848 |
aged 28 y'rs 9 mo |

> Blessed are the pure in heart, for
> they shall see God.

**J. Pierpont Camp** | son of | Joseph E. & Rhoda Camp | died |
Dec 3, 1817 | Æ 16½ |

> Art thou dear youth so quickly fled
> So quickly numbered with the silent dead
> Yet still on thee shall fond remembrance dwell
> And to the world thy worth delight to tell
> So may thy bright example fire each youth
> With love of virtue gentleness and truth.

**Rev. Joseph E. Camp** | the first | Pastor of the | Congrega-
tional | Church and Society | in this Place | having Sustained |
that office for | forty-two years | died May 27, 1838 | aged 72
years | Mrs Rhoda Camp | wife of | Rev J. E. Camp | died May
30, 1840 | aged 68 years |

> Friends in our joy, friends in our misery too,
> Friends given by God in mercy and in love
> Our Counsellors, our Comforters, and Guides.

Mr. David Camp | died Feb 25, 1814 | Æt 85 |

> And he died in a good old age
> An old man and full of years
> Spirit divine in Christ direct our way
> Through this dark world
> to worlds of perfect day.

Two sons of Merritt | & Clarissa Clark | died |
Edward | Dec 25, 1830 | || David L. | Jan 1, 1831 | Æt
Æt 3 yrs. & | 3 mo. || 15 mo. |

Lydia K. | daughter of | Merritt & | Clarissa Clark | died |
Mar 1, 1837 | Aged 5 years | & 8 months |

Amelia L. | daughter of | Merritt & | Amelia Clark | died |
Sept 7, 1838 | Aged 8 months |

Amelia E. | daughter of | Merritt & | Amelia Clark | died |
Oct 10, 1843 | Aged 5 weeks |

Ann Marsh | wife of | Joel Castle | died | Nov 14, 1887 |
Æ 74 |

Clarissa | wife of | Merritt Clark | died July 18, 1835 | aged
35 |

Lydia | wife of | Merritt Clark | died Oct 15, 1825 | Æt 31

Mary H. Catlin | born | Mar. 3, 1844 | died | Apr 12, 1846 |

Charles Curtiss | died | Jan 17, 1864 | Æ 53 |

Capt Eli Curtiss | died | May 25, 1867 | Aged 81 |

Nancy | wife of | Capt Eli Curtiss | died | Jan 9, 1860 |
Aged 72 |

In | memory of | Lois | wife of | Daniel Curtis | who died |
April 30, 1832 | aged 72 years |

In Memory of | Mr. Daniel Curtis | who died March 3d |
1803 in the 50th year of his age |

In | Memory of | Miss Sally Cook | who died | Dec 18, 1807|
Æ 30 |

Fanny | Wife of | Norris Way | Died at New Haven | Oct
8, 1865 | Æ 78 | Relic of Daniel Fox & | Jacob Turner |

Howard J. | son of | George & | Emeline Curtiss | died |
April 20, 1867 | Æ 5 mo |

Emeline P. Whitney | wife of | George Curtiss | Died Jan 6, 1870 | Æ 40 |

George Curtiss | born | June 3; 1821 | died | Nov 1, 1890 |

Jason Curtiss | died | Dec 1, 1875 | Aged 81 |

Phebe Turner | wife of | Jason Curtiss | died | Oct 9, 1887 | Aged 86 |

Daniel A. | son of | Jason & | Phebe Curtiss | died | Mar. 13, 1845 | Aged 8 years | 3 months |

Joseph D. | son of | Jason & Phebe Curtiss | died | Aug 11, 1844 | aged 2 years |

Eliakim Curtiss | Died | June 27, 1855 | Æ 85 |

Lucy | wife of | Eliakim Curtiss | died | Oct 25, 1834 | Aged 50 |

Martha | widow of Joseph Curtiss | of Wallingford | died | Jan 4, 1827 | Æt 94 |

Jane A. Olmsted | wife of | Joseph Curtiss | died | Dec 9, 1863 | Æ 37 |

Joseph Curtiss | died | Sept 15, 1864 | Æ 33 |

Julia A. | wife of | William Crosby | died | Jan 19, 1853 | Æ 83 |

In | memory of | William Crosby | who died | Nov 25, 1845 | Aged 81 |

In memory of | Uriah Catlin | & Rebecca his wife |
Uriah | died April 10, | || Rebecca | died Sept 14, 1808, Æ 73 | || 1806, Æ 61 |

Charles E. | son of | Miles & | Sarah Doolittle | died | Mar 4, 1843, | aged 4 years | & 4 mo. |

Martha | wife of | John M. Downs | died | Mar 3, 1850 | Aged 42 |

John M. Downs | died May 15, 1859 | aged 49 |

Twin children of | Wyllys and | Millissent Downs | Wyllys Z. | died Nov 27, 1829 | aged 3 mo. & 22 days | Lewis G. | died Jan 12, 1830 | aged 4 mo & 7 days |

Henry Decker | 1820, 1889 | Margaret A. Judd | his wife | 1826-1891 |

In | Memory of | Eliabeth Ann | Driver | who died May 27, 1834 | Æt 14 |

> Weep no more but court a smile
> Tho' from thy breast a chord is riven
> She was but lent to me a while
> That she might bloom more sweet in Heaven
> Erected by Mary Driver, her
>         mother.

Louisa Dickerman | died | Mar 5, 1850 | Æ 34 |

Guy B. Elliott | died | at Vernon, Ala. | Sept 12, 1835 | Æ 25 |

Stephen C. Elliott | died | at Newtown | Sept 18, 1840 | Æ 23 |

William Elliott | died | May 27, 1863 | Æ 81 |

Philinda Elliott | Died | Aug 4, 1894 | Aged 87 Yrs | 3 Mo's |

Nathan French | Died Feb 28, 1834 | Æ 87 | Lucy | His Wife | Died May 18, 1833 | Æ 77 |

Nathaniel French | died | Nov. 9, 1825 | Æt 22 |

Asa French | Died Nov 30, 1861 | Æ 85 |

Irena | wife of | Asa French | died June 15, 1849 | Æ 65 |

Louisa C. | daughter of | Nathan & | Susan French | died | Nov 21, 1851 | Æt 21 |

Mary I. | daughter of | A. N. & Huldah | French | died | Dec 2, 1874 | Æ 26 |

Asahel N. French | died | Mar 25, 1887 | aged 68 | Huldah Churchill | His wife | —— | FRENCH |

In memory of | Lucinda Fuller | wife of Chester Fuller | who died | May 22, 1823 | aged 33 |

> No man should be moved by these
> afflictions.

Nathan French | died | July 24, 1869 | Æ 68 |

Charles C. French | Died | Oct 2, 1863 | Æ 27 |

Laura | wife of | Isaac C. Fenn | died | March 9, 1877 | Aged 51 Y'rs |

Isaac C. Fenn | died | Nov 5, 1875 | Aged 54 |

In | Memory of | Samuel Frost | A native of Kent (Eng.) | who died Jan 13, 1807 | aged 67 years | A mortal Man's life's but a Span |

In memory of | Aaron Watson Fox | Who Died [ Nov 9, 1835 | Æ 26 |

In | Memory of | Sally Fox | wife of | Aaron W. Fox | who died | Dec 15, 1843 | Aged 30 |

Abner G. Fox | died | Dec 9, 1841 | aged 34 | Also Ann Eliza | daughter of | Abner G. & | Eliza I. Fox | died | Aug 12, 1841 | aged 1 year |

Anna | wife of | Abner G. Fox | & daughter of ] Truman Webster | died July 11, 1834 | Æt 23 |

Gurdon B. | son of | Walter & | Margaretta C. Filley | died | Aug. 12, 1863 | Æ 1 Y'r. |

Samuel Fenn | died July 3, 1823 | Aged 85 |

In | Memory of | Mrs. Sarah wife of | Mr. Samuel Fenn | who died March 13, 1822 | in the 85 year | of her age. [

In | memory of | Chloe, relict of | Linus Gilbert | who died | Mar 22, 1836 | aged 87 years |

Linus Gilbert | died Sept 19, 1820 | aged 74 |

Frances M. | wife of | Samuel H. Garnsey | died | Nov 21, 1846 | Aged 25 years | & 8 months |

> Farewell my distress and my woe
> Farewell dear Husband all is o'er.
> Farewell all dear friends here below
> Death's terrors appall me no more.

Samuel H. Guernsey | died | Aug 27, 1886 | Aged 66 | Ruth A. | his wife | Died Mar 2, 1885 | Aged 63 | GUERNSEY |

Estella A. | Curtiss | wife of | A. W. Goodwin | died | March 25, 1893 | Aged 39 | GOODWIN |

Hattie A. Goldsmith | wife of | Albert Goldsmith | died July 15, 1874 | Æ 27 | GOLDSMITH |

Jennie | daughter of | Linus T. & Lydia Gilbert [ died | Aug. 28, 1877 | Aged 11 Mo's |

Lydia Loveland | wife of Linus T. Gilbert | died ] Aug 16, 1892 | Aged 60 |

Linus T. Gilbert | died | Aug 17, 1877 | Aged 48 |

Maria Tolls | wife of | Linus Gilbert | Died Sept. 29, 1882 | Aged 83 | At rest |

Linus Gilbert | died | Aug 19, 1872 | Æ 82 |

Fred K. | Son of M. K. & E. J. Gray | died | Aug 25, 1883 | aged 15 Weeks |

John H. | son of | William & | Sarah A. Gill | died | June 29, 1872 | Æ 6 Y'rs 10 Mo's | & 13 D's |

Henry Gill | died | Aug 22, 1882 | Aged 66 |

In | Memory of | Sally Goodwin | wife of | David Goodwin | who died Oct 27, 1827 | aged 37 years |

In | memory of | Hannah wife | of Othniel Gillet | who died April 27, 1833 | aged 82 years 3 | mo & 9 days |

Noah Guernsey | died | April 16, 1873 | Æ 80 | Amanda | his wife | Died Mar 25, 1886 | Æ 91 |

Harriet A. | died Dec 6, 1851 | Æ 19 y'rs | Noah | died Aug 25, 1831 | Æ 3 y'rs | Children of | Noah & Amanda | Guernsey |

Rev. | William H. Guernsey | died at Savannah, Ga. | April 7, 1850 | Æ 33 || Syrena P. | wife of Rev. Wm H. Guernsey | died | May 28, 1859 | Æ 37 |

In Memory of | Laura wife of | Samuel Garnsey | who died May 6th 1810 | aged 26 years |

Samuel Garnsey | died | Mar 7, 1865 | Æ 90 |

Mabel | wife of | Samuel Garnsey | Died Aug 18, 1878 | Aged 97 Yrs & 8 Mo's |

John Guernsey | died | May 1, 1870 | Æ 81 |

Laura | wife of | John Guernsey | died | Aug 3, 1872 | Æ 81 |

Noah | Son of Noah & | Amanda Garnsey | Died | Aug 25, 1831 | Æ 3 yr-s |

An infant | daughter of | John & Laura Garnsey | died | Jan 20, 1830 | Aged 11, weeks |

Caroline | Daughter of | Capt Noah & Mrs | Hannah Garnsey | died Oct 31st 1801 | aged 4 years | and 8 months |

Three Children of | John & Laura Garnsey | John H. died April 20, 1837 | Aged 6 years & 5 months | Laura E. died April 26, 1837 | Aged 2 years & 5 months | Ralph G. C. | died April 28, 1837 | in his 13, year |

Elizabeth | daughter of | Joseph H & | Elizabeth C. | Garnsey | died | Sept 7, 1831 | aged 3 months |

In | Memory of | Capt Noah Garnsey | who died Sept 18, 1820 | Æt 74 |

In | Memory of | Thankful relict of | Capt Noah Garnsey | who died | July 11, 1845 | aged 94 years |

Luman Hale | died | May 8, 1826 | Æt 30 |

With my boys | Jane A. | Wife of | Henry Hall | Died Jan 14, 1886 | Æ 68 | George L. Hall | Died Nov 23, 1872, | Æ 24|

Blessed are the dead who die in the Lord

Eli S. Hall | Died | July 10, 1867 | Æ 20 |

> While on earth we deeply loved thee
> Much we wished to have thee stay
> But thy guardian early called thee
> To thy heavenly home away.

Laura Janett | daughter of | Henry & | Jane A. Hall | died Sept 7, 1849 | Aged 4 years | 5 mo & 12 d's |

> We lay thee in the silent tomb
> Sweet blossom of a day.
> We just began to view thy bloom
> When thou were't calld away.

Walter L. Hall | Died | March 26, 1863 | Æ 24 | Blessed are the dead that die in the Lord | Anna M. | his wife | Died May 13, 1860 | Æ 18 | Her troubles are all over | She is at rest |

Avis C. Heaton | wife of | Levi Heaton | Born Feb 20, 1810 | Died Sept 12, 1889 |

Levi Heaton | born Feb 18, 1810 | died | Apr 21, 1857 |

Frederick W. | son of | Henry & | Jane Hopkinson | died | April 9, 1874 | Æ 13 Y'rs & 6 mo's |

Hannah | wife of Andrus Hall | died | Dec 9, 1856 | Aged 56 |

Andrews Hall | Died | Jan 19, 1864 | Æ 66 |

Mrs. Elizabeth | wife of | Mr. Phineas Hitchcock | died April 16, 1819 | Æ 26 |

> Here she lies, oh could I once more view
> Those dear remains, take one more fond adieu
> Weep o'er that face of innocence & save
> One darling object from the noisome grave.

Father, Mother | Percy B. Hall | died | March 27, 1888 | Aged 75 | Olive | his wife | —— |

Ephraim Hall | died | Apr 6, 1870 | Aged 75 |

Dorcas | daughter of | Joseph & Dorcas | Hall | Sept 18, 1861 | Aged 61 |

Dorcas | wife of | Joseph Hall | died | Jan. 15, 1858 | Aged 90 |

Huldah | daughter of | Joseph & Dorcas | Hall | Jan. 6, 1872 | Aged 86 |

Melissa Alfred | wife of | Edward Hopkins | Died Mar 4, 1887 | Aged 85 Yrs | 7 Mos |

Edward Hopkins | died | Apr 25, 1876 | Aged 79 Years |

Katie E. | died | Oct 25, 1876 | Aged 5 Y'rs | & 3 Mo's | Our darling || daughter of | Joseph H. & Delia A. | Hopkins |

Marina | wife of | Wᵐ L. Hopkins | Died Aug 19, 1874 | Aged 70 || HOPKINS || Wᵐ L. Hopkins | Died | Sept 1, 1883, | Aged 80 |

HULME || Willis C. | son of S. & A. C. Hulme | Jan 20, 1874 | Aug 13, 1896 |Asleep in Jesus |

Gilbert L. Humphreville | died | Sept 20, 1869 | Æ 29 |

Albro M. Humphreville | died Feb 28, 1887 | Aged 77 | Hannah M. Andrews | his wife | —— | Mary Emma | their daughter | Died Sept 3, 1853 | Aged 9 |

Huldah J. Hopkins | a member of the | Rev. Mr. Camp's | family | died April 27, 1837 | aged 16½ years |

> Deep in their affections is her
> Memory embalmed
> She was mild and benevolent
> A most amiable and lovely youth
> May she remain a beauteous flower
> Again more lovely sweet to grow
> Forever may she bloom
> **In air untainted by the gales below.**

Bennet Humiston | died | Sept 6, 1876 | aged 81 years |
Emily | his wife died | Mar 8, 1889 | aged 84 years | HUMIS-
TON ||

In | Memory of | Lucy wife of | Charles Hall | resident of
Ohio | who died | at Plymouth | Sept 26, 1844 | aged 44 years |

Mr. | Joseph Hall | died | July 19, 1834 | Aged 68 years |

In | memory of | Phebe ¹ wife of | Joseph H. Hopkins | who
died | May 9, 1838 | aged 69 years |

In | memory of | Joseph H. Hopkins | who died | Feb 18,
1834 | Æt 69 years |

Thankful Hopkins | Died | Jan 28, 1864 | Æ 90 |

William Hopkins | Died | Mar 2, 1833 | Æ 66 |

In | memory of | Margaret | relict of | Capt. Harris Hop-
kins | who died | Dec 1, 1832 | Aged 91 |

In | Memory of | Capt. Harris Hopkins | who died | Dec
16, 1820 | aged 76 |

In | Memory of | Thomas J. Hotchkiss | who died | Mar 28,
1838 | Æ 31 years |

P. H. | Miss Patience Hotchkiss | daughter of Mr. Joel & |
Mrs. Abigail Hotchkiss | died March 3, 1814 Æt 36. |

Laura E. | daughter of | David & Welthy Hotchkiss | died |
Apr 20, 1842 | aged 18 years | & 5 months |
David Hotchkiss | died | June 6, 1849 | Æt 55 |

Wealthy Hotchkiss | died | Sept 13, 1869 | Æ 73 |

Fred'k S. Hotchkiss | died | Aug 10, 1854 | Æt 33 |

Amelia R. | daughter of | William L. & | Anarina Hopkins |
died | Mar 19, 1842 | Æ 5 years | & 4 mo's |

In | memory of | Abigail relict of | Joel Hotchkiss | who
died | Aug 15, 1837 | aged 83 years |

In | memory of | Joel Hotchkiss | who died Jan 29, 1816 |
Æt 64 |

In | memory of | Mary | wife of | Silas Humaston | who
died | June 1, 1842 | Aged 71 |

Mr Silas Humaston | died | Jan 24, 1838 | Aged 67 |

Mrs Lucy, wife of | Capt Noah Humaston | She died Sept
6ᵗʰ 1799 | aged 57 |

Capt | Noah Humaston | died Feb 2ᵈ | 1812 | Æ 66 |

> Mortal while here thou dost my ashes view
> Think on the glass that runs for you
> Thy most material business set about,
> Make thy peace before the sand runs out.

Joseph S. Hubbard | Co A. 2 Conn | Heavy Art. | died | April 10, 1875 | Æ 54 |

Silas | son of Henry | And Anna | Hartshorn | died May 14, | 1828, Æt 4 |

In | Memory of | Eliphalet | Hartshorn, Jr. | who died | Feb 18, 1830 | Æt 49 |

Levi Heaton | died | Aug. 12, 1844 | Æ 70 |

Anna Heaton | wife of | Levi Heaton | died | Dec 14, 1817 | Æ 38 |

In | Memory of | Iru Heaton | Son of | Mr Abraham & | Mrs. Mabel Heaton | who died | Sept 21ˢᵗ 1801 | aged 18 years |

In | Memory of | Infant Daughter | of J. Harris | Hopkins | & his wife | died in the birth |

In | Memory of | Rositta wife of | Seaman Hickcox | who died | Nov 5, 1806 | aged 30 years |

Hariet daughter to |Mr. Seaman & Mrs. Rositta Hickox | died Jan 7ᵗʰ 1804 | in the 4ᵗʰ year | of her age |

Jesse Hubbard | Died | May 8, 1885 | Aged 86 |

Sally | Wife of | Jesse Hubbard | Died Oct 12, 1869 | Aged 68 |

George son of | Gilbert & Sally | Vanhoesen died | Jan 1825 | Æ 2 years | Also | Gilbert son of | Jesse & Sally | Hubbard died | Sept 3, 1836 | Æ 6 mo |

Lieut. | Horace Hubbard | died | Sept 19, 1864 | Æ 33 | Nettie | Æ 6 Yrs. & 7 Mo. |

Thomas Hale | died | March 31, 1872 | Æt 52 | Walter | son of Thomas & | Mary A. Hale | of Co. C, 20 Reg't. C. V. | Killed at | Chancellorsville Va | May 3, 1863. | Æ 18 |

George Hubbard | died | May 11, 1863 | Aged 33 |

In | Memory of | Lemuel G. Humphreville | Who died | Aug 18, 1836 | in the 32 year of his age |

HUMASTON | Sherman died Mar. 1, | 1828 Æ 39 | Polly died Jan 6 | 1860, æ 69 | Belinda W. died at | New Preston Sept 10 | 1835 æ 15 | Phebe B. died at | New Haven Oct 19, | 1848 æ 25 |

In | memory of | Hannah wife of | John Humaston | who died | Nov 1, 1827 | in her 82 year |

In | Memory of | John Humaston | who died | April 30, 1822 | aged 80 years |

Mr | Eliphalet Hartshorn | died | April 25, 1831 | Æt 87 |

Rebekah | wife of | Eliphalet Hartshorn | died 'Oct 2, 1818 | Æt 68 |

Mabel | wife of | William Heaton | died | March 2, 1841 | Aged 93 |

Mr. Abraham Heaton | died | August 9, A. D. 1832 | Aged 87. |

Lemuel Humphreville | died | Nov 13, 1828 | in his 59 year |

Ursula | wife of Lemuel Humphreville | Died May 26, 1882 | Aged 102 Y'rs 3 Ms & 14 D's |

Bethia M. | Wife of | A. H. Ives | Died Nov 10, 1864 | Æ 53 |

John Jones | died | Jan 24, 1874, Æ 57 |

The Lord has given him rest |

In | memory of | Charles H. Judd | who died | Jan 13, 1842 | aged 27 years |

Lucy | wife of | Elisha H. Judd | died | Mar. 12, 1857 | Æ 64 |

In | memory of | Timothy Judd, Esq | who died | Jan 23, 1796 | Æ 82 |

Hulda Kilborn | of Plymouth | died | July 25, 1854 | Æ 85 |

Mr. | James Kellogg | died | Dec 28, 1828 | aged 74 |
David Kellogg | died in Burwick | Pennsylvania | Nov 30, 1814 | Æt 19 | Merritt Kellogg | died at | Staten Island | April 5, 1827 | Æt 18 |

In | Memory of Betty | Blackman wife of | Mr. Luke Lattin | who died Sept 16th | A D 1800 | aged 57 years |

Harriet M. Little | Æt 8 years | June 4th A D 1807 |

Caroline A. | died | Mar. 28, 1826 | aged 2 years | Amelia S. | died Dec 18, 1836 | aged 9 years | daughters of | Moses & | Caroline Moss |

In | Memory of | Moses Moss | who died | Feb 25, 1836 | aged 39 years |

In | Memory of | Mr. Levi Moss | who died | Mar. 6, 1825 | aged 78 |

In | Memory of | Martha | Wife of | Levi Moss | Who died | Aug 26, 1843 | aged 94 |

Ira H. Munger | died | Nov 20, 1858 | Æ 5 Y'rs |

Watson J. Morse | died | Oct 30, 1877 | Æ 34 | MORSE || Dwight W. Morse | Æ 2 m's || Linus G. Morse | died | Feb. 28, 1875 | Æ 61 | his wife | Angeline H. | —— ||

Dwight W. | son of Watson & | Hattie E. | Morse | died | Feb 23, 1874 | Æ 2 mo's |

Stephen Morse | died | Aug 18, 1868 | Æ 86 |

Louisa wife of | Stephen Morse | died | Mar 1, 1857 | Æ 63 |

Bede S. wife of | Stephen Morse | died | Apr 30, 1863 | Aged 67 |

Levi Andrews | son of Levi & | Thalie Morse | died Oct 2, 1821 | aged 7 years |

Tracy Marsh | died | Aug 21, 1849 | Æ 54 |

In | memory of | Lydia E. Marsh | who died | Mar. 22, 1835 | aged 28 years | wife of Col Tracy Marsh | Respected in life, lamented in death |

Andrew | son of | James M & | Lucia Morse | Oct 1, 1844 | Æ 2 yrs |

Jerod | son of Col. James & | Sarah Marsh | died Oct 15, 1819 | Æt 31 |

In | Memory of | Sarah Marsh | who died | Aug 1, 1832 | Æ 67 | wife of | Col James Marsh | Respected in life, lamented in death |

In | Memory of | two children of | Alvin & | Esther Morse | Belinda died | Sept 13, 1818 aged | 1 year 7 mo. & 7 ds. | George W. died | Feb 28, 1820, aged | 9 years |

Linus G. Moss | died | Feb 28, 1875 | Æ 61 |

In | Memory of | Lucretia Moss | wife of Jacob Moss | who died Sept 9, 1819 | aged 26 years |

Jacob Moss | died Nov. 1, 1862 | Aged 71 |

Harriet | wife of | Jacob Moss | died | March 1, 1882 | Aged 82 |

Roxy J. | Walk gently here my friends, | Pause and remember me. || Wife of | David Morse | died | Aug 8, 1858 | Æ 19 |

Susan A. | wife of | L. N. Murray | died | June 4, 1881 | Aged 28 |

> O! long expected day begin
> Dawn in these realms of woe and sin
> Fain would I leave this weary road,
> And sleep in death to rest with God.

Aaron Morse | died | Sept 17, 1875 | Aged 81 |

Rhoda Baldwin | wife of | Aaron Morse | Died Oct 12, 1890 | Aged 97 |

Horatio Morse | drowned | near Sacramento, Cal. | Aug. 19, 1853 | Aged 25 |

Twin children of | Mr. & Mrs. Ralph E. Morse |

Ira E. | died | Sept 23. || Ida M. | died | Oct 4, 1886 | 1886 | Æ 2½ Mo's | || Æ 3 Mo's |

Emeline Marsh | died | Aug 23, 1887 | aged | 58 Years |

Phebe | wife of | Lucius Marsh | Died Jan 1. 1884 | aged 61 |

Lizzie Marshall | wife of | Charles Didsbury | died July 23, 1887 | Aged 33 || MARSHALL || Josephine M. | daughter of | Samuel & Eliza | Marshall | died Mar. 30, 1883 | aged 18 Y'rs 2 Mo's |

Rev. Lewis Munger | died | March 21st, 1879 | Aged 39 Years |

Alma Heaton | wife of | William S. Munger | died | July 24, 1883 | Æ 75 Yrs |

William S. Munger | died | Aug 31, 1887 | Aged 75 Yrs |

Corp. Apollos C. Morse | Co. A 2 Ct H. A. | son of Lewis

H. & Jane E. A. Morse | Killed at Cold Harbor, | June 2, 1864 | Aged 20 |

Lewis H. Morse | Born at Litchfield | Feb 19, 1817 | Died at Litchfield | Aug 10, 1893 |

Eunice | Wife of | Samuel M. Merwin | Died Aug 25, 1863 | Æ 84 |

Samuel M. Merwin | died | May 31, 1864 | Æ 87 |

Cynthia Merwin | died | Jan 14, 1881 | Æ 78 yrs |

Mehetabel | wife of | Joseph Mason | died | Dec 7. 1828 | Æ 69 |

Joseph Mason | died | March 21, 1844 | aged 89 |

Mr. | David Morse | died | Aug 22, 1830 | Æ 85 |

Mrs. Eunice Morse | wife of | Mr. David Morse | who died Jan 7, 1830 | in her 80 year |

> Her last words were
> these: wait on the Lord
> for I shall still praise him.

Caleb Morse | died | Oct 24, 1853 | Æ 70 |

Ervin J. Marsh | died | Nov 2, 1841 | Æ 24 |

In | Memory of | Martha | wife of | Aaron Marsh | who died | May 14, 1837 | Æt 53 Y'rs |

Aaron Marsh | died | Aug. 5, 1863 | Æ 83 |

In | memory of | Jemina relict of | Samuel Merchant | who died | Nov. 17, 1838 | Aged 61 |

In | memory of | Samuel Merchant | who died | Aug 11, 1829 | aged 56 years |

In | memory of | Anna Eliza | Merchant | who died | Aug 15, 1835 | aged 18 years |

In | memory of | Caleb E. Moore | who died Sept 29, 1828 | aged 19 years |

J. In M. | memory of | Joshua Moore | who died | July 29, 1818 | aged 81 years.

In | Memory of | Phebe | wife of | Joshua Moore | who died Dec 22, 1822 | aged 51 years |

Mr | Jabez Mc Call | who died | May 12, 1810 | Æt 39 |

In memory | of Sarah | daughter of | Ebenezer & Permelia Miller | who died Feb 5, 1830 Æt 2 yea | rs & 6 months |

Harriet C. | daughter of | George & | Caroline Marsh | died | Feb 20, 1831 | Æt 2 years | & 7 months |

James G. | son of George & | Caroline Marsh | died Dec 2, 1826 | Æ 2 years & 7 mo |

In | memory of | Mrs Lucy wife of | Roger Marsh, Esq | who died May 18, 1806 | Æt 67 |

Roger Marsh, | Esq. | died April 13, 1818 | Æt 85 |

Moses Marsh | died | July 29, 1824 | Æ 42 |

In | memory of | Ursula | wife of | James Marsh | who died | July 21, 1835 | aged 64 |

James Marsh | died | April 25, 1858 | Æ 96 |

Charlie L. | son of | Leonard L. & | Lucy L. Munson | died | Jan 23, 1870 | Æ 4 yrs 5 mos |

Julia Ann | daughter of | Levi & | Abigail Merriam | died Nov 15, 1821 | Æt 2 years 7 months |

Ansel Kellogg | son of | David K & | Julia A. Merriam | Died | April 25, 1844 | Aged 2 years | 4 ms. & 26 d's |

Levi D. | son of | David K. | & Julia A. Merriam | died | Jan 7, 1860 | Æ 11 wks |

Joel Merriam | died March 22, 1807 | Æt 48 |

Theodocia | wife of | Joel Merriam | died Dec. 17, 1834 | Æ 72 |

In | memory of | Abigail | wife of | Levi Merriam | who died | March 29, 1839 | Aged 50 |

In | memory of | Levi Merriam | who died | Mar 22, 1850 | Æ 62 |

Sacred | to the memory of | Mary Ann Noble | who died | Feb 25, 1836 | Aged 24 |

Even so them also which sleep in Jesus
Will God bring with him.

Eugene Morse | Son of | I. S. & E. M. | Newton | Died April 10, 1855 | Æ 2 Y'rs & 3 Mo's | It is well |

Louisa | daughter of | George & | Sophia Newton | died | June 1, 1842 | Æ 7 years |

Ralph L. | son of | William & | Mary Newton | died | Jan 27, 1846 | Æ 8 y'rs & 12 d's |

Sophia | wife of | George Newton | Died Nov. 4, 1869 | Æ 61 |

In memory of | George Newton | who died | Aug. 18, 1840 | Aged 33 years |

Stop, friend, awhile, as you pass thoughtless by,
Ask well yourself, am I prepared to die
This stone now speaks from me beneath this sod
Give up the world and make your peace with God.

Polly | wife of | Isaac Newton | died | July 29, 1848 | Æ 66 y'rs |

In memory of | Isaac Newton | who died | April 3, 1870 | aged 88 years | and 2 mo's |

Our darling | Nellie May || daughter of | Anthony & Agnes | Newton | Died Apr 8, 1888 | Aged 1 Yr. 11 Mos. |

Charles Nightingale | died | June 7, 1892 | Æ 54 | Mary Ann | his wife | — | At rest | NIGHTINGALE || Charles H. | died March 17, 1871 | Æ 3 yrs. | Nellie M. | died July 31, 1876 | Æ 5 yrs 6 mos | children of | Charles & | Mary A. Nightingale |

Elizabeth | wife of | Joseph Nightingale | Died Oct 24, 1861 | Æ 55 |

Ransom Newton | died | Oct 16, 1885 | Æ 83 | Lucinda Woodward | his wife | — | NEWTON ||

Sarah Ann | wife of | George Nelson | Died Feb 13, 1880 | Aged 69 |

George Nelson | died | Mar. 1, 1888, | Aged 79 |

William Newton | died Nov 7, 1890 | Æ 80 | Mary G. Leavenworth | his wife | —— | NEWTON ||

Mabel B. | daughter of | C. E. & A. M. Parsons | born Aug 16, 1889, | died | Dec 22, 1889 |

Bertha | rest in peace || Bertha E. | daughter of | Thomas K | & Sarah J. | Pearson | Died Nov 29, 1874 | Æ 2 Y'rs & 6 Mo. |

In | loving remembrance of | Isaac B. Pond | Died Oct 24, 1886 | aged 66 |

Jeremiah Peck | born | Oct 4, 1805 | died | Feb 3, 1875 | PECK || Cornelia E. Dudley | wife of | Jeremiah Peck | Born in Guilford, Ct. | Aug 13, 1816 | Died May 8, 1878 |

Our | Maud | April 7, 1887 | (*Peck*).

In | Memory of | Sidney | wife of | Sherman Pierpont | who died | May 16, 1841 | Aged 55 years |

This stone is erected | to perpetuate the | memory of | William Pierpont | Who died | Feb 16, 1841 | aged 69 |

Henry Son of Wm & Huldah Pierpont | died | May 14, 1808 Aged 3 years |

In | Memory of | Mrs Huldah wife of | Mr. William Pierpont | who died | July 16, 1812 | Aged 38 years [

In memory of | Abigail | Wife of Wm. Pierpont | late relic of | Jacob Smith Who Died | Oct. 29, 1835 | Æ 64. |

Burdette F. Penfield | died | July 14, 1869 | Æ 26 | Sarah E. | his wife | —— | PENFIELD || Mary J. | daughter of | William & | Elizabeth Cooper | died Jan 29. 1866 | Æ 18 || William Cooper | died | Nov 1, 1889 | Æ 71 | Elizabeth | his wife | died Nov 4, 1861 | Æ 36 | Cooper ||

Lyman Pond | died | Sept 23, 1831 | Æt 35 |

Mr. Samuel Peck | died | Jan 7th 1803 | aged 96 |

In Memory of | Mr. Cornelius Peck | who died | Oct 31st | 1801 In the 89th | Year of his age |

In | Memory of | Mrs. Bethia Peck | who died | Oct. 27, 1816 | Æ 94 |

Mary | wife of Shenton Perkins | & daughter of | Lemuel Humphreville | died March 10 1833 | aged 25 years |

John D. | son of Daniel & | Mabel Roberts | died April 7, 1822 | Æ 14 months |

Annie E. Richardson | died | May 29, 1884 | Aged 17 | Daughter of | Wm & Emma Richardson |

Elizabeth N. | wife of | Abel W. Smith | died | Nov 3, 1874| Æ 46 | Cheerful in sickness |

Abel W. Smith | died | Nov 4, 1891 | Aged 70 |

Clarissa | wife of | William Stuart | died | January 7, 1871 | aged 70 y'rs |

Polly Smith | died | Aug 25, 1895 | Aged 86 Y'rs |

Esther Smith | died | Dec 7, 1887 | Aged 83 Y'rs |

In | Memory of | James Smith | who died | March 22, 1820 | in his 68, year |

In | memory of | Sarah wife of | James Smith | who died | July 21, 1850 | Æt 78 |

In | memory of | Horace Stevens | who died | Aug 21, 1841 | Æ 55|

In | memory of | Susan wife of | Horace Stephens | who died | Dec 10, 1832 | aged 36 years |

Henry Stevens | of Col. Swift's Regt. | died | April 16, 1851 | Æ 87 |

Mrs. | Ruth Stevens | wife of | Mr. Henry Stevens | died Jan 2, 1829 | Æ 57 |

Farewell ! | Clayton H. Smith | died | Feb, 8, 1873 | Æ 23 |

Bertha | daughter of | Herbert M. & Carrie L. Smith | June 24, 1884 | July 11, 1893 |

Joseph Senior | died | Dec 12, 1872 | Æ 39 | Hannah | his wife | —— | SENIOR ||

In memory of | James M. || And his wife | Sallie Tur-
Smith | April 6, 1826 | Feb || ner | Mar. 27, 1830 | ——
7, 1887 | ||

| SMITH |

Rosetta T. | daughter of | Levi D. & | Rosetta T. Smith | died | Aug 11, 1854 | Æ 3 y'rs 14 ds |

> God in his wisdom has recalled
> The precious boon his love had given
> And though the casket moulders here
> The gem is sparkling now in heaven.

Levi D. Smith | died | Feb 14, 1859 | Aged 41 |

In | memory of | Eliza Smith | who died | Oct 3, 1837 | aged 31 years |

John Smith | died | June 15, 1814, | æ 15 |

John A. | son of | Noah B. & | Fannie Smith | died | Feb 14, 1846 | aged 6 y'rs |

Fanny | wife of | Noah B. Smith | died | May 10, 1846 | Aged 42 |

Chloe | wife of | Samuel Sweet | died | Apr 9, 1854 | Æ 76 |

In | memory of | Philonia | wife of | Samuel Sweet | who died | Dec 31, 1820 | Aged 38 years |

Samuel Sweet | died | June 10, 1842 | Æ 63 |

> Wrapt in the shades of death
> No more that friendly face we see
> Empty oh, empty every place
> Once fill'd so well by thee.

Roswell Sweet | died | April 3, 1849 |Aged 39 |

Lewellyn | son of | De Witt C. & | Jane H. Smith | born July 31, 1869 | died | July 19, 1872 |

Harriet Smithers | wife of | John Smithers | died | Dec 9, 1875 | Æ 45 |

Esther Smith | died | April 1, 1846 | Æ 69 |

David Smith | Died Nov. 4, 1861 | Æ 84 | Anna | His wife | Died Sept 17, 1828 | Æ 44 |

Ellen | Francis | daughter of | Charles & | Catharine Smith | died Aug 27, 1844 | aged 2 y'rs 2 m. | & 7 d's |

In Memory of Rev. Lewis Smith | of the Methodist | Episcopal Church | who died | Oct. 19, 1846 | Aged 41 |

An infant Son | of | Dennis & Sally | Smith died | Nov 21, 1822 | aged two weeks |

Mr | Jacob Smith Jun. | died Feb 23, 1808 | Æ 37 |

> Dear wife and children do not weep
> I am not dead but here do sleep
> Beneath this solid lump of clay
> Until the resurrection day.

In | memory of | Mr. Jacob Smith | who died April 14th, 1807 Æ 69

In | Memory of | Mrs. Mary Smith | Relict of | Jacob Smith | who died Dec 30, 1823, | Æt 81 |

Levi Smith | died | Aug 1, 1833 | aged 52 years |

In | memory of | Pol'y wife of | Levi Smith | who died | April 7, 1836 | aged 53 |

L. S. | Lemuel Smith | died | Jan. 13, 1852 | Æ 77 |

Nancy | Relict of | Lemuel Smith | died | Jan 4, 1861 | Æt 83 |

In | memory of | Betsey J. | daughter of | Lemuel & | Nancy Smith | who died | April 18, 1838 | aged 15 years | & 6 months |

In | Memory of | Thankful wife of | Ziba Seymour | who died | Nov. 21, 1806 | aged 32 years |

Dennis Smith | died | Aug 19, 1880 | Æ 83 years | Sally | Wife of | Dennis Smith | died | Nov 9, 1841 |Æ 44 yrs |

Mrs. Sarah Sanford | wife of Mr. | Stephen Sanford | died Feb 6th, 1802 | In the 31st year | of her age |

Betsey | Dautr of Mr. Joseph | & Mrs. Hopy Sanford | Died Jany 7, 1807 | Aged 6 Months |

Caroline Jennett | daughter of | Truman & | Julia Ann Smith | died | Aug 3, 1844 | Aged 5 years |

In | memory of | Sarah | wife of Wm Scovill | who died | Dec 16, 1853 | Aged 90 y'rs |

Mr. | Stephen Sanford | died | April 12, 1827 | Æ 86 |

In | Memory of | Mrs. Abigail | wife of | Mr. Stephen Sanford | Died | Nov. 18th 1802 | aged 66 |

Arthur Taylor | —— | Eliza | his wife died | Jan 12, 1894 | Æ 42 | TAYLOR || Nellie | daughter of | Arthur & Eliza Taylor | died | July 30, 1887 | Æ 10 yrs |

In | memory of | Eber Tompkins | who died in Foresyth | Geo. | Oct 22, 1826 | in the 33 year | of his age |

In | memory of|Wm.Tompkins | who died | in Kent | Aug 25, 1827 | in the 22 year | of his age |

David Turney | died | Dec 17, 1874 | Aged 75 Y'rs |

Lois Newton | wife of | David Turney | died | January 28, 1871 | aged 66 y'rs |

In | memory of | Esther | wife of | John Turney | who died | April 13, 1841 | aged 69 y'rs |

Joel A. Tharp | died | Sept 23, 1881 | Aged 66 |

Mariah H. | Wife of | Joel A. Tharp | died | June 10, 1878 | Æ 68 |

Little | Widena | died | Aug 1, 1880 | Aged 4 Y'rs ] 6 Mo | (*In Tharp lot*).

Joel A. Tharp, Jr | died | Nov 17, 1895 | Age 25 Y'rs |

Carl G. | son of Lyman & | Fannie Tharp | died | July 19, 1884 | Aged 6 Y'rs |

Zeri Tharp | died | Apr 19, 1852 | Aged 67 | Sabra Tharp | died | Mar 19, 1853 | Aged 64 |

Rufus C. Tharp | died | Jan 4, 1884 | Aged 70 |

George W. Tharp | died | April 14, 1893 | Age 53 Y'rs |

Amos M. Tharp | died | Sept 24, 1892 | Aged 73 |

Abram Manning Turner | July 27, 1824 | May 22, 1888 | TURNER || Dwight Filley Turner | Mar 21, 1856 | Aug 14, 1875 | "With Christ, which is | far better" || Elizabeth Filley Turner | Feb 3, 1828 | Aug 19, 1894 ||

Melitta | wife of | Eber Turner | died | Aug 25, 1863 | aged 75 |

Eber Turner | died | Sept 20, 1857 | Æt 75 y'rs |

Isaac Turner | died Sept 3, 1836 | Aged 56 | Cynthia Mason | his wife | died Jan 12, 1871 | Aged 85 |

Jacob Turner | died | April 16, 1838 | aged 60 |

In | memory of | Sarah wife of | Jacob Turner | who died Dec 11, 1825, | Æ 47 |

Rhoda Adaline | Daughter of Mr Jacob | & Mrs. Sally Turner | died suddenly of a scald | May 4th 1810 | Aged 3 years & 2 months |

In Memory of | Deacon Ebenezer Todd | who died Feb 4th | 1798 In the 76th | year of his age |

Ebenezer Todd Jun | died March 7, 1811 | Æ 54 |

In | memory of | Patience relict of | Ebenezer Todd Jr. | who died | Dec 30, 1824 | aged 67 years |

Julius Todd | died | Dec 5, 1829 | Æt 32 |

Merritt Todd | Died | Jan 18, 1889 | Æ 66 |

Caroline | Wife of | Hiram Todd | Died Jan 28, 1871 | Æ 72 |

Hiram Todd | Died Dec 16, 1858 | Æ 63 |

Sophia | wife of | Titus Turner | Died Apr. 3, 1872 | Æ 70 |

Titus Turner | died | June 22, 1875 | Aged 73 |

Titus Turner | Born June 10, 1741 | Died Dec 25, 1828 |

In | Memory of | Mrs. Sara wife of | Mr Titus Turner | who died | May 28th 1809 | Aged 66 years |

Heman | a twin son of | Henry & | Sarah Whitlock | died | Aug 22, 1845 | aged 19 mo's & 14 d's |

Hiram Whitlock | died | Oct 19, 1866 | Æ 42 |

Sally | wife of | Zalmon Whitlock | died | Nov 25, 1859 | Aged 62 |

Zalmon Whitlock | died | Apr 18, 1852 | Æt 57 |

Rachel Williams | died | Dec. 31, 1848 | Æ 84 |

Edwin Way | died | Dec 15, 1824 | Æt 22 |

In | Memory of | Rebecca, wife of | Doct. | Reuben S. Woodward | who died | May 31, 1841 | In the 62 year | of her age |

Reuben S. Woodward M. D. | died | June 27, 1849 | Aged 83 |

Mrs. Minerva | Wife of | Sherman P. Woodward | died | Aug 22, 1837 | Æ 28 |

Lucy E. | daughter of | Sherman P. & | Hannah E. | Woodward | died | April 16, | 1841 | aged 1 year |

Sally C. | Wife of | John Worrall | Died Aug 29, 1861 | Æ 51 |

Gilbert. I. Wooster | born | March 21, 1822 | died | Jan 9, 1893 | Not lost, but gone before |

Frederick H. | son of | Daniel T. & | Eliza A. | Wooster | died | Dec 29, 1846 | Æ 11 mo's & 3 d's |

Joseph H. | son of | Daniel T. & | Eliza Wooster | died | Nov 11, 1851 | Æ 4 ye & 11 da |

So fades the lovely blooming flower.

Ruth J. | adopted daughter of | Daniel T. & Eliza A. | Wooster | Died June 30, 1871 | Æ 13 |

Daniel T. Wooster | February 6, 1820 | August 1, 1890 | Eliza A. Stevens | his wife | June 4, 1820 | —— |

Jennet Sharp | Wife of Geo. W. Wooster | Died Aug 17, 1856 | Æ 26 |

Anner Ford | wife of | Truman Wooster | Died Oct. 9, 1890| Aged 95 |

Truman Wooster | Died | April 15, 1864 | Æ 67 |

Aurilla Tolls | wife of | Truman Wooster | died | May 25, 1849 | Aged 49 |

Sergt. David B. Wooster | Co. D. 2 C. H. A. | Killed in Battle | at Fishers Hill | Sept 22, 1864 | Aged 36 |

Mary | eldest daughter of | David B. & | Sarah A. Wooster| died | Jan 15, 1875 | Æ 16 Yrs 7 mo's |

Isaac Wakeman | died || Oct 27, 1888 | Æ 80 Y'rs 8 mo |

Mary | wife of | Isaac Wakeman | died | Sept 3, 1860 | Aged 41 | Also an Infant buried by her side |

Julia K. | died Feb 6, 1861 | Aged 10. | Emily G. | died | Feb 7, 1861 | Aged 7 | Children of | I. & Mary Wakeman |

Clarissa Wakeman | died | Mar. 21, 1883 | Aged 27 |

Oh! how we miss thee! | Charles H. | son of | George & Martha | Wright | Died Sept 11, 1877 | Aged 15 | We shall meet again |

Mary Wildgoose | Born in Sheffield, Eng. | June 4, 1838 | Died | Feb 27, 1891 |

Kirby M. Webster | died | Sept 4, 1868 | Æ 36 |

Eliza Warner | born | Oct 25, 1797 | died | Aug 24, 1863 |

Lyman Warner Jr. | died | at Essex, Oct, 9, 1833 | Æ 26 | of a wound received by | explosion of Steam-Boat | New England. |

Miss. | Elvira Warner | died July 11, 1818 | Ælt 23 |

Electa Blakeslee | wife of | Ard W. Warner | died | July 16, 1849 | Ælt 44 |

Elvira Electa | daughter | of | Ard W. & | Electa Warner | died | Mar 5, 1851 | Aged 22 |

Ard Walton Warner | died | Sept 24, 1864 | Æt 63 |

Mr. | Ara Way | died June 29th | 1811 | Æ 50 |

Lydia | wife of | Ara Way | died | Sept 3, 1852 | Æt 84 |

Mr. | Thomas Way | died | Jan 20, 1818 | Æ 90 |

In | Memory of | Mrs. Zillah Way | wife of | Mr Thomas Way | who died | Oct 8, 1801 | aged 68 years |

In Memory of | Mrs Lydia Way | wife of | Mr Thomas Way Jun. | who died Dec 2d 1801 | In the 34th year | of her age |

In Memory of | James Way | who died Sept 10th 1802 | aged 32 years |

In | memory of | Thomas Way | who died | Aug 9, 1848 | Aged 80 years |

In | Memory of | Orril Daughter | of Mr. Thomas & Mrs. | Lydia Way who died | March 8, 1813, aged | 13 years |

Sarah | Wife of | Elihu Webster | Died April 9, 1869 | Æ 66 |

In Memory of two | Son of Truman | & Dema Webster | Stephen Sanford died | Nov 2d, 1799 | aged 3 | years and 4 months | David died Nov 1 st | 1799 aged 16 months |

> In tender years we were not spared
> To follow us O be prepared.

In memory of | Diadema | wife of | Truman Webster | Who Died | Aug 10, 1839 | Aged 65 |

In | Memory of | Truman Webster | who died | Sept 18, 1844 | aged 74 |

Annis Welton | wife of | Lyman Warner | died | July 11, 1844 | Aged 71 |

Lyman Warner | died | May 17, 1850 | Aged 82 |

Annah Warner | relict of | Chauncey Warner, Esq | died | July 12, 1857 | Aged 84 |

In | memory of | Chauncey Warner | who died | Feb 1, 1849 | Æ 79 |

Ann Elizabeth | Died June 9, 1872 | Aged 15 Mo's | Alice Louisa | Died Sept 5, 1877 | Aged 5½ Yrs | Children of | James & Sarah A. | Ward |

# MILTON

A thorough search of the land and town records reveals no definite clew toward determining when this burying ground was first consecrated to the dead, but the dates on the oldest stones would indicate that it was near the Revolutionary period.

On July fifth, 1813, the selectmen of Litchfield bought half an acre of David Welch from the south part of his farm for a burying ground, but this was very clearly an addition to one already in existence. It is spoken of in a deed of 1790 to Justus Seelye.

In 1872 Mrs. Clarissa Seymour Welch sold to the town over three acres to be used as an addition to Milton yard, excepting the family burial place therein.

This ground lies nearly a mile west of the village of Milton, in a sheltered valley, and is now enclosed by a substantial wall of quarried stone.

WEST CEMETERY—PAUL PECK

# INSCRIPTIONS.

Loueisa Ambler | died | Feb 23, 1877 | Æ 72 |

In | Memory of | Esther | wife of | Isaac Baldwin | who died | Feb 15, 1848 | Æ 80 |

Hiram Bissell | died | Mar 6, 1876 | Æ 93 |

Beata | wife of | Hiram Bissell | died | March 12, 1847 | Aged 63 years | & 6 mo |

In | Memory of | Benjamin | Bissell son | of Hiram & | Beata Bissell | who died | Dec 9, 1823 | Æ 16 years |

Daniel Beach | died | Dec 28, 1859 | Æ 71 |

Alice | wife of | Daniel Beach | Died Jan 18, 1880 | Aged 89 |

Lorenzo Beach | died | Jan 11, 1847 | Æ 21 |

Martha Beach | died | Sept 5, 1862 | Æ 34 |

Anna Beach | died | Jan 26, 1883 | Aged 83 Y'rs | BEACH || Daniel Beach | died | Apr 1, 1838 | Aged 82 Y'rs || Susan B. Ranney | died | Oct 28, 1821 | Aged 35 Y'rs || Susanna Beach | died | Jan 4, 1836 | Aged 78 Yrs |

Rev. Benjamin Beach | departed his life | July 12, 1816 | in the 79 year of his age |

Mercy Beach | wife of | Rev Benjamin Beach | departed this life | Nov 21, 1812 | being 75 years old to a day |

In | memory of | Mary | daughter of | Smith & | Lucia Beach | died June 26, 1834 aged | 8½ hours | .

Eunice | wife of | Damon Beecher | died | March 15, 1874 | Æ 76 |

Simeon Beach | died | Jan 26, 1849 | Æ 68 |

Mary | wife of Simeon Beach | died | July 20, 1876 [ Æ 85 |

Albert H. Birge | died | Oct 10, 1842 | Æ 45 | Lois | his wife | died | May 23, 1871 | Æ 69 |

Samuel Bishop | died | Oct 8, 1841 | aged 37 |

Jane | daughter of | Samuel & | Mary Ann Bishop | died |
Dec 27, 1846 | Æ 17 |

Anson Beach | died | Nov 12, 1846 | Æ 70 |

In | Memory of | Albert Blake | who died | April 24, 1855 |
Æ 58 years |

In | memory of | Harriet Blake | wife of | Albert Blake |
who died | Aug 8, 1844 | Æ 47 |

In | memory of | Martha Blake | daughter of Albert | &
Harriet Blake | who died | Sept 10, 1844 | Æ 22 |

Jerome | son of Albert & | Harriet Blake | died | Dec 7,
1851 | Æ 23 |

In | Memory of | Mary wife of | Amizi Beach | who died |
April 2, 1853 | aged 33 years |

In | memory of | Amos Bishop | who died | June 16, 1849 |
Æ 80 |

In | memory of | Lois wife of | Amos Bishop | who died |
Sept 17, 1837 | aged 65 years |

Anne Bishop | wife of | Noah Bishop | died Aug 11, 1822 |
aged 86 years | & 3 months |

In | memory of | Noah Bishop | who died | Feb 13, 1824 |
aged 85 |

Annis Bishop | died | July 2, 1876 | Æ 83 |

Amos G. Bishop | died | Nov 1, 1881 | Æ 71 |

Almira Bishop | born | Oct 15, 1800 | died Oct 17, 1890 |

Sarah M. | daughter of | Joseph & | Sarah M. Birge | died |
Dec 4, 1840 | aged 1 year | & 3 mo |

In | memory of | Ira Buell | who died | March 4, 1778 | in
the 34 year | of his age |

In | Memory of | Prudence relict | of Ira Buell | who died |
Oct 30, 1828 | in the 88 year | of her age |

BASSETT | Laura B. Coe | Died | Oct 12, 1871 | Æ 77 |
Samuel F. Bassett | Died | Oct 24, 1873 | Æ 60 || Mehetable
Buell, | Wife of | Nathan Bassett | Died | March 9, 1848 | Æ
74 || Henry | Died | at Sandusky City | Ohio | Sept 12, 1834 |
Æ 25 | Frederick | Died | at Gilead, Ohio | Jan 10, 1839 | Æ
27 | Sons of Nathan & Mehetable Bassett || Nathan Bassett. |
Died | Oct 6, 1862 | Æ 93 |

In | memory of | David Baldwin | who died | July 10, 1819|
Æ 73 yrs | Also his wife | Ruth Baldwin | who died | April 14,
1840 | Æ 88 y'rs |

Nancy | daughter of | Aner & | Annis Baldwin | died April
12, 1815 | aged 2 years | & 3 months | Her death was occas- |
ioned by a scald |

Betsey | daughter of | Aner & | Annis Baldwin | died March
21, 1809, Æ 8 weeks |

Died | Jan 15, 1830 | Dea. Aner Baldwin | in the 53, year |
of his age |

In | memory of | Sarah | wife of | Nathan Benedict | who
died Aug 27, 1825 | Æ 66 |

Mr. | Nathan Benedict | died Sept 13, 1807 | aged 48 |

In | Memory of | Mary Bissell | died April 14, 1807 | in the
45 year | of her age |

In Memory of | John Bissell | died July 27, 1819 | in the 59
year | of his age |

Amanda Jennett | wife of | Capt William Bissell | died |
Dec 29, 1892 | Aged 81 Y'rs & 8 Mo |

Henrietta E. | daughter of | William & | Amanda J. Bissell |
died Jan 18, 1883 | Aged 50 |

Rosanna B. | daughter of | William & | Amanda J. Bissell |
died | April 23, 1850 | Æ 6 y'rs 7 mo | & 23 d's |

L. Carrie | daughter of | William & | Amanda J. Bissell |
died | April 5, 1866 | aged 27 y'rs | 1 mo & 13 d's |

Frank L. | son of | William & | Amanda J. Bissell | died |
Nov 8, 1869 | aged 18 years | 3 mo & 11 d's |

Elizabeth Benedict | died | Oct 4, 1870 | Æ 81 |

Silas Benedict | died | Feb 19, 1868 | Æ 81 | Polly | his
wife | died | Feb 13, 1861 | Æ 66 |

Seymour Beach | died | Jan 19, 1856 | Æ 57 |

Myron L. | son of | Amzi & Chloe I. | Beach | Aged 21 ]|
was killed | Jan 8, 1879 |

Heman Beach | died | Mar 25, 1881 | Aged 68 | Eliza his
wife | died | Dec 10, 1849 | Aged 34 | Mary R. Beach | died |
May 16, 1888 | Aged 61 | BEACH || Eugene | died | Oct 21,

1854 | Aged 12 | H. Wesley | died in Kansas | July 22, 1870 | Aged 25 | Eliza J. Frisbie | died | Nov 6, 1877 | Aged 28 Children of Heman & | Eliza Beach | Jennie | Daughter of | Eliza J. Frisbie | died | June 18, 1872 | Aged 7 mo |

Smith Beach | Born Apr 10, 1809 | Died —— | Lucia | his wife | Born Sept 9, 1813 | Died June 2, 1881 |

Annie | daughter of | Daniel L. & Mary | Beach | died | Oct 3, 1881 | Aged 5 Y'rs |

Daniel L. Beach | died | Feb 25, 1886 | Aged 37 |

Robert J. Blake | died | Oct 30, 1891 | aged 22 yrs 5 mos |

Anson B. Beach | died | Mar 19, 1885 | Æ 81 | Elizabeth | his wife | Died May 25, 1885 | Æ 78 | BEACH ||

Noah W. Beach | born | June 24, 1816 | died | Oct 28, 1880 |

James Blake | born | May 18, 1825 | Jane L. Seelye | his wife | Born May 24, 1825 | Died Feb 11, 1891 | BLAKE || Edward W. Blake | Born July 8, 1857 | Died May 13, 1867 |

In memory of | Cicero | son of | Lyman & | Ann Carter | who died | by drowning | May 23, 1836 | aged 3 years |

In memory of | Cicero | son of | Lyman & | Ann Carter | who died | Sept 1, 1827 | aged 2 yrs & 3 mo |

In | Memory of | Lucretia wife of | Lyman Carter | who died | May 10, 1823 | Æt 25 |

In | Memory of | Onner | wife of | Lyman Carter | who died | June 18, 1821 | Aged 21 |

Hiram Clark | died | Aug 4, 1867 | Æ 39 |

Leman Clark | died | April 20, 1864 | Æ 25 |

George S. | died | Feb 1, 1860 | Æ 25 d's | Salmon C. | died| May 28, 1866 | Æ 2 y'rs & 11 mo | Children of Shelden | & Melissa Clark |

Henry Clark | died June 22, 1881 | aged 13 years|CLARK|| Caroline | daughter of | Jaleel | & Susan | Clark | died Jan 25, 1831 | aged | 5 Yrs 8 Mos |

In | memory of | George Clark | who died | Nov 21, 1841 | in his 90 year |

In | memory of | Lydia wife of | George Clark | who died | July 22, 1841 | in her 85 year |

In | memory of | Jaleel Clark | who died | Aug 16, 1851 | aged 66 years |

In | memory of | Susan | wife of | Jaleel Clark | who died | Feb 8, 1872 | aged 86 years |

George O. Clark | died | Feb 27, 1856 | Æt 33 Y'rs |

Elisha Clark | died | May 18, 1867 | Æ 68 |

Irene | wife of | Elisha Clark | died | Mar 26, 1858 | Æt 60 |

Lyman Clark | died | June 27, 1873 | Æt 84 |

Alvira | wife of Lyman Clark | died | Sept 20, 1856 | Æt 71 |

Betsey O. Clark | died | Jan 20, 1860 | Æ 32 y's & 8 mo |

Caroline | wife of | Heman L. Cummings | died March 29, 1828 | aged 29 |

In Memory of | Mr. Isaac Catlin | Who died July | yᵉ 12ᵗʰ A. D. 1786 | in the 77ᵗʰ year | of his age |

In | Memory of | Harriet Loisa | daughter of | Elijah & | Anna Comings | deceast | March 16, 1818 | Æ 17 |

Sacred to the | Memory of | Mary Ann wife of | Calvin Collins | and Daughter of | Jonathan & Thankful Wright | Who departed this life | Jan 25, 1814 | aged 20 years |

Ann | wife of | David Catlin | died April 11, 1834 | Æ 69 years | 6 mo & 12 d's |

Betsey | daughter of Phineas | & Irene Cook | died Oct 26ᵗʰ 1810 | aged 3 years | & 3 months |

In | memory of | Jonathan Churchill | who died | Feb. 6, 1829 | aged 79 years |

In Memory of | Capt Daniel Cook | who died on his birth | day August 14, 1809 | Aged 49 Years |

In | memory of | Chloey Ann | Dare | who died | Aug 27, 1832 | a'd 2 y's |

Sarah B. | Wife of | Anson Dickinson | died July 14, 1852 | Æ 73 y'rs |

Anson Dickinson | died | Mar 9, 1852 | in the 74 year | of his age |

Reuben Dickinson | died Nov 5, 1818 | aged 102 | Sarah Dickinson | died March 9, 1816 | aged 90 |

Francis F. | son of Amos & | Sally Dickinson | died Aug 8, 1832 | Æt 10 months |

Ithamar P. Dickinson | died | Sept 29, 1845, | Æ 21 |

Sarah P. | wife of | Amos Dickinson | died | Nov 20, 1849 | Æ 53 |

Amos Dickinson | died | Feb 9, 1867, | Æ 77 |

In Memory of | Mr. William | Dickinson he | Died Sep^t y^e 10^th | 1776 in y^e 41^st year | of his Age |

In Memory of | Mr. Oliver Dickinson | who Departed this | Life Jan 29, A. D. 1783 | in the 59^th year of his | age | Memento Mortis |

In | Memory of | Mary Dickinson | relict of | Oliver Dickinson | who died | April 1, 1809 | aged 70 years |

In Memory of M^r | David Dickinson who | Departed this Life | Nov 21^st 1788 in the | 24^th year of his age | Memento Mori |

Oliver Dickinson | born | July 10, 1757 | died Mar 23, 1847| his wife | Anna Dickinson | born April 19, 1760 | died Christmas 1849 |

Ambrose | died | June 26, 1806 | Æt 23 | Anna | died | Sept 12, 1792 | Æt 8 Mo's || Children of | Oliver & Anna Dickinson |

In | Memory of | Mehetable Deming | relict of David Deming | who died | Oct 24, 1817 | aged 97 years |

In | Memory of | Rhoda Dickinson | consort of | David Dickinson | died April 5, 1795 | Æt 28 |

In Memory of | Lois Dickinson | wife of | So'omon Dickinson | who died | April 12, 1798 | aged 30 years |

Delia E. | wife of | W^m E. Dickinson | & daughter of | Gerrit P & Clarissa Welch | born | Dec 10, 1829 | died | May 27, 1855 | Aged 25 |

Harriet E. | wife of | E. P. Dickinson | Died Jan 6, 1876 | Aged 48 |

Gilbert A. | son of | E. P. & Harriet E. | Dickinson | died | Jan 24, 1873 | Æ 9 Y'rs |

Lois Hartwell |wife of | Peter Ferver | died | May 21, 1866| Æ 88 |

Peter Ferver | died | June 1, 1835 | Æ 56 |

George Ferver | died | Aug 25, 1850 | Æ 36 |

Polly Ferver | died | Aug 10, 1830 | Æ 28 |

Consecrated | to the Memory of | Dotha daughter of | Peter & Lois Farvour | & intended consort of | Adouiram French | who departed this life | Aug 25, 1821 | aged 17 y. 9 m. & 27 d.|

Lois C. | Wife of | O. B. Frisbie | Died | July 19, 1861 | Æ 29 |

S. Elias | died Sept 26, 1862 | Æ 3 y's & 4 m's | Hattie E. | died Sept 20, 1862 | Æ 1 y'r & 10 m's | Children of | O. B. & Lois C. Frisbie |

Abby | wife of | Sherman Frisbie | died | Nov 16, 1879 | Æ 78 |

Sherman Frisbie | died | May 14, 1863 | Æ 65 |

Mehetible Parsons | wife of | Charles Ferniss | died | Sept 27, 1880 | Aged 75 |

Charles Ferniss | died | Dec 15, 1883 | Aged 79 |

In | memory of | Thomas F. Gross | who departed | this life | Nov 3, 1846 | Æt 75 |

In | memory of | Lydia | wife of | Thomas F. Gross | who died | July 23, 1864 | Aged 91 |

Moore Gibbs | died April 5, 1834 | aged 77 years |

Patience | wife of | Moore Gibbs | died | Apr 25, 1853 | Æ 91 |

Mrs. Salome S. | wife of | Birdsey Gibbs | died | May 30, 1828 | aged 30 |

Elizabeth Gibbs | died | April 25, 1852 | Æ 60 |

Emma E. | died | Mar 10, || Rosa | died | Nov 24, 1851 | 1850 | Æ 2 y'rs |           || Æ 6 mo | Children of Emma M. | & Willis Gibbs |

Frederick Griswold | Aged 77 |

Benjamin Griswold | died | Mar 24, 1862 | Æ 83 | Sally | wife of | Benjamin Griswold | died | April 10, 1836 | Æ 62 |

Alice Marian | Adopted Daughter | of | H. H. & S. J. Guild || died | May 3, 1859 | Æ 5 y'rs |

In memory of | Frederick F. Guild | who died | Sept 21, 1854 | Æ 51 |

Theresa M. | daughter of | Jarvis & Susan | Griswold | died | Nov. 9, 1867 | Æ 27 |

Melissa Jane | daughter of | Jarvis & Susan | Griswold | died | Oct 14, 1844 | Æ 16 y'rs |

Susan P. | wife of | Jarvis Griswold | born | March 17, 1807 | died | April 5, 1878 |

Jarvis Griswold | died | Jan 16, 1881 | aged 80 |

Charlotte P. | wife of | Benjamin Griswold Jr | died | Feb 28, 1837 | Æ 24 |

Ella | daughter of | Benjamin & | Nancy Griswold | died | Apr 16, 1856 | Æ 1 y'r & 6 mo |

Asahel Griswold | died | Aug 7, 1828 | Æ 85 | Hannah his wife | died | Aug 9, 1827 | Æ 77 |

Asahel Griswold | died | Feb 16, 1859 | Æ 83 |

Desire | wife of | Asahel Griswold | died | Mar 3, 1860 | Æ 83 |

In | memory of | Mary O. | daughter of | Benjamin & Sally Griswold | died | Dec 19, 1833 | aged 31 |

In | Memory of | Betsey Griswold | wife of Julius Griswold | and daughter of | Nathan Stuart | who died Dec'r 20, 1809 | in the 26 year | of her age | Nathan S. Griswold | their son | died March 6th 1810 | Aged 7 months |

Nancy | wife of | Benjamin Griswold | died | July 27, 1867 | Æ 51 |

Mary E. | daughter of | Benjamin & | Nancy Griswold | died | May 2, 1864 | Æ 22 |

Tabitha Gibbs | died Sept 1807 | Æt 84 |

H. G. || S. G. (ibbs) (*footstone*)

In memory of | Submit | Wife of | Gershorn Gibbs | Died Nov 1, 1833 | Æ 82 |

William J. | son of P. G. & | H. E. Guild | drowned | July 7, 1859 | Æ 2 Yr & 6 Mo |

Mary H. | daughter of | Penfield G. & Harriet Guild | died | Nov 18, 1867 | Æ 5 y's & 11 mo. |

In Memory of | Gad Guild | who died | May 16, 1860 | Æ 78 years |

In | memory of | Sarah | wife of | Gad Guild | who died | Dec 2, 1852 | aged 67 years |

In memory of | M^rs Anna Guild | wife of M^r Gad Guild | who died July 5^th 1807 | in the 27^th | year of her age |

In | Memory of | Eunice | wife of | David D. Guild | who died | Apr 30, 1849 | Æ 37 |

David D. Guild | died | July 31, 1885 | Æ 77 |

In | Memory of | Hannah Guild | wife cf | Jeremiah Guild | died May 9, 1800 | Æt 44 |

In | Memory of | Jeremiah Guild | died January 30 | 1822 Æt 76 |

In | Memory of | Lucinda | wife of | Jeremiah Guild | who died Feb 22, 1849 | aged 80 years |

Martha J. wife of | Earl S. Guild | died | Oct 29, 1862 | Æ 20 |

Harriet D. wife of | Earl S. Guild | died | Apr 26, 1861 | Æ 25 |

Laura | wife of | Jeremiah Guild | died | May 18, 1863 | Aged 68 years |

Jeremiah Guild | died | Aug 18, 1859 | aged 67 years |

John Griswold | died | Sept 30, 1871 | Æ 86 |

In memory of | Jeremiah Griswold Esq | who died on the 29^th | of March 1790 in the | 78^th year of his age |

Lieutenant John Griswold | born 29 Jun : 1758, died 22 Dec. 1847 | a soldier of the American | Revolution | Rhoda his wife daugh^r | of M^r David Wetmore | born 25 December 1765 | died 30 January 1848 || Dotha, daughter of | John Griswold | born 25 July 1787 | died 14 September 1867 ||

Julius Griswold | Born Jan 11, 1784 | Died May 13, 1868 | Asenath Hall | his wife | Born Mar 1, 1789 | Died Aug 25, 1885 |

Truman Guild | born | Apr || Lamira Catlin | born | Jan 19, 1806 | || 10, 1809
Married Feb 21, 1830.
died | Mar 2, 1890 | | died | Dec 31, 1883 |
GUILD

Nellie L. | daughter of | Truman & | Lamira Guild | died | July 23, 1866 | Æ 22 |

Alban Guild | died | May 2, 1874 | Aged 90 |

Roxana | wife of | Alban Guild | Died Nov 4, 1874 | Aged 88½ |

Charles L. Guild | died | Apr 27, 1893 | Aged 31 y'rs 8 mo's |

Sarah Delphine | daughter of | Abner & Roxana O. Gilbert | died | Feb 15, 1871 | Æ 27 |

Mary Elizabeth | Daughter of | Abner & | Roxana O. Gilbert | died | Oct 17, 1867 | Æ 22 |

Henry S. | Griswold | died | May 6, 1883 | aged 76 years || Nancy | Perkins | wife of | Henry S. Griswold | died Sept 13, 1851 | aged 43 years || To the memory of | Helen M. | Whittlesey | wife of | Darius P. | Griswold | who died | Sept 17, 1897 | aged 66 years | and 6 months |

Horatio Page Griswold | Died June 29, 1892 | Aged 55 Y'rs |

| GRISWOLD |

Charles S. | Died Jan 20, 1860 | Aged 6 Y'rs | Emma C | Died May 4, 1863 | Aged 5 Y'rs | Mariah A. | Died Nov 12, 1865 | Aged 14 Y'rs |

Sylvester C | Died Jan 28, 1892 Aged 78 | May A | Died May 31, 1859 | Aged 35 Y rs | Sarah E | Died April 3, 1878 | Aged 43 Y'rs | Wives of | Sylvester C. Griswold |

William O. Died Aug 31, 1883, Aged 27.

Lucius Griswold | died | Feb 24, 1876 | Aged 64 |

Arthur Griswold | died | Apr 16, 1877 | Aged 22 |

Cornelia L. Bissell | wife of | Otis E. Gillette | Born Sept 11, 1841 | Died Feb 5, 1900 |

Norman Hall | 1805-1852 | his wife | Emily Merriman | 1807-1886 || Geo. W. Seelye | 1840-1886 || Eliza A. | 1834-1855 | Electa C. | 1832-1854 |

Eliza A. Hall | died Oct 15, 1855 | Æ 21 Y'rs | Electra C. | wife of J. W. Cook | died at Chicago, Ill. | July 16, 1854 | Æ 22 Y'rs | Daughters of Norman | & Emily Hall |

Norman Hall | died | Oct 14, 1852 | Æ 47 |

WEST CEMETERY—EUNICE BUEL

In memory of | Desire | Wife of Daniel Hall | died | May 6, 1875 | aged 93 years |

Daniel Hall | died | May 22, 1862 | Æ 86 |

Sally B. Hall | died | April 10, 1843 | aged 24 years |

William Hall | died | Feb. 7, 1836 | aged 32 |

John Hall | died | Apr 4, 1848 | Æ 94 | Damiras wife of | John Hall | died | Jan 4, 1849 | Æ 93 |

In | memory of | Reuben Hart | who died | May 22, 1836 | Æ 75 | Ruth wife of | Reuben Hart | died Aug 29, 1843 | ⌐ 82 |

Elias Hart | died | Jan 19, 1867 | Æ 60 |

Julia A. Page | wife of | Elias Hart | died | Oct 17, 1886 | aged 80 |

Jennette wife of | Seelye Hart | died | Nov 16, 1867 | Æ 34 |

Mrs. Eva J. Hart | died | Sept 16, 1882 | Aged 24 Y'rs |
Dora M. Hart | daughter of | Isaac C. & Mary E. | Hart |
died | Nov 28, 1892 | Age 17 Y'rs |

Sarah | wife of | Charles W. | Hotchkiss | died Sept 20 | 1883 | aged 25 y'rs | HOTCHKISS |

Frederick T. Jennings | Co A, 2. Regt H'vy Art'y C. V. | died | Dec 16, 1878 |

Helen M. | daughter of | Frederick T. & | Claricy G. | Jennings | died | May 11, 1850 | Æ 6 days |

David T. Jennings | died | Sept 9, 1848 | Æ 18 |

Leverett A. Jennings | died | Aug 1, 1863 | Aged 28 |

Lucinda Jennings | wife of | Josiah Jennings | Died July 4, 1881 | Aged 80 |

Josiah Jennings | died | Nov 20, 1876 | Aged 76 |

Sal'y Jennings | died | Aug 22, 1848 | Æ 45 |

Burritt Jennings | died | Feb 22, 1848 | Æ 90 | David T. | died | Dec 3, 1811, Æ 5 |

Mrs Ruth | wife of | Burritt Jennings | died | Oct 20, 1828 | Æ 61 |

Mary Jewett | died | Aug 19, 1864 | aged 13 Mo's & 29 d'ys|

Lewis W. Jones | Co. C. 10 Regt. | Maryland Vols | died |
Apr 22, 1889 |

Sarah J. Skiff | wife of | Levi N. Jacus | born | Apr 25,
1837 | died | Apr 23, 1895 | Æ 58 Y'rs |

Levi N. Jacus | died | Jan 14, 1890 | Æ 55 |

Mr. Roger Kirby | died | June 12, 1793 | aged 95 years |

Mary Jane Clark | wife of | Edw. Kimberly | died Aug 1,
1886 | Æ 63 Y'rs 6 Mo 6 Dys | KIMBERLY || Edward Kim-
berly | died | Oct 16, 1895, | Æ 69 Yrs |

Ethan Kilbourn | died | Mar 7, 1888 | Æ 84 | Thankful |
wife of | Ethan Kilbourn | died | Dec 30, 1876 | Æ 74 |
KILBOURN || John Jennings | died | Dec 10, 1879 | Æ 83 |
Polly his wife | died | May 20, 1881 | Æ 84 || William H.
Jennings | died | Sept 19, 1877 | Æ 46 | JENNINGS || Hiram
D. Jennings | died in Sparta, Wis. | Aug 24, 1862 | Æ 34. | J.
Wesley Jennings | a member of Co K 1 Wis. Cav. | died in
Cleaveland, | East Tenn. | April 22, 1864 | Æ 25 |

Cynthia | daughter of | Marcus & | Ruth | Leonard | died |
Feb 19, 1838 | Æ 5 mo's |

Isaac P. | son of | Marcus & | Ruth Leonard | died | June 6,
1828 | Æ 7 Y'-rs |

Louese S. | daughter of | Charles F. & Theresa | Lorber |
died Sept 30, 1874 | Æt 19 |

John B. | son of | James B. & | Catherine Lyons | died | Jan
9, 1863 | aged 6 mos |

Abigail Morris | died | Sept 24, 1862 | aged 69 years |

In | memory of | Augustus Morey | died | April 19, 1867 |
Æ 73 |

In | Memory of | Harriet | wife of | Augustus Morey | who
died | Jan 23, 1847 | Æ 47 |

Asa T. | aged 2 years || Diadama | aged 5 years | who
died Sept. 11, 1778 | Son & Daughter of | Dea. John & Lydia
Munson |

In | memory of | Isaac Morey | who died | Dec 15, 1799 |
Æ 26 years |

Henry S. Morehouse | Co H. 2 Regt H'vy Art'y C. V. |
died | June 7, 1886 |

In | memory of | Abigail | wife of | Horace Nichols | who died | May 30, 1853 | aged 39 years |

William Newcomb | died June 8, 1842 | aged 74 years | Artemesia | his widow | died Aug 3, 1845 | aged 81 years |

In Memory of | M$^r$ Joseph Osborn | who died August 25$^{th}$ | A. D. 1809 in the 65$^{th}$ | Year of his age |

Died | April 7, 1829 | Delia | daughter of | Manly & | Hannah L. | Peters | aged 13 mo. |

Died | Oct 8, 1837 | Martha H. | daughter of | Manly & | Hannah L. | Peters | aged 7 y'rs | & 6 mo |

Daniel Perkins | died | July 3, 1847 | aged 66 years |

John Page | son of | Roswell & | Philomela Page | died | Sept 4, 1846 | Æ 21 |

Sarah E. | daughter of | Daniel & Ursula Page ] died | Sept 1, 1857 | Æ 31 |

Ursula | wife of | Daniel Page | died | Apr 19, 1861 | Æ 66|

Daniel Page | died | July 6, 1881 | Æ 88 |

In | memory of | Miss Huldah Parsons | who died | June 1849 | Æ 47 |

In | memory of | Phebe Parsons | who died | Nov 1, 1841 | aged 41 years |

In | memory of | Eliphaz Parsons | who died ] Dec 12, 1841 | aged 72 |

Mrs. | Caroline Page | wife of | Daniel Page | died | Oct 23, 1846 | in the 87 year | of her age |

Mr. | Daniel Page | died | Dec 1, 1834 | aged 78 |

In | Memory of | David Page | who died | Nov 19, 1829 | Aged 52 |

In | Memory of | Rhoda | wife of | David Page | who died | Mar 11, 1843, | Æt 66 |

In | Memory of | Mrs Abigail wife of | Capt Eliphaz Parsons | who departed this life | Feb 22$^d$ 1799 | In the 57$^{th}$ year | of her age |

> In memory of life that's past
> In hopes of life to come.
> The Husband of the deceased
> Doth consecrate this Tomb.

Died | Aug 29, 1835 | Aaron son of | Henry & | Lovina Peck | aged 9 mo |

In Memory of | Lieunt Jehiel | Parmele he died | Jan^{ry} y^e 15^{th} 1776 | in ye 58^{th} year of | his Age |

In Memory of | Mr. Jehiel Parmele | he died July y^e 17^{th} | 1777 in y^e 25 | year of his Age |

In | memory of | Daniel Perkins | who died | Aug 15, 1841 | æ 91 years |

In | memory of | David Page | who died | Feb 2, 1820 | aged 84 |

In Memory of | Anna Page | wife of | David Page | who died | August 6, 1813 | aged 74 years |

Amelia | daughter of | David B. & Alfaetta | Parmelee | died | June 13, 1888 | Æ 4 Y'rs & 19 D's |

Susan King | wife of | S. D. Page | Died Feb 10, 1885 | Aged 56 |

John A. Page | died | Aug 21, 1881 | Aged 32 |

Carrie S. | daughter of | Samuel D. & Susan K. Page | died | June 23, 1872 | aged 13 years |

Nelson G. Parmeley | died | Jun 21, 1891 | Aged 44 |

Elsie A. | Wife of | William Parmeley | died | Mar. 16, 1878 | Æ 71 |

Eli Perkins | died | Dec 15, 1864 | Aged 48 |

Children | of | Eli & Emeline | Perkins || Octavia U. | died | Sept 23, 1854 | Æ 2 yrs & 2 mo | Daniel B. | died | Oct 4, 1849 | Æ 2 y'rs & 2 mo. | Dwight F. | died | Sept 2, 1862 | Æ 18 Y'rs & 5 Mo |

Daniel Perkins | died | July 3, 1847 | Æ 66 | Rachel | his wife | died June 13, 1876 | Æ 95 | PERKINS. |

Ithamar Page | 1804-1885 | PAGE || Children of | Ithamar & Jennett | Page | David | 1832-1847 | Marcella W. Parker | 1829,-1865 |

Died | May 3, 1850 | Olive | daughter of | Horace & | Sally G. Page | aged 11 years | 7 mo. & 15 d's |

Sally G. | wife of | Horace Page | died | Aug 6, 1881 | Aged 77 |

Horace Page | died | June 22, 1856 | Aged 54 |

Gilbert Page | born | Jan 13, 1835 | Entered into rest | Dec 3, 1884 |

Ira Page | died | Dec 11, 1885 | Æ 53 |

Charles Page | died | June 6, 1882, Æ 48 | Orlie | son of C. & Mary P. | Page | died | July 23, 1875 | Æ 11 |

Mary wife of | Charles Page | died Jan 5, 1865 | Æ 26 || Roswell Page | died | Nov 12, 1875 | Æ 77 | Philomela H. Page | died | Apr 16, 1883 | Æ 88 | PAGE || John | son of Roswell & | Philomela Page | died | Sept 1, 1846 | Æ 21 |

Mary Ann | wife of Beecher Perkins | died | Sept 1, 1875 | Aged 60 |

Beecher Perkins | born | May 3, 1811 | died | Aug 20, 1882! Aged 71 |

Ralph ! Son of | Daniel & Eva | Perkins | Died Apr 4, 1885! Æ 4 Mo's |

Ella Perkins | died | Oct 18, 1859 | aged 2 yrs 9 mos | 18 days || Only daughter of | Orlando & | Sarah A. Perkins |

In | Memory of | Harmon jr. | Son of Harmon | & Maria Seeley | who died | March | 10, 1820 | Æt 10 Mo |

In Memory of Mrs | Martha, wife of Mr | Nathan Stewart, who | Died November 27th | A. D. 1786 in the 43rd | year of her Age | Also | In Memory of Jarid Stew | art their Son who Died | at New York January 26th | A D 1777 in the 16th | Year of his Age |

In Memory of | Eunice | wife of | Nahan Stewart | who departed this life | Sept 12, 1819 | Æt 69 |

Burrill | Son of Samuel W. | & Lucretia Spencer | died Dec 11, 1802 | aged 6 weeks | Jabez B. | died June 21, 1811 | aged 2 years & 9 months |

In Memory of | Mr William Stewart who | departed this life Janry | 17th 1800 in the 94th year | of his age |

In Memory of | Mrs Mary wife of | Mr William Stewart | who departed this life | Feby 17th 1799 in the | 74th year of her age |

**Sarah Stewart** | (*footstone*).

In Memory of | Jared Stewart | Son of Mr Na | than Stew-art & | Martha his wife | who Died Oct 2 ( ?) | A D 1779 Aged 8 | months |

Virginia M. | daughter of | Horace & Harriet | Seeley | died | Nov 17, 1864 | aged 22 y'rs | 7 mo & 13 d's |

Harriet R. | wife of | Horace L. Seelye | died | Nov. 23, 1866 | aged 52 years |

Horace L. Seelye | died | Apr 15, 1887 | Aged 70 |

Benj. N. Starr | died | July 12, 1873 | aged 13 y'rs & 11 mo's | son of | Rev. Geo. J. & Elizabeth Harrison |

William H. Jr. | son of | Wm. H. & | Charlotte A. Snyder | died | Oct 22, 1867 | Æ 10 y's & 2 mo |

Julia Anna | Daughter of | Wm H. & | Charlotte A. Sny-der | died | Oct 17, 1867 | Æ 7 y's & 8 mo |

Alva D. Sharp | died | Aug 25, 1869 | aged 60 Y'rs |

Lucy Sharp | wife of | Alvah D. Sharp | died | Aug 30, 1884 | aged 72 years |

Andrew P. Smith | died | Nov 5, 1864 | Æ 56 || Almira P. | wife of | Andrew P. Smith | died | Dec 27, 1868 | Æ 59 || Abbie J. | wife of | Seth Whiting | died | Jan 23, 1869 | Æ 35 |

Seymour Stevens | died | Jan 15, 1873 | Æ 71 |

Emeline L. | wife of | Seymour Stevens | died | Sept. 12, 1881 | Aged 71 |

Anson C. Smith | died | Mar 26, 1883 | Aged 70 y'rs & 16 Ms |

Justus | Seelye | 1795 |

W. S. | 1793 | (*Seelye?*)

William Tuttle | died | Jan 7, 1853 | Æt 74 |

Mrs | Polly Tuttle | wife of | Mr William Tuttle | died Dec 16, 1811 | Aged 30 years |

Mrs. | Hannah Tuttle | wife of | Mr William Tuttle | died Feb 13, 1823 | aged 42 years |

In | Memory of | Mr Jonathan Taylor | who died at Corn-wall | July 6, A. D. 1809 | aged 56 years 8 months & | 14 days|

In | memory of | Ruanna | wife of | Lyman Thomas | de-ceased | who died | Jan 31, 1850 | aged 71 years |

Rev. Richard Thompson | died | July 26, 1857 | Æt 59 |

Mary E. | wife of | Richard Thompson | died | May 23, 1877 | Aged 19 Yrs |

John M. West *M. D.* | Let the dead rest. |

Laura Ann | Daughter of | John M. & Sophia | West who died | March 7, 1813 | Aged 3 Months |

John Welch | died | Dec 26, 1844 | aged 85 |

Rosanna Welch | wife of John Welch | died March 22, 1830 | aged 64 |

David Welch | died March 26th, | 1815 Æ 91 |

Irene Welch | died May 14th | 1814 Æ 77 |

Irene Welch | daugher of | John Welch | died March 20, 1821 | aged 34 |

Gertrude E. Williams | died | May 6, 1850 | Æ 24 |

In | memory of | Sarah L. | daughter of | Noble & Jerusha Ann | Wetmore | who died | Oct 10, 1842 | Æ 19 |

Jerusha Ann | wife of | Noble Wetmore | died Sept 21, 1844 | Æ 39 |

Noble Wetmore | died | Aug 30, 1855 | Æ 56 |

Polly | wife of | Noble Wetmore | died Sept 19, 1886 | Æ 84 yrs |

Here lies the body | of Mr. David Wetmore | who deceased the 15th | of June A. D. 1774 in the | 46th year of his age. | Mrs Sarah wife of | Mr David Wetmore & only child of the | late Henry Stanton | Esq. of Wallingford | died —— |

In | Memory of | Elihu Wetmore | who died | Sep 14th 1841 | Æ 52 |

In | Memory of | Angeline daughter of | Elihu & | Polly Wetmore | who died | Oct 20, 1843 | aged 20 years |

Rosanna Welch | Born Aug 31, 1801 | Died March 30, 1848 | aged 47 years |

In | Memory of | Samuel West | who died | Dec 8, 1821 | in the 72 year | of his age |

In memory of | Jonathan Wright | who died | April 15, 1836 | aged 90 years |

Thankful | wife of | Jonathan Wright | died | Feb 25, 1831 | aged 74 |

In Memory of | M^rs Tryphena Wright | wife of Jonathan Wright | who departed this life | Nov^r 26^th, 1786 | aged 38 | years |

In Memory of | Mrs Leah Wright wife | of Jonathan Wright | who departed this life | June 11, 1782 aged 35 |

In Memory of | M^r Jonathan Wright | 2^nd who Died Dec 14, | 1799 Aged 32 years |

In Memory of | Mrs Honour Wife of | M^r Jonathan Wright | 2^nd who died Aug 24^th | 1803, Aged 35 years |

In | Memory of | Mrs Almira wife of | Capt Jonathan Wright | & daughter of | John Griswold | who died May 4, 1821 | in the 29 year | of her age |

Samuel Wright | died | March 12, 1875 | aged 86 | Desdemona | his wife | died | May 26, 1871 | aged 81 | WRIGHT || Everett H. Wright | born | Nov 21, 1823 | Died Jan 29, 1883 ||

Seth Guild | son of | E. H. & L. S. Wright | died | Aug 30, 1865 | Aged 1 Y'r 1 Mo | & 14 D.s |

Samuel Landon | son of | E. H. & L. S. Wright | died | Sept 26, 1862 | Aged 1 Yr & 8 Mo |

Wolsey Woodin | died | Jan 18, 1875 | Æ 49 |

William Wishart | died | Mar 18, 1874 | Æ 27 |

Clarissa | wife of | Gerritt P. Welch | died Feb 26, 1888 | Æ 86 y'rs |

Gerritt P. Welch | died | Nov 15, 1847 | aged 52 years |

Irene M. | daughter of Gerit P. & | Clarissa Welch | born July 3, 1826 | died Oct 24, 1847 | Aged 21 years |

Maria W. | daughter of | G. P. and | Clarissa Welch | died | June 13, 1842 | aged 7 years |

Caroline E. | daughter of | G. P. & C. M. Welch | died | Oct 10, 1828 | aged 15 months |

John H. Welch | died | May 5, 1878 | Æ 46 Y'rs 7 M's |

HEAD QUARTERS.

Albert Anson | died | May 19, 1891 | Aged 77 Y'rs |

Myron Benson | died | Oct 10, 1880 | Æ 82 | Betsey | his wife died | Mar 27, 1884 | Æ 82 |

Allen Benson | died | June 2, 1885 | Aged 64 |

Betsey E. | wife of | Joseph Bradley | Died Sept 24, 1869 | Æ 84 | Julia M. Dains | wife of | Nathaniel Roraback | Died Oct 28, 1869 | Æ 28 |

Lillie R. | daughter of | Morton & | Mary A. Benson | died | Mar 16, 1876 | Æ 15 y'rs | & 6 mo |

Etta J. | daughter of | Morton & | Mary A. Benson | died | Feb 24, 1889 | Æ 26 yrs |

George W. Bement | died | April 2, 1896 | Aged 65 |

Mary Jane Tuttle | wife of | George W. Bement | died | Sept 2, 1886 | Aged 53 |

Laura Granniss | wife of | Julius W. Bement | died | Apr 16, 1883 | Aged 82 |

Joseph Birge | died | Sept 24, 1854 | aged 86 years |

Marcella Birge | died | Oct 24, 1846 | Aged 78 |

James P. | son of | Cornelius G. | & Sarah W. Birge | died | Apr 22, 1848 | Æ 8 mo. & 3 d's |

Cornelius G. Birge | died | Jan 27, 1869 | Æ 55 |

Abigail Birge | Daughter of Harvey | and Thankfull Birge | died Aug 2, 1844 | aged 22 |

Harvey Birge | died | Nov 29, 1860 | in his 79 year |

In memory of | Thankful | Wife of | Harvey Birge | Who died | Dec. 8, 1838 | Æ 54 |

James Birge | died | Feb 10, 1850 | Æ 91 |

In | memory of | Sally | wife of | James Birge, Esq | who died | June 13, 1835 | aged 76 years |

Orrin Birge | died | June 20, 1847 | Æt 63 |

In | memory of | Hannah L. | daughter of | Harvey & | Thankful Birge | who died | Jan 19, 1832 | aged 22 years |

In memory of | Mr Benjamin Birge | who died March | 17th A D 1796, in the | 34th year of his | Age |

Lucinda H. | wife of | Erastus Bates | died | Jan 23, 1847 | Æ 26 |

Betsey E. | wife of | Thomas Cummings | died | June 4, 1877 | Æ 59 Y'rs & 3 Mo |

Mrs. | Philana Catlin | wife of | Mr Pierc Catlin | died | May 13, 1816 | Æ 23 | Jane Catlin | their daughter died | March 17, 1816 | Æ 5 months |

Sacred to the memory of | Samuel Carter | who departed this life Jan | 20, 1812 | Aged 48 | Also In Memory of | Diana his wife | who departed this life | Jun 28, 1804 | Aged 36 |

Lydia | wife of | Wm. H. Dudley | died | May 15, 1862 | Æ 68 |

William H. Dudley | died | Oct 25, 1872 | Æ 76 |

William Dudley | died | Sept 16, 1849 | Æ 89 |

Mrs | Abigail Dudley | wife of | William Dudley | Died | Aug 24, 1827 | Æt 65 |

In memory of | Augustus B. Dudley | Son of Mr William & | Mrs Abigail Dudley | who died May 1st, 1807 | Aged 14 Years |

In | Memory of | Chauncey Denison | Who died | July 18, 1838 | aged 78 years |

In | memory of | Sarah | wife of | Chauncey Dennison | who died | April 1, 1850 | aged 90 years |

Wilmot N. Dains | died | May 16, 1853 | Æt 43 y'rs |

Sally M. Benedict | wife of | Willmot N. Dains | died | July 17, 1886 | Aged 11 |

In | Memory of | John Denison | son of Chancy & | Sarah Denison | who died Aug 5, 1793 | aged 4 years | & 2 months |

In | memory of | Charles I. | son of | Noah & | Polly Frisbie | who died | May 4, 1839 | aged 2 y'rs | & 9 mo |

Margery Frisbie | died July 23, | 1815 Æ 82 |

Noah Frisbie | died May 12, | 1812 | Æ 64 |

Mr. | Jonathan Frisbie | died | July 7, 1814 | aged 53 years |

In | Memory of | Caroline Frisbie | died Dec 28, 1816 | aged 3 yrs | daughter of Levi | & Abby Frisbie |

Ellen Eliza | daughter | of | Henry & Betsey M. | Frisbie | born | Mar 3, 1850 | died | Sept 30, 1855 |

In | memory of | Friend H. Frisbie | who died | Aug 20, 1843 | aged 75 years |

In | memory of | Betsey | daughter | of Friend H. & | Lucy Frisbie | who died | March 13, 1826 | Æ 15 |

Elizabeth | wife of | Jonathan Frisbie | died May 27, 1830 | aged 66 |

Levi Frisbie | died | Oct 3, 1841 | Æ 58 |
Mrs. | Nabby D. | wife of | Levi Frisbie | born | Dec 11, 1790 | died | June 30, 1866 |

Freelove C. | wife of | Frederick Frisbie | died | Mar 25, 1853 | Æ 29 Y'rs |

Charlie | son of | Jerome & | Edna Granniss | died Sept 29, 1886 | aged 9 y'rs |

Joseph K. Granniss | died | May 22, 1858 | Æt 31 |

Emeley O. | daughter of | John E. & | Delia Granniss | died | April 15, 1861 | Æ 21 |

Capt. | John E. Granniss | died | Sept 15, 1873 | Æ 57 |

Annie A. | Daughter of | Andrew & Rebecca | Granniss | died | Jan 25, 1887 | Aged 24 |

Andrew W. Granniss | died | Aug 19, 1864 | Æt 45 Y'rs |

Ellen G. | daughter of | Andrew W. & | Rebecca Granniss | died | May 24, 1871 | Æ 17 Y'rs & 6 M's |

Eri T. Granniss | died | Dec 1, 1869 | Aged 45 |

Cicero T. Granniss | died | Mar 18, 1894 | Æ 61 | GRANNIS || Emeline | wife of | Cicero T. Granniss | died | Dec 16, 1887 | Æ 59 |

Geo. W. Granniss | died | Oct 16, 1870 | Æ 50 |

Polly Hays | wife of | Geo. W. Granniss | died | Dec 3, 1869 | Æ 46 |

Dwight H. Granniss | died | Nov 23, 1875 | Aged 20 |

Clarissa I. | wife of | Thomas S. Granniss | died | Oct 14, 1881 | Æ 74 |

Thomas S. Granniss | died | May 6, 1869 | Æ 62 |

Thomas Granniss | died | Sept 17, 1859, | Æ 89 |

Ruth | his wife died | Sept 10, 1857 | Æ 78 |

A. L. Granniss | born | ‖ Sally Potter | his wife | born |
Jan. 1, 1814 | died | Jan 13, ‖ Dec. 15, 1821 |
1894 |                        ‖

## GRANNISS

Ernest C. ‖ son of | F. M. & | Ella M. Granniss | died |
Oct 29, 1887 | Æ 5 Mo 20 D.'s |

Our little Willie ‖ son of | F. M. & | Ella M. Granniss |
died | Aug 5, 1877 | Æ 4 months |

Eri Granniss | died ‖ July 22, 1853 | Æ 66 |

Aurilla | wife of | Eri Granniss | died | May 11, 1874 |
Æ 81 |

Susan S. ‖ daughter of | Harry & | Lucinda Granniss |
died | Sept 14, 1857 | Æ 18 |

Asa W. ‖ only son of | Harry & | Lucinda Granniss | died |
Oct 16, 1857 | Æt 7 Y'rs |

Maria C. | wife of | Samuel H. Glover | died | Dec 10,
1872, | Aged 48 |

Electa | Wife of | John Griffin | Died May 1, 1868 | Æ 77 |

John Griffin | died | July 15, 1871 | Aged 86 |

Chester M. Goslee | died | Feb 22, 1873 | in his 38th year |

Elisha Glover | son of | Edward & | Hannah Glover ⌡ died |
Jan 25, 1841 | Æ 47 |

Sidney S. | son of | Elisha & | Ruth Ann Glover | died |
Mar. 13, 1841 | Æ 21 |

Hiram W. Griffin | Died Oct 2, 1874 | Aged 61 | Harriet
B. His wife | Died May 2, 1876 | Aged 56 |

John S. | Son of Hiram W. & | Harriet B. | Griffin | died |
Dec 17, 1856 | Aged 10 Y'rs |

Truman Gilbert | died | Aug 8, 1864 | Æ 77 |

Selima | wife of | Truman Gilbert | died | Jan 31, 1866 |
Æ 74 |

Francis C. Gilbert | Co E 8, Regt | Conn Vols | died | **Mar**
21, 1871 |

Aaron Granniss | died Jan 10, 1845 | Aged 79 | Hannah his wife | died Jan 28, 1846 | Aged 75 |

Henry W. | son of Nial & | Sally Granniss | died | Mar 14, 1836 | aged 3 y'rs | & 2 mo |

Nial Granniss | died | Feb 7, 1870 | Æ 80 | Sally his wife | died | Jan 27, 1836 | Æ 44 |

In Memory of Mr | William Granniss | who departed this | life March the 27th, |1792; in the 58th year of his age |

> Sleep on dear friend, till Jesus comes
> And Gabriel's trump shall bust the tombs;
> Then all immortal thou shalt rise,
> And may thy death instruct us to be wise.

In | Memory of | Sarah | wife of | William Granniss | who died | May 30, 1809 | Æt 76 |

Maria | wife of | Charles D. Granniss | Died May 23, 1883 | Aged 67 Y'rs & 9 Mo |

Charles D. Granniss | died | March 14, 1872 | Æ 63 |

George De | son of | Charles D. & | Rozetta Granniss | Died May 19, 1862 | Aged 19 Y'rs |

Charles Ai | son of | Charles & | Rosetta Granniss | died | Aug 30, 1855 | Æ 17 |

Rosetta | wife of | Charles D. Granniss | died | May 1, 1849 Æ 33 |

Henry W. | son of | Charles D. & | Rozetta Granniss | died | June 13, 1846 | aged 9 y'rs 3 m | & 4 d's |

Sarah E. | Wife of | John Hull | died Feb 29, 1884 | Æ 61 |

John Hull | died | Dec 17, 1869 | Æ 66 |

Charlotte E. | daughter of | John & | Sarah Hull | died | June 3, 1858 |

Corne'ius S. | son of John & | Sarah Hull | died | Dec 8, 1852 | Æ 3 y's & 7 mo |

Sarah A. | wife of | John Hull | died | Mar 11, 1843 | Æ 31 |

Died | Feb 24. 1850 | Ann Jennett | wife of | Joseph Hubbard | aged 20 years |

Josephine J. | daughter of Joseph & | Hannah Hubbard | died | May 23, 1851 | Æ 11 y'rs & 7 mo |

Lovina | wife of | Zera Keeler | died | Oct 14, 1870 | Æ 77|

Lucy B. | daughter of | Zelotas A. & | Dorcas Kidney | died|
June 5, 1874 | Æ 9 Y'rs |

Salmon Moulthrop | died | Dec 30, 1859 | Æ 88 | Polly his
wife | died Oct 25, 1846 | Æ 70 |

Miss Melinda Moulthrop | died | Feb 13, 1881 | Æt 72 |

William Moulthrop | died Feb 6, 1850 | Æ 80 | Mary his
widow | died | May 15, 1850 | Æ 76 |

In Memory of | Thalia Moulthrop | who died Sept 3, 1800 |
aged 1 year | Jacob died Sept 1, | 1801 Aged 3 yrs & 5 mo |
Anna died Aug 28, 1805 | aged 1 yr & 9 mo | Orrin died Nov
7, 1806 | aged 12 yrs | William Jr. died Jan 19, 1819 | aged
6 yrs & 7 mo | children of William & | Mary Moulthrop |

Mamie | daughter of | W. B. & Jennie S. | Morgan | died
June 28, 1874 | Æ 16 Mo's |

Truman Moulthrope | died | Jan 22, 1869 | Æ 64 |

Solomon Moulthrope | died | Jan 6, 1872 | Æ 71 |

Emeline | wife of | Solomon Moulthrop | died | July 20,
1850 | Æ 47 |

In | memory of Mary Merriman | who died | July 15, 1838 |
aged 33 years |

In | memory of | Joseph Merriman | who died | Nov 15,
1829 | aged 59 years |

In | memory of Betsey | wife of | Joseph Merriman | who
died | June 11, 1840 | aged 68 y'rs |

Solomon Noble | Died Dec 6, 1868 | aged 75 | Sarah A. |
his wife | Died Feb 24, 1843 | aged 36 |

In | memory of | Mrs. Polly | wife of | Jesse Osborn | who
died | Aug 18, 1819 | aged 36 years |

Cynthia J. | wife of | Curtis F. Platt | died Mar 6, 1859 |
Æ 37 y'rs 8 mo's | Eva J | their daughter | died Jan 3, 1856 |
Æ 3 Mo's |

Mr. | Joel Potter | died | July 18, 1827 | aged 66 |

Clarissa Irene | Daughter of | Curtis S. & Abigail W. | Pot-
ter died | June 30, 1831 | aged 9 years | Also | Truman Cur-
tis | their son, died | Feb 26, 1833 | aged 6 months |

Hermon Potter | died | Sept 26, 1863 | Æ 74 Y'rs ] Philana
D. | wife of | Hermon Potter | died Sept 25, 1863 | Æ 70 Y'rs|

Julius | son of Orrin | & Rhoda Potter | died | March 13,
1822, aged 2 years |

In | memory of | Parmelia Potter | died Oct 21, 1818 | aged
33 | wife of Hermon Potter |

Frozen | Dec 17, 1827 | William D. | son of D. & | N. Pritch-
ard | aged 3 years | 3 mo & 4 d's |

Polly Patterson | Born | Jan 28, 1799 | Died | Jan 11, 1891 |

Died | June 6, 1819 | Desire wife of | Aaron Page | aged
79 |

In Memory of Israel | Son to Cap^t Israel & | Mr^s Mary Pot-
ter | died O^ct 12^th 1785 | aged 1 year, the first | in this burying
ground. |

Enos Potter | died Feb 8, 1826 | aged 44 | Augustus Potter |
died Aug 1829 | aged 26 | Dorleska E. Potter | died April 14,
1826 | aged 4 | Wyllis S. Potter | died April 24, 1826 | aged
6 |

In Memory of | Polly Potter | wife of Enos Potter | who
died Nov 18, 1811 | Aged 30 years |

Mr. | Israel Potter | died March 9, 1815 | Aged 77 |

Lucy Benson | wife of | Egbert See | died | Octr 8, 1881 |
Aged 58 |

Horace Smith | died | Jan 11, 1867 | Æ 76 |

Almeda | Wife of | Horace Smith | died | July 22, 1860 |
Æ 67 y'rs |

In | memory of | Hannah | wife of | Hicks Smith | who
died | July 16, 1838 | aged 73 y'rs |

In | memory of | Hicks Smith | who died | Oct 14, 1830 |
aged 65 years |

Sidney | Son of Mr Hicks & | Mrs. Hannah Smith | Died
Dec 31^st 1804 | Æ 2 Years & 6 | Months |

In | memory of | Hannah M. | daughter of Hicks | & Han-
nah Smith | who died | Feb 27, 1826 | Æ 21 years |

In | Memory of | Ira Smith | who died | July 1, 1849 | Æ
49 y'rs & 15 days |

In | Memory of | Fanny B. | daughter of Job | & Arcena Simmons | died June 25, 1818 | Æt 4 yrs & 4 mo |

In | Memory of | Mrs Eliza Sherman | who died | March 26, 1845 | aged 48 years |

In Memory of M<sup>rs</sup> | Polly wife of M<sup>r</sup> | Hezekiah Smith | daug<sup>tr</sup> to Cap<sup>t</sup> Israel | Potter; died Oc<sup>t</sup> 27<sup>th</sup> | 1793 in the 23<sup>d</sup> year | of her age |

> Here my dear polly lies
> Obscur'd in the dust
> Thus all but virtue dies
> Whose memory cannot rust.

In memory of | Arseneth | wife of | Job Simmons | who died | Feb 23, 1869 | Æ 86 |

In memory of | Job Simmons | who died | June 20, 1855 | Æt 76 y'rs |

Eugene E. Wells | died | Dec 16, 1872 | Æ 21 |

Emma S. | wife of | Eugene E. Wells | Died Feb. 26, 1875 | Æ 25 |

Abbie B. | daughter of | Norman & | Selima Wetmore | died | Nov 20, 1871 | Æ 23 |

Hannah E. | aged 7 years | George S. | aged 1 y'r & 3 mo's | Children of Norman | & Selima Wetmore |

Elsie P. | daughter of | John & Sarah Wilson | died | Aug 5, 1854 | Æt 1 year |

# MORRIS

The town of Morris was originally the parish or society of South Farms in Litchfield, and it was not until 1859 that its extensive area was incorporated into a separate town. This is the reason why the two burying grounds of Morris are included in this book.

1 Litchfield Town Records 81.

"At a Meeting of the Inhabitants of the Town of Litchfield according to Law Decm^r 8^th A D 1747 ........ voted Liberty to the Inhabitants in the South Farms to have one quarter of an Acre of Land laid out by any two of the Select Men where they shall judge convenient for the use of a Burying Place for the Inhabitants of the Town."

No record has been found that the two selectmen ever carried this out, but four miles south of Litchfield, on the road to the meeting house in Morris lies this ancient burying ground on a hillside sloping to the south. The oldest stones are very near the road. Within a hundred years enlargements have brought the area of this burial place to three acres, and it has been well cared for.

# INSCRIPTIONS

Chauncey H. Alvord | died | May 11, 1881 | Aged 77 |

Elizabeth Smith | Wife of | Geo. N. Atwood | Died Feb 19, 1885 | Aged 56 |

Lucius S. Benton | Emma J. | his wife | 1851-1891 | BENTON ||

Leman H. Benton | 1830-1889 | BENTON || Lucius Allen | 1887-1888 | Herbert Webster | 1884-1890 | Bessie Benton | 1880-1890 | Children of | E. W. & S. E. Ensign || ENSIGN ||

Blanche E. | Burgess | died | Aug 4, 1888 | Aged 1 Month |

Willie D. Burgess | Died | Apr 26, 1871 | Aged 3 Mo's |

Frederick J. Burgess | Died | Aug 31, 1884 | Aged 26 |

Wm. L. Burgess | 1823— | Sarah A. Buel | his wife | 1828-1898 |

John Babbitt | died | Nov 1, 1869 | Æ 52 years.

Arthur Babbitt | died | May 15, 1874 | Æ 19 Y'rs & 3 Mo |

Herbert S. Babbitt | died | Sept 6, 1878 | Æ 31 |

Hattie A. Camp | wife of | Herert S. Babbitt | died | Nov 24, 1889 | Æ 39 |

Arthur J. | son of | Herbert S. & Hattie A. | Babbitt | Died Aug 28, 1895 | Æ 20 |

Amanda J. | wife of | Edwin Bierce | died | Sept 12, 1872 | Æ 37 |

David Benton | died | Apr 10, 1888 | Aged 88 |

Amy H. Orvis | wife of | David Benton | died | Oct 27, 1884 | Aged 80 |

The grave | of | Two little daughters | of | Alva M. & Mary A. | Bristol || Lucy | died | Sept 20, 1860 | Aged 5 Years | & 4 Months || Mary Jane | died | Sept 21, 1860 | Aged 9 Years | & 5 Months |

BLAKEMAN || J. D. Blakeman | 1815-1896 || Amy | **wife** of J. D. Blakeman | Born Sept 5, 1819 | Died Jan 16, 1888 ||

Capt John Pulaski | Blakeman | of the 20th U. S. C. T. | Died of Typhoid Fever | at New Orleans | Aug 5, 1864 | Æ 25 | His remains were brought to his | home and intered New Years 1865 |

Carrie | wife of | James D. Blakeman Jr. | died | April 26, 1876 | Æ 27 |

In | memory of | Samuel Barnard | who died | Oct 10, 1838 | aged 50 years |

In | memory of | Weltha S. | daughter of | Henry & | Ann Barnard | who died | Oct 30, 1834 | aged 20 years |

Isaac Bristol | died | July 12, 1862 | Æ 77 yrs |

In | memory of | Fanny wife of | Isaac Bristol | **who died** | Aug 28, 1839 | aged 55 yrs |

John R. Bradley | died | May 4, 1867 | Æ 68 |

Julia A. | wife of | John R. Bradley | died | Feb 3, 1860 | Aged 57 |

Dennis Bradley | died | Dec 26, 1861 | Aged 88 |

In | memory of | Mabel | wife of | Dennis Bradley | who died | Dec 14, 1845 | Æ 72 |

Infant child | of B. & E. | Barnard | Nov 3, 1822 |

In memory of | Henry | son of Benton & | Elizabeth Barnard | who died | Feb 14, 1821 | aged 17 months & | 20 days |

William Rea | son of Benton & | Elizabeth Barnard | died March 27, 1816 | aged 1 year & | 6 months |

Elizabeth R. | wife of | Benton Barnard | died | Dec 3, 1853 | Æt 69 |

Benton Barnard | died | March 25, 1855 | Æt 69 |

James | son of | William & | Mary Barnard | died | Oct 20, 1845 | aged 1 year |

Marietta L. | daughter of | William B. & | Mary Barnard | died | Oct 1, 1849 | aged 8 years |

William H. | son of | William B. & | Mary Barnard | died | Feb 7, 1857 | Æ 5 y'rs 7 mo | & 21 d's |

William B. Barnard | died | Aug 21, 1871 | Aged 53 |

Mary Barnard | died | Aug 1, 1873 | Aged 56 |

In | memory of | Drusilla wife of | Pattron M. Blackman | who died | Dec. 12, 1822 | aged 48 years |

In | memory of | Sarah wife of | Pattron M. Blackman | who died | June 19, 1845 | aged 65 years |

Pattron M. Blackman | died | Apr 19, 1850 | Æt 75 Y'rs |

In Memory of | Miss Lucy Bradley | the amiable Daughter of | Mr. Zina & Mrs. Molly | Bradley who died August | 24th A. D. 1798 in the 21st | year of her age |

In | memory of | Mrs. Mary Bradley | who died | March 13, 1827 | Æ 81 |

In Memory of | Mr. Zina Bradley | who departed this life | Nov 19th 1802 | in the 55th year | of his age |

In | memory of Polly | wife of | Wheeler Beacher | who died | Aug 27, 1848 | Æ 75 | Also an Infant of | Anson & Nancy Beecher | who died | Sept 25, 1833 | Æ 4 weeks |

In memory of | Mary Barnard, wife | of Samuel Barnard Jr. | Mother of Chauncey & Benton | Barnard, daughter of Ebenezer | & Amy Benton who died July | 23, 1786 | aged 23 years |

> Sleep on dear mother, take thy rest,
> Thy age at twenty three was set
> When from thy friends thou wast removed
> Forty and three have since elapsed
>
> ———
>
> And now thy son thine infant babe
> For whom thy care so much was paid
> Sets forth his love afresh to thee
> By this a marble memory.

Joel Bostwick | Born | in New Milford | Feb 2, 1778 | Died | Sept 29, 1860 |

Nancy Stone | wife of | Joel Bostwick | died | April 24, 1841 | Æ 55 |

june ye 8 | in 1768 died | Abigial Barns | wife. of. Enos | Barns. age: | . 39: |

Mrs Amy Benton | relice of Ebenezer Benton | died | May 17, 1827 | Æ 88 |

In Memory of | Mr. Ebenezer Benton | who died October 31, A. D. | 1813 in the 86 year | of his age | Here the weary are at rest. |

In Memory of | Leman & Joel Benton | Brothers | who were drown'd in | Long Island March 8, 1819 | Leman aged 28 | Joel 25 |

Amos Benton | died | Apr 11, 1859 | Aged 88 |

In memory of | Rachel | Wife of | Amos Benton | Who died | Feb 25,1841 | aged 65 |

Phebe Lucretia | daughter of | Erastus & | Anna Benton | died April 22, 1825 | Æ 54 years |

Anna Rea | relict of | Erastus Benton | & widow of | Daniel Lampson | died | Aug 5, 1856 | Æt 60 |

In | memory of | Erastus Benton | who died | Dec 26, 1829 | Æ 34 |
No age nor sex can death defy
Think, mortal, what it is to die.
Erected by D. Lampson.

In | Memory of | Saba wife of | David Benton | who departed this Life | Aug 5, 1830 | Æt 33 |

Ebenezer Benton | died | Jan 26, 1849 | Æt 82 |

Lois Benton | widow of | Ebenezer Benton | died | Aug 18, 1857 | Æt 91 |

Ebenezer Bates, Esq | died | Oct 10, 1868, | Æ 93 Y'rs & 8 M's |

Anna Mead | wife of | Ebenezer Bates | died | Nov 25, 1858 | Aged 86 |

........Memo.... | .... Sarah, wife of | Doctor Seth Bird | Who Died July yͤ 10, | 1766 In yͤ 29 yr o | her age |

In Memory of | Mrs. Hannah Bird | Wife of Doct Seth | Bird Died July the 30th | 1803 in the 66 Year | of her ....e.

This is the Grave of | Seth Bird physician | who died on the first October | One thousand eight hundred & | five in his seventy third year | Those whose pains have by his | skill and care been alleviated, | or whose lives have been | protracted; will give a more sincere | eulogiuin than can Marble | *Posuit Filius* |

Mrs. | Deborah Baldwin | wife of | Ashbel Baldwin | Died | Dec 24, 1834 | Æ 82 |

In | memory of | Ashbel Baldwin | who died | May 18, 1828 | Aged 77 |

In Memory of | M^rs Phebe Morris | wife of M^r Tim Barns & Dea^n Ja^s | Morris who Di- | ed April 15^th 1793 | in the 81^st year of | her age |

In Memory of | Mr Timothy Barns | who | Departed this | Life Oct 10, 1750 | in the Forty first year | of his age |

In Memory of M^rs Abagiel  Wife | of M^r Abel Barns | & Widow of M^r | James Stoddar She | Died octob^r y^e 3 | A D 1757 | Aged 36 years |

In | memory of | Samuel Barnard 2^d | who died | May 29, 1828 | aged 65 years | Also his wife | Weltha | died Feb 16, 1836 | aged 70 years |

In | Memory of | Brainard Barnard | who died [ Feb. 9^th, 1809 | Æ 32 |

My time was short my days were few
And I have bid this world adieu.

In Memory of the two unfortunate | youths, who were drowned Dec 16, 1812 |

| Willam Bennett | a native tive of Georgetown | S Carolina | departed this life | in the 16 year | of his age | | William M. Ensign | Son of Mr. Isaac & | Mrs Subra Ensign | departed this life | in the 15 year | of his age |

| By foreign hands thy dying eyses were closed | See here a Father's rising hope a Mother's fondest joy |
| By foreign hands thy decent limbs composed | An unseen hand this flower did crop |
| By foreign hands thy humble grave adorned | And their fond hope destroy A Father's prayers, a Mother's tears |
| By strangers honored and by strangers mourned | Could not prolong his tender years. |

Gone home | Robert M. | Son of | Silas & Camyntha | Catlin | Died Feb. 4, 1883 | Aged 11 Y'rs |

Stanley Carpenter [ died | Jan 17, 1876 | Aged 26 |

Frank J. Cook | son of | Joseph & Althea | Cook | Died Nov 6, 1884 | Aged 21 |

Joseph B. Cook | 1800-1887 | Althea M. Foster | his wife | 1834 — | COOK ||

Alvah Clark | died | Feb 22, 1876 | Æ 72 | CLARK || Children of | Edwin H. & Arabella L. | Clark | Herbert M. Died Mar 9, 1874 | Aged 4 Mos. | Henry W. Died Sept 19, 1874 | Aged 9 Mos. & 9 D's | Edwin F. Died Sept 13, 1881 | Aged 4 Y'rs 3 Mos. & 13 D's |

Dea. Phineas W. Camp | died | May 25, 1881 | Aged 72 |

Louisa B. McNeil | wife of | Phineas W. Camp | Born Jan 14, 1812 | Died May 9, 1895 |

Sylvia Amanda | Daughter of | Charles & Sylvia | Cook | Born Apr 18, 1851 | Died Sept 20, 1864 |

Mary A. | Daughter of | Charles & Sylvia | Cook | Born July 12, 1844 | Died May 10, 1861 |

Harriet | daughter of | Wm. H. & Lucy Catlin | Died June 6, 1868 | Æ 18 |

George W. Canfield | 1820-1902 | Sarah Pierpont | his wife| 1824-1899 | CANFIELD |

Edward Cowles | died | Apr 4, 1849 | Æ 53 |

Wealthy Maria Downs | wife of | Edward Cowles | Who died Jan 31, 1839 | Æ 41 |

Edward Sanford | son of | Edward & Rhoda | S. Cowles | died Feb 26th | 1846, Æ 2 Yrs | 5 Mo. & 7 d's |

Sophronia H. | wife of | Joseph W. Crossman | died | March 1, 1859 | Æ 48 |

Joseph W. Crossman | died | Nov 13, 1848 | Aged 37 |

Julia | Daughter to | Dan. and Pamola | Clark Died March | 18, 1804 in the | third Year of her | Age |

Anna Collins | died | Jan 15, 1852 | Æt 92 Y'rs |

In Memory | of | Mrs Anne Wife of Mr Charles | Collins Who | Departed this | life April 20th | 1787 in the 58th | Year of her Age |

In memory of | Mr Charles Collens who | Departed this | Life August the | 17th A D 1796 Aged 69 years |

In Memory of M^rs Rebecca Chase | Consort of y^e Rev^d Amos Chase | Daughter of y^e Rev^d Levi Hart | Grand daughter of y^e Rev^d Joseph Bellamy | She died Feb^y 25^th 1791 In y^e 26^th year of her age |

> Early bright transient as morning dew
> She sparkled was exhaled and went to heaven.

Rhoda Ann | Wife of | Job Clark | died Aug 25, 1851 | Æ 35 |

In | memory of Abel Clark | who died | Mar 25, 1842 | aged 77 years |

In | Memory of | M^rs Susan Camp | Wife of M^r Ezra Camp | who died February 17, | 1812 in the 56 year | of her age |

In | memory of | Ezra Camp | who died | Dec 23, 1838 | aged 76 years |

In | Memory of | Julia Ann Camp | Daughter of | Mr Ezra and Mrs. | Susan Camp who died Feb 18, 1812 in | the 17 year of her Æ |

> Ye young and gay
> Tho thoughtless pass me by
> Come view my tomb
> And learn to die.

Albert O. | Son of Samuel & | Phelenia Clock | died Oct 16, 1846 | aged 3 years | also | an infant daughter | aged 15 weeks | died July 9, 1842 |

Meroa A. | daughter of | Samuel & | Harriet Clock | died | Nov 13, 1839 | aged 12 y'rs |

Harriet M. | Wife of | Samuel Clock | died | July 4, 1836 | Æ 25 | Zendavesta, their Daughter | Died Feb 19, 1836 | aged 1 y'r & 3 mo's |

Philenia G. | Wife of | Samuel Clock | died | July 4, 1876 | Æ 64 |

Samuel Clock | died | Feb 26, 1884 | Aged Yrs |

In | Memory of | William Cable | who suddenly | departed this life | Dec 7, 1818 | aged 53 years |

James T. Cable | died | Sept 16, 1873 | Aged 64 Y'rs |

In | memory of | Lucy | wife of | James Cable | who died | April 5, 1835 | aged 18 years |

Lucy Jane | daughter of | James & | Louisa Cable | died | Jan 22, 1851 ⌈ Aged 9 Yr's | & 9 Mo's |

> But again we hope to meet thee
> When the day of life is fled
> Then in heaven with joy to greet thee
> Where no fare well tears are shed.

In | memory of | Meliscent Camp | wife of | Abel Camp | who died | Dec 27, 1824 | aged 74 years |

In memory of | an infant | Son of Mr Abel | & Mrs Sabra | Camp who die<sup>d</sup> | Sept 23<sup>d</sup>, 1791 |

In | memory of | Mr. Abel Camp | who died | May 8<sup>th</sup> 1825 | Æt 77 |

In Memory of | Mrs. Sabra, consort of | Mr. Abel Camp | who departed this life | May 19, 1807 in the 59<sup>th</sup> | Year of Her Age |

In | Memory of | Phineas Camp | Son of | M<sup>r</sup> Abel and ⌈ Mrs. Sabra Camp | who Departed this | Life Nov<sup>r</sup> 18<sup>th</sup>, A. D. | 1794 in the 18<sup>th</sup> year | of his age |

Daziah | wife of | Abel Camp | Died Aug 26, 1876 | aged 87. |

Dea. Abel Camp | died Aug 26, 1826 | in his 39<sup>th</sup> year |

> He was a good man
> and full of the Holy Ghost
> and of faith.

Henry E. Daley | Died July 25, 1864 | Aged 69 Y'rs | his wife | Maria M. | Died Dec 18, 1873 | Aged 73 Y'rs | DALEY || Mary E. Daley | Died Sept 11, 1826 ⌈ Aged 1 Y'r 6 Mo's | George H. Daley | Died Dec 21, 1862 ⌉ Aged 40 Y'rs | Mary J. Daley | Died Sept 2, 1869 | Aged 36 Y'rs || TURKING- TON || Nettie Turkington | Died Aug 31, 1858 | Aged 2 Y'rs 10 Mo's |

Cornelia M. Dunning | died | April 22, 1873 | Aged 35 |

Benjamin Dunning | died | Feb 5, 1870 | Aged 84 | Al- mena | His Wife | Died Feb 22, 1880 | Aged 89 |

Andrew B. De Wolfe | died | Sept 10, 1867 | Æ 73 ⌈

Levi De Wolfe | died | Jan 23, 1849 | Æ 85 |

Huldah Stanley | Widow of | Levi De Wolf | Died Jan 15, 1857 | Æ 91 |

Mr. | Reuben Dunning | Died | April 1, 1838 | Æ 82 |

In memory of | Abigail Dunning | wife of | Reuben Dunning | who died Jan 30 | 1829 | Æ 76 |

In memory of | Mr. John Dodgester | who died decemb^r 15^th AD. 1789 in the | 80^th Year of his age |
Terrestial things cannot content us.

In memory of | Mrs. Mary Dod | gester Relict of Mr | J. D. She died - oct | 20^th 1795 in the | 71^st Year of her age |
Who does the best his circumstances allow does well acts nobly Angels could no more.

Phila M. Skilton | wife of Wells D. Davis | born Jan 1, 1827 | died Dec 26 1853 | one angel more | in heaven |

Mrs. | Lydia Dewey | Died Sept 3, 1855 | Æ 85 | Phebe S. Wife of | James Waugh | Died Aug 24, 1868 | Æ 85 |

Elmore C. Emmons | died | Sept 29, 1892 | Aged 41 Y'rs | & 9 Mo's |

Lucy S. Ensign | died | Mar 6, 1871 | Aged 70 |

Cornelia | wife of | Charles A. Ensign | died | July 28, 1882 | Aged 66 |

Dea. William M. Ensign | died | Aug 19, 1878 | Aged 66 |

Phineas Emmons | died | June 13^th 1825 | Aged 70 |

In Memory | of | Mr Arthur Emons | Who Died Aug 26, 1804 | Aged 73 |

In | Memory of | Wid. Sarah Emons | relict of Mr. Arthur | Emons who died | January 8, 1816 | Æ 83 |

Ozias G. Ensign | of Rochester, N. Y. | Died in Morris | Nov 14, 1865 | Aged 66 |

Electa | relict of | Jesse Ensign | died | July 17, 1851 Æ 78 |

Jesse Ensign | died | April 8, 1846 | Aged 71 years |

Abigail | relict of | Samuel Ensign | died | Sept 1, 1853 | Æt 85 |

Samuel Ensign | died | Sept 10, 1839 | Æt 72 |

Esther G. | Daughter of | Samuel & | Abigail Ensign | died | May 25, 1831 | Aged 25 |

Abigail A. Ensign | died | Oct 2, 1849 | Aged 50 |

Lewis William | son of | Charles A. & | Cornelia Ensign | died | Oct 28, 1852 | Æ 10 y'rs |

Charles Harmon | son of | Charles A. & | Cornelia Ensign | died | Nov 28, 1860 | Aged 13 |

Walter | Infant son of | Samuel M. & | Jane Ensign | died | Mar 30, 1844 | aged 3 mo |

Clinton | son of | Sam'l M. & | Jane Ensign | died | Dec 25, 1848 | Æ 3 mo & 15 d's |

Cornelia G. | only Daughter of | Samuel M. & Cornelia | Ensign | Died Sept 12, 1853 | Æ 18 Years & 11 Mo's |

Cornelia De Forest | wife of | Samuel M. Ensign | died April 22, 1842 | Æ 32 |

Jane De Forest | wife of | Samuel M. Ensign | died | Jan 13, 1857 | Aged 39 |

Rebecca | Schleucker | wife of | Samuel M. Ensign | died | March 6, 1875 | Aged 53 |

Henry P. | Son of | Wᵐ M. & Laura E. | Ensign | Died Feb 14, 1855 | Æ 10 Y'rs 2 Mo's | & 5 D.'s |

Frank Henry | son of | Wᵐ M. & L. E. | Ensign | died Jan 23, 1861 | Æ 11 Mo & 10 D's |

Laura E. Ensign | wife of | Wm. M. Ensign | died | Aug 31, 1863 | Aged 46 |

Edward O. Ensign | son of N. & A. Ensign, Died | suddenly of diphᵃ | in Pittston, Pa. | Oct 18, 1860 | Aged 27 Y'rs | 10 ms. & 22 D's |

Emily A. | daughter of | Newton & | Angeline Ensign died | Jan 22, 1843 | Æ 4 y'rs |

Lewis W. | son of Newton | & Angeline | Ensign, died | Feb. 9, 1843 | Æ 7 y'rs |

> It is the Lord Jehovah's hand
> That blasts our joys in death
> Changes the visage once so dear
> And gathers back the breath.

Angeline | wife of | Newton Ensign | Died Mar 31, 1866 | Aged 67 |

Newton Ensign | died | Feb 12, 1872 | Aged 71 |

In Memory of Mrs. | Elesebeth Wife | of Mr Arter emons junr | Who Died may | the 4th A D 1792 | in the 39th year of | her age |

In Memory of | Mrs Mary E ...... | Consort of Mr .... | Ensign who Di .... | 1807 in the ...... | of her age |

In | Memory of | Mr. Samuel Ensign | who died | Dec 30, 1819 | Æ 79 |

In Memory of | Rhoda Daughter of | Mr Samuel & Mrs Mary | Ensign who Died Jan | 7, 1811 | in the 32 year | of Her Age |

Emily | daughter of Isaac | & Sabra Ensign | died Feb 25, 1823 | Æt 10 years & 10 mo |

> If worth departed e'er deserved a tear
> Oh! gentle stranger pay the tribute here

Dea. Isaac Ensign | died | Aug 1, 1848 | Æ 79 | Sabia, Wife of | Dea Isaac Ensign | died | May 19, 1848 | Æ 77. |

Phebe M. Farnam | died | Nov 7, 1891 | Æ 86 |

In | Memory of | Asenath wife of | Seth Farnam | died | Mar 19, 1861 | Æ 83 |

In memory of | Mr. Seth Farnam | who died | April 9, 1831 | Æ 54 |

> Sad is the home to those who live
> When earthly props are rent away
> But guided by the light of truth
> Faith points us to a brighter day
> Yes, thanks to God, the eye of faith.
> Sees far beyond this mournful scene
> Where mortal forms so loved on earth
> Now flourish in immortal green.
> Then let us dry all useless tears
> Since this blest hope inspires our breast
> That he who sleeps benath this mound
> Has entered on the promised rest.

In memory of | Almira | daughter of | Mr Martin & Mrs H. Foot | Middlebury Vt | who died 5, March 1817, | aged 19 years, & 5 months |

> Let each who has a soul to save
> Extend their views beyond the grave
> And while salvation still is nigh
> To Christ the friend of sinners fly.

In | memory of | Sally Farnam | who died | July 25, 1831 | Æ 45 |

In | Memory of | Meriam wife of | Joseph Farnam | who died | July 4, 1820 | aged 39 . years |

Joseph Farnam | died Feb 15, 1843 | Æ 64 |

In | Memory of Lamira P. Daughter | of John & | Hannah Farnam | who died | April 28, 1812 | Aged 8 years |

Sleep my sweet child, and take thy rest
God took thee when he thought it best.

In Memory of | Ethel T. Farnam | son of | John & Hannah Farnam | who died | Oct 9, 1815 | Aged 17 years |

Mr. John Farnam | died | March 20, 1824 | Æ 54 |

In | Memory of | Pamelia H. Daughter | of Joseph & | Merriam Farnam | who died | Oct 8, 1809 | Aged 16 months |

In | Memory of | Mr. Seth Farnam | who died | April 13, 1820 | Æ 86 | Also | Mrs Dinah wife of | Mr Seth Farnam | who died | Jan 2, 1816 | Æ 75 |

F . | DYᵈ AUG :Yᵉ 5 : | AGE : 30 : 1756 : | (Farnam)

In memory : of 'yᵉ . | body - of John | Farnam who died | Iuly yᵉ 22 - 1758-in | the 66 year of | his age |

In | Memory of | Mr. Gad Farnam | who died | Sept 8, 1819 | Æ 83 |

Blessed are the dead
Who die in the Lord.

In | Memory of | Jane Farnam | relict of Gad Farnam | who died | June 24, 1827 | in her 85, year |

Dea. Kasson Goodwin | born | Mar 24, 1800 | died | Nov 12, 1878 |

Marie De Wolfe | Wife of | Dea Kasson Goodwin | died | Oct 18, 1872 | Æ 64 |

Leonard Goodwin | Born July 1ˢᵗ, 1848 | Died May 26, 1865 |

In | Memory of | Lois Gibbs | Wife of | Reuben Gibbs | Who Died | June 24, 1835 | Æ 44 |

Mr | Reuben Gibbs | Died | July 22, 1829 | Æ 67 |

In | Memory of | James Gibbs | who died | March 11, 1819 | Æ 23 |

Anna Goodwin | wife of En<sup>s</sup> | Thomas Goodwin | who died August | 19, 1813 in the 83 | Year of her age |

Ens | Thomas Goodwin | who died Nov 6, 1807 | In the 79 year of his | Age |

Abigail | Daughter of | Thomas & Anna | Goodwin | Died May 18, 1858 | Æ 86 |

In | memory of | Uri Goodwin | who died | April 12, 1830 | in the 67, year | of his age |

Martha B. Guernsey | wife of | Capt Anthony | Guernsey | died Aug 15, 1868 | Æ 54 |

Dea. Nathaniel Goodwin | died Apr 15, 1841 | aged 81 | Rhoda | his wife died | Dec 28, 1839 | aged 73 |

Mrs Rhoda Goodwin | wife of | Col° Nath¹ Goodwin | died 27, Oct. 1796 in | the 34, year of her age |

As a tribute of respect & esteem
This monument is here placed.

In | Memory of Mrs. | Elizabeth Goodwin | Relict of Capt.| Nathaniel Goodwin | who died | Dec 14, 1802 | in the 74<sup>th</sup> year | of her age |

In Memory of | Olive wife of | Capt Erastus Goodwin | who died March 6, 1817 | aged 42 | Also their three children | Chloe Eliza, died Nov 10, 1806 | aged 17 months | Edmund Sanford, died | Nov 24, 1806 aged 3 years | An infant son died May | 30, 1808, aged 15 days |

Phebe Beach | relict of | James Thomas | & wife of | Capt. E. Goodwin | died | Sept 3, 1852 | Æt 70 |

Friends nor physicans could not save
This mortal body from the grave
The grave cannot retain it here
When Christ her Saviour doth appear.

Erastus Goodwin | died | Nov 3, 1853 | Æt 81 |

Clarissa Goodwin | died | May 18, 1856 | Æt 42 |

In | memory of | Cyrennis y<sup>e</sup> | son — of | Caleb . and | Marjeret. | Gibbs - who died | Feb - y<sup>e</sup> - 1<sup>th</sup> - 1768 | age - 2 year - old |

In | Memory of | Mr Lemuel Gibbs | who died | Jan 3, 1827 in the 90 | year of his age |

> The sweet remembrance of the just
> Shall flourish when he sleeps in dust.

In | Memory of | Esther wife of | Mr Lemuel Gibbs | who died | Feb 27, 1805 | in the 68 year | of her age |
Capt Wᵐ Gibbs Jur | died | Oct 22ⁿᵈ 1818: | aged 33 years |

> Farewell my friends my
> work is done.
> I sleep in dust till
> Christ doth come.

Mrs. Amy | wife of Wᵐ Gibbs | died | April 13ᵗʰ 1819 | aged 78 |

In memory of . | Miriam . Gibbs | daughter . of | Warham Gibbs | who died | February 17 | 1765 age 9 | years |

In | Memory of | Mʳˢ Dinah | Gibbs wife of | Capt Benjamin | Gibbs who De | parted this Life | Septʳ 14ᵗʰ AD. | 1796 in the 85ᵗʰ | year of his age |

In Memory of Cap | Benjamin Gibbs | who Departed this | Life Septʳ 25ᵗʰ A D | 1798 in the 89ᵗʰ year | of his age |

Sibel Gibbs | daughter of | Aeron Gibbs | age 14 m |

Miriam Gibbs | age - 7 | years |

Zebulon | Gibbs | died Febuʸ | 20, 1768 | Age 31 |

Ruth Gibbs | age 8 m |

In | memory of | Betsey | relict of | Medad Gibbs | who died | Dec 12, 1833 | aged 55 years |

> Here sleeps our mother in the silent dust
> By all our sorrows all our love unmov'd
> Sleeps till the solemn summons of the just
> Bid her awake and meet the God she loved.

In Memory of | Mr. Medad Gibbs | Who died | Jan 25, 1828 | Æ 65 |

> Tho wife & children friends & neighbors mourn
> Unto our kindred dust we must return.

In | memory of Mʳˢ | Elenor Consort of | Mr Medad Gibbs | who died Oct 26ᵗʰ 1800 | in the 35ᵗʰ year of her age |
Lizzie I. Hall | daughter of | Lewis B. & Sarah M. | Hall | died March 24, 1883 | Aged 16 Yrs |

Sarah M. Ingersoll | wife of | L. B. Hall | died Oct 31, 1879 | aged 42 yrs |

Hiram Hotchkiss | died | May 7, 1877 | Æt 58 |

Laura C. Whittlesey | wife of | Rollin H. Harrison | Born Apr 6, 1842 | Died June 20, 1874 | Aged 32 |

Wᵐ H. Harrison | Died | Jan 17, 1870 | Æ 1 Yr 3 M'os |

Elbert | son of | Nathan B. & | Julia A. Hinman | died | June 28, 1862 | Aged 2 years |

Flora L. | died | May 1, 1872 | Æ 16 Y'rs | Carrie O. | died| April 29, 1872 | Æ 6 y'rs & 7 mo | daughters of | Nathan B. & Jalia A. | Hinman |

Serj. Henry B. Hill | son of | Rev. William And | Mary B. Hill | Co D 27ᵗʰ Regt C. V. | died Jan 13, 1863 | of wounds received at | the battle of Fredericksburgh | Dec 13, 1862 aged 18 years |

The Grave of | Mary | wife of | Rev William Hill | who departed this life | at New Haven | Mar 15, 1862 | Aged 44 Y'rs & 6 M'os |

The | grave ⌈ of | Rev. William Hill | born at Huntington, L. I. | Mar 12, 1814 | died at Bristol, Conn | July 31, 1851 | Æt 37 |

Mary Anna Robertson | Wife of T. M. Hills M. D | Daughter of | Rev Wm. & Mary B. Hill | Born at Newburgh N. Y. | July 26, 1843 | Died at Norfolk Va. | Jan 16, 1864 ⌉ Minnie Morton | daughter of T. M. & M. A. Hills | Born at Norfolk, Va. Dec 6, 1863 | Died Jan 6, 1864 |

Susan R. daughter of | Wm & | Harriet L. | Hamlin | died | Apr 2. 1847 | Æ 18 || Harriet L. | wife of | Wm. Hamlin | died | Nov 10, 1844 | Æ 43 || Henry | was buried ⌉ in New Jersey | where he died | Dec 13, 1846 | Æ 26 | William A. died | Oct 5, 1849 | Æ 19 | sons of Wm & | Harriet L. Hamlin |

Anthony | son of | Wᵐ & Harriet | Hamlin died | April 13, 1825 | Æt 3 mo's | Also an infant | son died Dec 30, Æt 4 days |

Eleanor | (Hall )

Alanson Hall | died | Sept 20, 1858 | Æ 55 yrs 9 mo |

Elizabeth C. | wife of | Alanson Hall | died | Aug 28, 1885 | Æ 78 y'rs |

Simeon G. Harrison | Born | Oct 27, 1813 | Died July 28, 1852 | Susan R. Jackson | His Wife | Born Apr 5, 1819 | Died Apr 3, 1840 | HARRISON || Asahel Harrison | Born | June 18, 1778 | Died Mar 31, 1823 | Miriam Harris | His Wife | Born June 11, 1786 | Died Mar 31, 1868 || Charles W. Harrison | Died | Nov 9, 1870 | Aged 59 |

Zeruiah | relict of | Joel Hubbard | died | May 26, 1842 | aged 81 years |

In | Memory of | Joel Hubbard | who died April 23, 1813 | in the 54 year | of his age |

Linus Hubbard | died | April 29, 1864 | Aged 68 |

Selina | wife of | Linus Hubbard | & daughter of | Levi & Huldah De Wolfe | Born April 23, 1799 | Died Dec 29, 1890 |

Joseph Hubbard | died Nov 27, 1888 | Æ 51 |

Rollin Hubbard | Died at Bridgeport | Aug 30, 1856 | Æ 24 |

Ithamar Hubbard | died | Jan 3, 1875 | Æ 79 |

Lavina B. | wife of | Ithamar Hubbard | died | May 7, 1876 | Æ 76 |

In | Memory of | Sally, Wife of | Ralph Hall | who died April 8, 1819 | in the 28 year of | her age |

In | Memory of | John M. son of | Anson & | Betsey Hubbard | who died | July 13, 1869 | Æt 5 years |

In | Memory of | Mrs Abigail Hare | who died [ June 15, 1814 | Æ 82 |

Anna Sperry, | wife of | Roswell Harrison | died May 17, 1819 | Aged 49 |

My flesh long waited thy command
To sink into the dust
Jesus to thy dear faithful hand
My naked soul I trust.

In | memory of | Serviah, wife of | Roswell Harrison | who died | Feb 26, 1841 | aged 62 years |

Wrapt in the shades of death,
No more that friendly face we see
Empty oh empty every place
Once fill'd so well by thee

In | memory of | Sarah, wife of | Roswell Harrison | who died | Sept 23, 1851 | aged 78 years |

Roswell Harrison | died | Dec 29, 1859 | aged 87 years |

Stephen S. Harrison | died | Dec'r 2, 1880 | Aged 76 | Lucretia C. Churchill | 1902 | HARRISON |

Julia | daughter of | Mr Levi & Mrs | Anna Hoyt ⌈ died Jan 16, 1817 | aged 1 year & | 14 days |

In Memory of | Thomas Harrison | Esq$^r$ he died June y$^e$ | 16$^{th}$ 1758 in y$^e$ 65$^{th}$ | year of his Age |

In memory | of the Widow | Hannah Harri | son consort of | Thomas Harrison | who Died April 27 | 1790 in the 95$^{th}$ | year of her | Age |

In memory of | M$^r$ Thomas Harri | son who Died Dec | the 23$^{rd}$ 1791 in the | 69 year of his | Age |

Sybil Shervoy | wife of | Thomas Harrison | died ⌉ Dec 13, 1835 | Æt 97 Y'rs |

In | Memory of | David Harrison | who died ⌉ April 13, 1812 ⌊ Aged 61 |

Lyman Hotchkiss | died | March 15, 1861 | Æ 80 |

Clarissa | wife of Lyman Hotchkiss | died | March 7, 1855 | Æt 70 |

Mrs. Lydia Hotchkiss | Wife of | Elihu Hotchkiss | Died | June 2, 1836 | Æ 93 |

Mr. | Elihu Hotchkiss | Died | May 12, 1835 | Æ 93 |

In Memory of | Alex. Hamilton | Harrison | son of the late | Simeon and Hannah | Harrison | born Sept 1, 1804 | died June 3, 1875 | Æ 71 |

In | Memory of | W$^m$ H. Harrison | who died | March 17, 1830 | Æ 33 |

> Like other tyrants Death delights to smite
> What, smitten, most proclaims the pride of power,
> And arbitrary nod. His joy supreme
> To bid the wretch survive the fortunate
> The feeble wrap th' athletic in his shroud
> And weeping Faathers build their children's tombs.

Hannah Elizabeth | daughter of | W$^m$ H. & | R. Harrison | died | Dec 23, 1826 | aged 15 days |

In | memory of | Hannah consort of | Simeon Harrison | who died | March 3, 1824 | in the 53 year of his age |

In memory of | Simeon Harrison | Who Died | June 3, 1835 | Æ 67 |

In | memory of | Abigail wife of | Dan Harrison | who died| March 4, 1839 | aged 67 |

D. H. | In | Memory of | Mr. Dan Harrison | who died June 4, 1811, Æt 42 |

In | Memory of | Capt Elihu Harrison | who departed this life | May 3$^d$ 1806 | in the 67$^{th}$ year | of his age |

In | Memory of Theda | wife of | Elihu Harrison | who died Nov. 5, 1815 | aged 74 years |

In | memory of | Josiah Hubbard | who died | Aug. 7, 1829 | Aged 77 years |

In | Memory of | Polly Hubbard | who died | Dec 31, 1830 | aged 55 years |

Ann Eliza | daughter of | Benj. & Polly Hubbard | Died Mar. 28, 1867 | Æ 17 |

> The midnight stars are beaming
> Upon her silent grave
> Now sleeping without dreaming
> The child we could not save.

In Memory of Wid | Hannah Harriso$^n$ | Died January 11, 1804, in | the 75 Year of her Age |

In memory | of Lieut Ephra | Harrison | who Died Nov | 7$^{th}$ 1791 in the | 65 year of his | Age |

Ella E. Turkington | wife of | C. M. Judd | Aug 22, 1863 | Mar 22, 1897 |

Clara E. Beecher | Wife of | Herbert D. Janes | died | August 24, 1883 | Aged 69 y'rs |

Moses Lyman Judd | died | Oct 19, 1870 | Æ 28 Yrs 4 Mos | & 19 D's. |

In | memory of | Amy, wife of | George Johnson | who died | July 6, 1851 | Æ 39 |

Stephen Johnson | died | Aug 8, 1853 | Æ 53 |

Elizabeth S. | wife of | Stephen Johnson | died Feb 11, 1856 | Æ 56 |

Cornelia Watson | daughter of | John O. & Harriet Judd | died | Sept 8, 1843 | aged 10 mo |

Little | Addie | Aged 2 Y'rs | & 3 Mo || son of | John O. & | Harriet Judd | died. Feb 27, 1859 |

Lucy | wife of Ezra H. Judd | died | Feb 15, 1854 Æt 59 |

Ezra H. Judd | died | Apr 16, 1867 | Æ 72 |

Annis H. Judd | wife of | Ezra H. Judd | died Mar 20, 1861 | Aged 70 years |

In | Memory of | Amos Johnson | who died Aug 31, 1837 | aged 58 years |

Sally | wife of | Amos Johnson | died | Sept 10, 1856 | Æt 72 |

Almon | Son of | Almon L. & | Sarah L. Johnson | Died July 20, 1856 | Æ 12 W'ks |

In | Memory of | Elizabeth Relict | of Edward | Johnson who | died jan 17th, 1800 in | the 91st year of her age |

Maria | wife of | Martin Johnson | died I July 22, 1880 | aged 35 |
"Meet me in Heaven."

Charles G. Kirchberger | 1828-1889 | Catherine Kurth his wife | 1833-1893 | KIRCHBERGER |

Edith L. | daughter of | Rollin F. & | Louisa M. Kilborn | Died Jan 29, 1872 | Æ 4 Y'rs |

Catharine R. Smith | wife of | Leonard Lane | died | July 26, 1893 | Aged 65 Y'rs |

Clark Stone Loveland | Sept 20, 1840 | Apr 24, 1895 | Mary Catharine Kilborn | his wife | Nov 19, 1841 | — | LOVE-LAND || Clara Jane Loveland | Mar 20, 1868 | Mar 10, 1888 | daughter of | C. S. & M. C. Loveland |

Sarah M. Lyman | Daughter of | Benjamin Dunning | Born | Aug 3, 1818 | Died | April 5, 1858 |

Wm. H. Laire | Co. F. 3 Regt. | Conn. Vols. | died | May 16, 1878 |

Mary E. Blakeman | wife of | J. W. Lane | died Feb 11, 1842 | Æ 23 |

Mary | daughter of | J. W. & | Mary E. Lane | died | Sept 28, 1845 | Æ 2 weeks |

Willis W. Loveland | Died | March 30, 1863 | Æ 50 |

Edwin Willis | son of | James L. and | Maria Loveland | died | July 7, 1860 | Aged 8 years | & 7 mo |

Maria | wife of | James L. Loveland | died | June 22, 1872 | Æ 62 |

James L. Lovelannd | died | Oct 1, 1882 | Aged 71 |

Sarah Jane | Wife of | Nathaniel G. Loveland | died | March 6, 1863 | Æ 47 |

Nathaniel G. Loveland | died | June 3, 1853 | Æt 38 |

Lydia, wife of | Clark Loveland | died | Sept 21, 1850 | Aged 75 years |

Clark Loveland | died | July 17, 1851 | aged 86 years |

Mrs. | Lois Loveland | wife of | Joseph Loveland | died | Dec 18, 1828 | Æ 88 |

In | Memory of | Joseph Linsley | who died | June 30, 1821 | aged 86 |

In | Memory of | Lydia wife of | Joseph Linsley | who died | Dec 13, 1799 | aged 70 |

Mrs | Lois Lampson | wife of | Daniel Lampson | died | Feb 8, 1833 | Æ 68 |

Daniel Lampson | died | Oct 6, 1852 | Æt 98 y'rs 7 mo's | & 6 d's |

In | Memory of | the body of | Abigail the wife | of Benjamin | Landon who died | November y$^e$ 18 | 1765 in y$^e$ 22 y$^r$ | of hur age |

In | memory of | Mrs. Mary Lyma$^n$ | Dau$^{tr}$ of M$^r$ David | and M$^{rs}$ Mary | Lyman she died | Mrc$^h$ the 21 1776 | in the 21$^{st}$ year | of her Age |

William Monson | died | Aug 6, 1887 | Æ 94 | Alice Emmons | his wife | Died May 1, 1821, Æ 30 | Polly Benton | his wife | Died Sept 30, 1875 | Æ 84 | MONSON || Elizabeth L. Monson | died | Jan 19, 1895, | Æ 67 |

Andrew W. Marsh | died | Oct 2, 1883 | aged 75 yrs |

Charles | Son of | W$^m$ H. & Julia | Munson | Died Feb 8, 1879 | Aged 21 |

Lucius E. Munson | died | Apr 14, 1896 | Æ 87 | Sally B. Orvis | his wife | died | Mar 12, 1895 | Æ 86 | MUNSON ||

James M. Marsh | died | Jan 26, 1879 | Aged 68 |

In | memory of | Asenath | wife of | Daniel Marsh | died | Apr 22, 1862 | Aged 83 |

Daniel Marsh | died | May 19, 1854 | aged 80 |

John Marsh | died | Aug 30, 1869 | Æ 69 |

Martha E. | Daughter of | N. B. & A. H. | Munger | died Aug 27, 1854 | Æ 4 Y'rs |

C. C. M. | son of N. B. & A. H. | Munger | died | Aug 8, 1855 | 9 m & 13 ds |

Ann Kezia Allen | his wife | || Frederick A - Marsh | died| died | Feb 9, 1846 | aged 36 | || Nov 14, 1879 | Aged 76 |

Electa B. | Relict of | Horace Marsh | died | Sept 2, 1857 | Æ 74 |

Horace Marsh | died | May 21, 1844 | aged 72 |
H. Clark Marsh | Brother | Died Aug 26, 1864 | Æ 59 |

Lyman Colby | son of | Charles L. & Lucy C. | Munger | died June 11, 1855 | Æ 7 Y'rs |

Joseph W. Mason | died | Apr 4, 1886 | Aged 85 |

In | Memory of | Lucretia | wife of | Joseph W. Mason | Died May 15, 1877 | Aged 75 |

Joshua Mason | only son of | Joseph W. & Lucy C. | Mason | died in Charleston S. C. | Sept 1, 1858 | Aged 27 |

The grave of | Mrs. | Lucy C. Mason | wife of | Joseph W. Mason | who died | Sept 14, 1839 | aged 30 years |

Edward E. Mason | died | Jan 14, 1839 | Æ 5 months |

Frederic J. Mason | died | Oct 30, 1838 | Æ 2 years & 8 months |

Cornelia | Daughter of | Joseph W. & | Lucy C. Mason | died | Dec 15, 1832 | Aged 3 years |

Leonard | son of | George & | Eunice Merchant | died | Aug 5, 1841 | aged 1 year | & 6 months |

Capt. | Joseph Mansfield | died | June 6, 1821 | Æt 84 |

Fond memory lingers round this turf
Recalls his words, his useful life,
The hero brave, the parent kind
Are legasies that's left behind.

Mrs | Hannah Mansfield | died | Aug 22, 1826 | Æ 86 |

Mrs. Esther Murray | relice of | Philliman Murray | died |
Oct 6, 1831 | Aged 86 |

In memory of Mr. Philemon Murry | Who Died Jan^y 25^th |
1791 in y^e 45^th Year of | his Age |

                      ness vied
In aspect, dignity & frank
. . . . . . . . . . . . . . . . . . . .

In | Memory of | Allice Munson | wife of | W^m Munson |
died | May 6, 1821 | Æt 31 |

An Infant of | W^m & | Allice Munson | died Oct 1819 |

Julius | Son of | William & | Alice Munson | died | Feb 17,
1819 | Æt 1. |

In Memory of | Samuel son of | Mrs Betsey and | James
Morris Esq^r | who died Dec 22^d AD | 1793 in the 6^th year of
his age |

Mrs | Elizabeth Morris | consort of | James Morris Esq |
died Sept 9 A D 1814 | Æt 63 |

James Morris | died | Apr 20, 1820 | aged 68 | Rhoda F.
Wheeler | consort of | James Morris | & Samuel Wheeler |
died | Jan 11, 1860 | aged 79 || Jane E. Morris | died | Oct 22,
1832 | aged 16 y'rs & 9 mo |

In | memory of | Richard T. Munson | who died | Sept 7,
1842 | Aged 50 years |

H. M. | Huldah Murray | wife of | Hezekiah Murray |
died | March 28, 1844 | Aged 67 |

In | Memory of | Mrs Eunice wife of | Mr Hezekiah Mur-
ray | who died Oct 19, 1813 | aged 39 years |

A pleasing form a generous gentle heart
A good companion honest without art;
Just in her dealings faithful to her friend
Beloved through life, lamented in her end.

Hezekiah Murray | died | Jan 12, 1849 | Æ 75 |

Alice E. daughter of | Alison & Mary | **Morse** | **Died Aug 29, 1873** | Æ 7 Y'rs & 2 Mos |

> Gone in the springtime of life
> From those who loved her
> From the hearts that
>     had grown to her own
> She has crossed the river of death
>     She is with the angels now
> The cross is laid aside
> The crown is on her brow.

In Memory of | Deacon James Morris | who departed this life June | the 6th AD 1789 in the 68th | Year of his age |

> here?
> Reader all hail why downcast visage
>                                     war ( ?)
> If Death you dread Base Conduct be-
> .... Immortal .............its span!

S. MARCH | 1747

Mary Ann | wife of | Joseph Mansfield | died | Feb 2, 1848| Æ 78 |

Mr. Abner Northrop | born | July 28, AD 1788 | died | Oct 4 AD 1829 |

Mrs Ruth Northrop | wife of | Mr. Abner Northrop | died Dec 1, 1826 | Æt 34 |

> If worth departed e'er deserved a tear
> Oh! gentle stranger pay the tribute here.

> ———

> Go home my friends and dry your tears,
> I must lie here till Christ appears

In | Memory of | Anna wife of | Joseph Osborn | who died | May 22, 1822 | aged 79 years |

Truman Potter | buried at Hamden | Apr 30, 1831 | Æ 33 | Rebecca Booth | his wife died | Dec 25, 1871 | Æ 76 |

Susan E. Parmelee | died | Sept 28, 1871 | Æ 39 |

Asa Peck | died | May 17, 1818 | Æt 74 | Erected by the Rev. | J. M. Peck of Illinois |

PIERPONT. James M. Pierpont | died Nov 27, 1839 | Aged 39 | Sila M. Harrison | His Wife Died Apr 19, 1882 | aged 80 || Sarah H. daughter of | G. W. & S. P. Canfield | died July 7, 1876 | Aged 17 || Lucy M. daughter of | J. M. & S. M. Pierpont | died Sept 1, 1865 | Aged 30 | James M. son of| J. M. & S. M. Pierpont | died Oct 15, 1868 | Aged 29 || Robert Pierpont | died April 9, 1894 | aged 66 |

Sidney Peck | 1805-1891 | Catharine Catlin, | his wife | 1810-1862 | PECK || Julius Jay |1837-1846 | Sidney Jr. | 1842-1865 | Maria R. | 1840-1866 ||

Mary L. Partree | died | Oct 9, 1841 | aged 9 years |

James Pierpont | Died April 23, 1840 | Aged 79 | Lucy his wife | Died Feb 20, 1835, Aged 57 | Their remains were laid beneath | this stone | The remains of | Sherman, his oldest son, are | buried in the city of Sandusky, | on the shore of Lake - Erie, in which | he was drowned May 7, 1836 | Aged 53 |

Mrs | Elizabeth, wife of | Mr James Pierpont | died July 28, 1815, | Æt 59 | James Son of James & | Elizabeth Pierpont | died Nov 30, 1793, Æt 4. | Sally, Daughter of | James & Elizabeth Pierpont | died July 11, 1794 Æt 7 |

Mrs Lydia | wife of | Samuel Porter | Died | Dec 19, 1822 | Æ 36 |

Willie H. Picket | Died Mar 12, 1863 | Æ 16 Y'rs 2 Mo & 26 D's | — | Died at Washington, D. C. | May 10, 1863 | Sargent Birdsey Pickett | of Co G, 14 Regt C V | Æ 21 Y'rs 1 Mo & 8 D's |

Smith | Son of | R. S. & S. A. | Pickett | Died Sept 27, 1861 | Æ 14 Mo's & 17 D's |

Sweet little child of love
The savior has taken him home.

Rufus S. Pickett | died | Oct 12, 1869 | Æ 52 Y'rs 5 Mo | & 5 D's |

Rufus Pickett | born | July 22, 1784 | died | May 14, 1870 |

Paulina | wife of | Rufus Pickett | died Nov 3, 1855 | Æ 70|

Sarah E. Pickett | wife of | Rufus Pickett | died | Nov 1, 1869 | Æ 77 |

E. Clark Pickett | died | Oct 12, 1853 | Æ 19 |

Marietta | daughter of | Alanson J. & Marietta | Pickett | died Dec 9, 1840 | aged 8 mos. 9 dys |

Marietta | wife of | Alanson J. Pickett | died | July 12, 1840 | aged 29 years |

> "Yea though I walk through the
> valley of the shadow of death, I will
> fear no evil: for thou art with me;
> thy rod and thy staff they comfort me."

Alanson J. Pickett | died | Dec 16, 1880, | aged 72 years |

Doct. Joseph Parker | died | Feb 6, 1830 | Æ 70 | PARKER || Lydia Harrison | wife of | Doct. Joseph Parker | died | Sept 17, 1806 | Æ 41 || Sarah Moss | widow of | Jerry Blackman | and wife of | Dr. Joseph Parker | died Sept 7, 1847 | Aged 73 |

In Memory of | Mrs Mary consort of | Mr. ... per .... perkins | who Died May 3ᵈ | 1790 (?) ...... 76 .... | .... Age |

Edward A. Root | Co E. 5 Regt | Conn. Vols | died | Oct 1, 1883 |

McKenzie Root | died | Mar 10, 1878 | Æ 64 |

Fredie M. | son of | McKenzie & | Flora Root | died | Oct 29, 1877 | Æ 3 y'rs |

Dannie M. | son of | Henry L. & | Mary E. Root | died | Nov 6, 1877 | Æ 9 y'rs |

Jennie | daughter of | Evander & Margarett | Roots | Died Oct 27, 1878 | aged 2 Y'rs 3 Mo. | & 7 D's |

Isaac Ray | died | Feb 18, 1849 | Æt 54 Y'rs |

Miss | Sally Ray | Died | April 22, 1863 | Æ 80 |

In | memory of | Mr William Rea | who died Oct 6, 1813 | Aged 58 years |

In | memory of | Hannah Rea | Wife of | William Rea | who died | Dec 29, 1830 | Æ 73 |

In Memory of | Mr. David Rea | Who Died | Oct 13, 1827 | Æ 46 |

Phebe W. Rea | wife of | David Rea | died | April 18, 1855 | Æ 75 |

John Ray | died | Feb 14, 1850 | Æ 64 |

Charlotte P. | Wife of John Ray | Died May 26, 1866 Æ 73|

David | son of John & | Charlotte Ray | died | May 17, 1852 | aged 24 years |

William Ray | died | Jan 6, 1869 | Æ 76 | Nancy Blackman | his wife | died | Nov 28, 1848 | Æ 54 | RAY || Henry R. Ray | died | May 7, 1872 | Æ 48 | Lydia Ann | wife of H. R. Ray | died | March 17, 1866 | Æ 41 || Lemuel B | son of Wm. & Nancy Ray | died | July 31 | 1852 | Æ 27 |

Nancy L. | daughter of | Richard Ryder | died | March 25, 1867 | Æ 13 y'rs | Nancy E. | died | Aug 1, 1849 | Æ 3 mo |

Samuel W. Skilton | 1814-1894 | Mary White, his wife | 1829-1904 | SKILTON || children of | Samuel & Mary | William S. Skilton | 1847-1849 | Joel W. Skilton | 1851-1851 | Buried in Woodbridge |

Georgie A. | son of Truman O. & | Julia M. Sanford | died| April 13, 1872 | Æ 8 Mo |

Ella | Daughter of | Truman & Julia | Sanford [ Born July 1, 1863 | Died July 18, 1868 |

> The bud within its little cup
> Disclosed so sweet a blossom
> The Savior kindly took it up
> And pressed it in his bosom.

Truman O. Sanford | died | Sept 29, 1881 | Aged 38 | He enlisted at the age of | 18 years in the 2nd Ct Heavy [ Artillery, served three years | where he contracted the disease | of which he died, consumption | Home at last |

Joseph Sanford | died | July 13, 1871 | Æ 51 |

Betsey A. Potter | wife of | Joseph Sanford | died | Nov 30, 1893 | Æ 70 y's & 9 m's |

John P. Sanford | died | June 29, 1893 | Æ 36 y's |

Erasmus R. Sperry | died | Feb 22, 1858 | Æ 67 | Sally Sperry | His Wife Died | May 20, 1877 | Æ 93 |

Simeon Smith | died | June 18, 1880 | Æ 92 | Esther Clark| his wife | Died Aug 7, 1838 | Æ 51 | SMITH || Abraham Clark Smith | son of Simeon & | Esther Smith | Died Jan 19, 1869 | Æ 56 | Elizabeth Harrison | his wife | — | Mariette C. Smith | their daughter | Died Nov 10, 1869 | Aged 6 Yrs & 8 Mos || Sarah, widow of | Caleb Smith | Died Feb 3, 1840 | Æ 93. | Daughter of | Caleb & | Sarah Smith, | Naomi | Died Oct 10, 1817 | Æ 31 | Sally | Died Aug 25, 1850 | Æ 82 [

Amie J. Bkaleman | Wife of | Starr L. Sutcliff | Died Mar 16, 1876 | Æ 33 | Lewis S | Their infant son | Æ 8 D's |

Thala Sherman | died | Dec 30, 1849 | aged 50 years |

Jabez Sherman | died | Feb 9, 1848 | aged 81 years |

Silas Stockman | 1817-1890 | Sarah E. Whittlesey | his wife | 1828 — | STOCKMAN |

Ora E. | daughter of | S. & S. E. | Stockman | died | June 12, 1866 | Æ 3 Y'rs |

Gardiner Stockman | died | May 28, 1864 | from disease contracted in the army | Aged 21 Y'rs | & 14 D's |

Weltha S. | wife of | Alanson Stoddard | Died Dec 4, 1869 | Æ 49 |

The Grave of | Everetta | daughter of | Alanson & | Weltha S. Stoddard | who died | Dec 15, 1857 | Æ 9 y's 6 mo | & 8 d's |

Mary E. | daughter of | Alanson & | Weltha S. | Stoddard | died | April 24, 1844 | aged 3 y's |

Andrew F. Smith | died | July 12, 1860 | Æt 27 |

Lydia Ann | Daughter of | Ethanan & | Abigail Spooner | Died | Jan 24, 1832 | Æ 8 y-rs & 8 mo-s |

Julia E. | Daughter of | William L. & | Julia C. Smedley | died Feb 19, 1842 | aged 11 mo's |

Eunice | wife of | Ozias Sanford | died | June 1, 1869 | Æt 77 |

Ozias Sanford | died | Sept 7, 1856 | Æ 72 |

In | Memory of | Mr. Joseph Sanford | who died Dec 13, 1813 | Aged 68 years |

Sidney E. | son of | Joseph & Betsey A. | Sanford | Died Nov 22, 1854 | Æ 8 y'rs |

Lucy Sanford | died | Nov 9, 1892 | Æ 82 y's |

In memory of | Eunice | daughter of | Phineas & | Eunice Spaulding who died | April 28, 1825 | Æ 9 yrs |

In | memory of | Eunice Spaulding | wife of Phineas Spaulding | who departed this life | Dec 21, 1824 | aged 49 |

In Memory | of | Mr Jonah Sanford | Jr Son of Mr Jonah, and | Mrs Rhoda Sanford | who died the 28 of Aug- | ust 1806. Aged 33 |

In | Memory of | Mr Jonah Sanford | who died | Jan 21, 1817 | in the 82 year | of his age |

In Memory | of | Mrs. Rhoda Wife of | Mr Jonah Sanford | Who Died the 11 of July | 1807 Aged 65 |

Simeon Sanford | died | June 23, 1846 | Æ 71 |

Elizabeth Sanford | wife of | Simeon Sanford | died | May 25, 1853 | Ælt 72 y'rs. |

Tabitha Skilton | died | Oct 30, 1878 | Æ 87 Y's & 6 Mo |

Henry Skilton | Aug 5, 1847 | Æ 64 | Henry M. Skilton | Son of Henry & Maria M. Skilton | Died in Arkansas Aug^t 3^d 1846 | Æ 30 |

Maria Marshall | wife of | Henry Skilton | died | Sept 10, 1863 | Aged 72 | Faithful in life, trustful in death | One Mother more in Heaven |

Parthenia | daughter of | Henry & | Mariah Skilton | died | Dec 29, 1830 | Æ 9 years |

Chloe Stevens | wife of | Dea. Ira Smith | of Prospect | died | Oct 5, 1857 | Æ 86 |

Abigail | wife of | Amos Smith | died | Aug 21, 1850 | Ælt 85 yrs |

Amos Smith | died Aug 31, 1845 | Aged 81 |

In | Memory of | Martha daug't. | of Amos & | Abigail Smith | who died | June 16, 1820 | aged 26 years |

> A pale consumption gave the fatal blow
> The Stroke was certain; but the effect was slow.
> With lingering pain heaven saw me sore oppress'd
> Pity'd my sighs and kindly gave me rest.

Mr. | Rufus Smith | died March 5, 1815, | in the 26 year | of his age |

> His steady eye surveyed the happy shore
> Where grief & pain & sickness are no more
> He view'd the mighty ransom that was given
> To waft the immortal soul in peace to heaven.

Anna H. | daughter of | Nathan D. & | Mary Ann Smith | died | Sept 23, 1840 | in the 19, year | of her age |

Stephen H. Smith | Son of Nathan | D. Smith Died | Aug 17, 1837 | had he lived until | the day of the | erection of this Stone | Oct 7 6 years would | have been his age |

"Father, I want to kiss you."

Mary-Ann | Wife of | Nathan D. Smith | Died | Jan 25, 1836 | Æ 37 yr-s | & 4 mo-s |

The form that was laid here once clothe$^{d}$
a heart which beat as high and thrill-
ed as warmly as our own . She hoped
and feared, enjoyed and sorrowed, loved
and hated even as we do, and now
lies here inanimate clay.

Nathan Smith | died | May 29, 1868 | Æ 77 |

Henry N. Smith | died | June 14, 1876 | Æ 37 |

Joshua Smith | died | May 7, 1862 | Aged 29 |

Julia B. Hand | Wife of | Isaiah H. Smith | Died Sept 27, 1887 | Aged 73 |

Caroline Catlin | Wife of | Isaiah H. Smith | Died Apr 17, 1848 | Aged 38 |

Isaiah H. Smith | Died | Nov 16, 1892 | Aged 83 Yrs 5 Mos |

Job Smith | 10-17-1777 | 5-17,-1851 | Elizabeth A. Smith 5-7-1783 | 12-14-1867 |

Lucy | daughter of | Lester N. & Abby | Smith | Died May 6, 1852 | In the 22 Year | of her age |

Ah! dearest Lucy, how short thy stay
On this frail earth of sin & woe
How soon thy soul pursued its way
And left thy weeping friends below.

Lester N. Smith | died | Jan 5, 1861 | Aged 57 |

Empty ah! empty every place
Which once was filled so well by thee

Abby Catlin | Wife of | Lester N. Smith | Died Sept 15, 1870 | Aged 64 |

Prosper W. Smith | died | April 27, 1866 | aged 41 yrs | 1 mo. & 16 d's |

Rufus Smith | died July 31, 1886 | aged 67 | SMITH ||
Mary Ann McNeil | wife of | Rufus Smith | 1818-1892 ||
Julia M. Hall | daughter of | Rufus & Mary Ann | Smith 1850-
1892 ||

.... DY. | M-S 1755 |

In memory of | Naomi Smith | who died | October 10th,
1817 | aged 34 years |

In | memory of | Sarah | widow of | Caleb Smith [ who died |
Feb 3, 1847 | aged 93 years | In | memory of | Sarah Smith |
died | Aug 25, 1850 | aged 82 years |

James Stoddard | died July 28, 1825 | aged 45 years |

Bryant Stoddard | died | Feb 17, 1824 | Æ 84 Y'rs |
Phebe, | Wife of | Bryant Stoddard | died | June 7, 1825 |
Æ 90 Y'rs |

Ann Barnard | Wife of | John N. Sanford | Died in Hart-
ford | Jan 15, 1857 | Æ 50 ]

> Ishall see thee no more Mother,
> till we meet around the throne.

Mary Steele | wife of Samuel Stearns | Died Jan 20, 1883 |
Æ 69 Y'rs | & 8 Mo's |

Henry Steele | died | June 20, 1874 | Æt 69 |
Menzies Steele | died | April 4, 1863 | Æt 56 |
William Steele | died July 22, 1860 | Æt 58 |
Frederick Steele | died | Dec 13, 1851 | Aged 78 ]
Huldah Maria Steele | died | Oct 15, 1844 | Aged 26 |

Huldah wife of | Frederick Steele | died | Oct 4, 1838 | Aged
63 |

Lucy M. daughter of | Charles & | Sally Steel | died | May
7, 1830 | aged 3 years | Charles Son of | Charles & | Sally
Steel | died | Mar 17, 1830 | aged 1 year. |

Robert M. Treat | Oct 19, 1815 | Dec 14, 1896 | H. Maria
Whittlesey | his wife | May 3, 1816 ] July 4, 1898 | Frederic
W. their son | Co A. 23, Regt C. V. | Apr 2, 1840 ] Aug 15,
1863 | Died at New Orleans |

In memory of | Anna Trumbull | Died july 7th 1802 | Aged
38 Years |

Ezekiel Trumbull | died | Nov 27, 1838 | aged 79 |

Gilbert W. Titus | Co. G. 23, Regt. | Conn. Vol's | died Aug 13, 1885 |

In memory of | Ruth Trumbull | Died March 25th 1784 | Aged 22 Years |

Lurah | wife of | John G. Titus | died | Jan 29, 1850 | Aged 48 y'rs |

David W. Whittlesey | died | Aug 12, 1898 | aged 82 Years |

Dolly Averill | wife of | David W. Whittlesey | Died June 4, 1879 | Aged 62 |

Henry H. Waugh | born June 22, 1819 | died Feb 1, 1892 | WAUGH || Martha M. | wife of | Henry H. Waugh | born Feb 16, 1831 | died Aug 10, 1854 | buried in Harwinton | Susan E. | wife of | Henry H. Waugh | born May 13, 1834 | died Aug 23, 1863 |

WAGNER || Flora A. Wagner | born | July 9, 1857 | Died Dec 29, 1866 | Æ 9 Y'rs & 6 Mo's | Harris W. Wagner | Born Nov 15, 1859 | Died Dec 30, 1866 | Æ 7 Yr's & 1 Mo. |

Caroline | wife of | Hiram C. Waldron | & daughter of | Levi & Clarissa Parmelee | died | Sept 28, 1857 | Æ 21 |

Frederick Whittlesey | died Jan 5, 1873 | Aged 81 | Hannah Rea | His Wife | died Aug 9, 1866 | Aged 78 |

W. L. Woodruff | died | Oct 30, 1852 | Æ 31 |

Caroline B. Waugh | died | Feb 15, 1885 | aged 83 yrs |

Jabez Whittlesey | died | Feb 10, 1850 | aged 64 years |

Nancy Parker | wife of | Jabez Whittlesey | died | Dec 23, 1853 | in the 66 year of | her age |

The Grave of | Edward C. Whittlesey | who died | on his passage from Mexico | Dec 16, 1834 | aged 21 years |

> Oh think on the stranger tos'd on the billow
> Afar from the Home of his childhood and youth
> No Mother to watch o'er his sleep-broken pillow,
> No Father to counsel, no Brothers or Sisters to sooth.

Dea. Henry Whittlesey | died | at New York | Apr 26, 1879 | Aged 88 Y'rs & 10 Mo's |

Abby R. Whittlesey | wife of | Dea Henry Whittlesey | died | at New York | Nov 1, 1860 | Aged 70 |

Henrietta A. | youngest daughter of | Henry & | Abby R. Whittlesey | died at New York | July 13, 1842 | Æ 7 Y'rs & 4 mos |

L. Amanda | wife of | George W. Weed | & daughter of | the late | Thomas B. Whitmore | died | Oct 11, 1847 | Æ 24 yrs |

Charles F. | son of | Hiram & Orrena | Weed died | Dec 27, 1827 | Æt 1 year | & 11 mo's |

Orrena | Wife of | Hiram Weed | died | April 7, 1839 | Æ 39 | Cordelia | Died July 13, 1832 Æ 2 y'rs | Joseph | Died Feb 24, 1837 Æ 6 m's | children of | Hiram & Orrenna Weed |

Deborah-Ann | daughter of | Roselle & | Mary-Ann Weed | died | Sept 25, 1841 | Æ 18 |

In | Memory of | Philo Woodruff | son of | Philo & Huldah Woodruff | who died Dec 16, 1810 | in the 22 year | of his age|

John Waters | died | Feb 1, 1890 | Aged 83 |

Katie H. | wife of | Edmund Waters | died | Jan 7, 1879 | Aged 33 Yr's & 26 D's |

In | memory of | Jacob Woodruff, Esq | born A. D 1717 | died | Dec 21, A.D. 1790 |

In | Memory of | Jacob Woodruff | who died April 23, | 1818 in the 67 | year of his age |

The Grave of | Dea. Roger N. Whittelsey | who died | March 15, 1835 | Aged 81 |

In | memory of | Mrs. Ann, wife of | Dea. Roger N. Whittelsey, | who died | March 7, 1825 | in her 69. year |

In Memory of | Mrs. Margaret wife | of Mr. John Waugh | who departed this | Life Feb yᵉ 15, 1773 | Æ 74 |

> Here lies intere'd an house of clay
> That yields to worms an easy prey
> Yet Christ my Lord this tomb shall burst
> And raise again the sleeping dust

In Memory of | Mr. John Waugh who | Departed this Life | Sept the 6 A D 1781 | in the 95ᵗʰ year of his | age |

In | Memory of | James Woodruff | Son of Morris | and Candace | Woodruff | who died Jan 15 | 1813 aged 15 days |

> "From death's arrest
> No age is free."

I. SANFORD DART

II. COL. BENJAMIN TALMADGE

III. GEN. MORRIS WOODRUFF

IV. GEN. FRANCIS BACON

In | Memory of M^r | James Woodruff | who died | April 3, 1813 | in the 64 year | of his age |

In Memory of | Mr^s Lucy consort of | M^r James Woodruff | who departed this life | April 28^th 1790 in | the 35^th year of her | age |

In | memory of | Mrs Sarah Woodruff | widow of | Mr. James Woodruff | who died | Mar 2, 1855 | Aged 86 y'rs |

Lieut Charles Woodruff | died Sept 12^th, 1802 | In the 85 year | of his age |

> Death is a debt to nature due
> Which I have paid and so must you.

Here Lyes The | Bod^y of John | Woodruff son of | Ens ( ?) Charles Wood | . . . . died Ap^r ( ?) 10 | 1769 Æ ( ?) 20 Y |

Maria H. | wife of Enoch J. Woodruff | Died Oct 28, 1864 | Æ 71 |

WOODRUFF || Enoch J. Woodruff | died | Aug 9, 1855 | Æ 71 || Catharine M. | wife of | Enoch J. Woodruff | died | Sept 8, 1823 | Æ 32 |

---

## LITCHFIELD EAST CEMETERY (Additional.)

Cyrus Catlin July 17, 1801-Oct 6, 1872

Emeline Wetmore His wife Dec 30, 1806-July 9, 1886.

Their daughter-Mary C. Catlin Sept. 8, 1828

Sept 29, 1901

### CATLIN

Arthur D. Catlin June 17, 1830.—

Eliza M Buel, His wife. Apr 27, 1829-Feby 13, 1859

Julia Benton, His wife July 8, 1839. Oct 16, 1866.

Clarissa A. Stoughton. His wife July 2, 1833.

### PRESCOTT.

George R. Prescott 1817-1903. Elizabeth R His wife 1819-1894

Eliza B. Fish. 1806—1871.

# FOOTVILLE

Under date of December fifteenth, 1776, the following town vote in reference to the yard at Footville or West Morris appears upon the records at Litchfield.

"Upon the Petition of sundry of the Inhabitants of the Southwest Part of Litchfield voted that the Select Men be empowered to buy of Mr. Thomas Waugh Half an acre of Land about Twenty Rods South of Joseph Waugh's Dwelling House for the Sum of Thirty Shillings for the Purpose of a public Burying Place for the Town of Litchfield And in Case said Thomas Waugh doth give & execute a Deed of said Half Acre of Land to the Inhabitants of the Town for the use of a public Burying Yard then said Thomas Waugh his Heirs & Assigns shall have good Right foreuer to inclose said Burying Yard and use it for Pasturing provided he or they shall keep & maintain convenient Bars for the People to pass and repass for the Purpose of burying their dead."

This bit of ground, lying some two miles west of Morris Meeting House, and southwest of Bantam Lake, was conveyed to the town nearly ten years afterward on November thirteenth, 1786. Since then another half acre has been added.

# INSCRIPTIONS

Diana Hall | Wife of | Elijah T. Abbott | & Daughter of | David & Phebe Hall | Died | June 16, 1848 | Æ 40 |

James son to | Hezekiah & | Sabra Agard | died Feb 8, 1791 | aged 1 year |

Rufus Ames | died | Nov 4, 1856 | Aged 57 |

Mary Ames | wife of | Rufus Ames | died | Jan 17, 1850 | Aged 42 |

> Dearest mother thou hast taught us
> Nine in number for to feel
> That 'tis God that hath bereft us
> He can all our sorrows heal.

> Peaceful be thy silent slumber
> Peaceful in the grave so low.

Olive Ames | Wife of | Rufus Ames | Died | April 24, 1831 | Æ 30 |

> To kindred earth she's gone
> And in her folded arms
> Her infant child just born
> Sleeps safe from all alarms
> One half the tree has dropped
> To show the partner's gone.*

Phebe B. | Daughter | of Rufus & | Olive Ames | Died Aug 14, 1829 | Æ 3 yrs |

Julia Ann | Daughter of | Rufus & | Olive Ames | Died | Dec 10, 1830 | Æ 1 y-r |

---

*(Referring to the weeping willow, sculptured on the stone.)

Orange B. Ames | Son of Rufus & | Olive Ames Died | July
1, 1842 | Aged 14 y'rs |

> The topmost branch has dropt
> To show the mother gone
> Three tender limbs are lopt
> That show her daughters gone.
> The others represent her sons
> One is dropt to represent one*

AMES | R. Smith Ames | died Mar 4, 1864 | Æ 29 | Behold
I have finished the work thou | gavest me to do. | Andrew J.
Ames | of Co. I. 5 Regt C. V. | died in Frederick | City Md.
Oct 23, 1862 | Æ 20 |

> In the midst of life we are in death.

Helen Clara | daughter of | Wᵐ B. & | Clara L. Ames |
died | Sept 20, 1863 | Æ 2 y's & 8 ms |

Olive Sarah | eldest child & only | daughter of | Wᵐ B & |
Clara L. Ames | died | Oct 19, 1864 | Æ 14 Y's & 2 Mo. |

> Oh may each heart
> That misses most thy happy smile of mirth.
> Ere long rejoin thee in thy heavenly birth
> No more to part.

Mrs | Olive Barnes | wife of | Orange Barnes | died | Jan
15, 1851 | Æt 90 |

Mʳ | Orange Barnes | died | Sept 30, 1823 | Æt 61 |

Here lyes The | Body of Mary | Barns The Wife | of Enos
Barns who | Departed this Life | January 30ᵗʰ A D 1790 | in
the Seventy year | of her Age |

In memory of | Enos Barnes | who died the 2ᵈ | day of
March A D | 1798 Aged 75 |

> With calm resignation he
> put off the frail agoniseing
> Garb of mortality for
> the Heavenly Robes of
> Immortal Glory.

Eber Barnes | died Oct 3ᵈ, 1800 | Æ 8 years |

---

*(A weeping willcw sculptured on the stone shows four branches on one side
all broken and falling down; three on the other, the lowest one broken off.)

In memory | of Urial Blake | who died March 14 | 1808 Aged 28 Years |

In | Memory of | Joseph Burgess | Who died | Sept 5, 1845 aged 72 |

In memory of | Mrs Lydia Burgess | Wife of Mr. James Burgess | who departed this life | January 12th, 1815 in the | 71st Year of her age |

Ezra Burgess | died Oct 1, 1848 | Aged 71 | Nabby | his wife | died | Oct 21, 1861 | Aged 83 |

Julia Waugh Bristol | died | May 28, 1884 | Aged 76 |

Junius Burgess | 1801-1873 | Sarah Eliza Treat | his wife | 1802-1873 |

William H. Baldwin | Co F, 6 Regt | Conn Vols | died | Mar 12, 1893 |

In Memory of | Judith Wife of | Deac Abel Comstock Di- | ed Dec, 19, 1803 | Aged 76 |

Wilburt Judson | son of | Wm. F. & Ruth | A. Carpenter | Died Sept 28, | 1848 Æ 7 mo- | nths & 18 days |

In | Memory of | Alden Carpenter | Son of Benjamin | & Caroline Carp- | enter Who died | Oct 6, 1843 | Aged 18 years |

Benjamin Carpenter | died | June 1, 1828 | Æ 36 | Caroline | wife of | Benjamin Carpenter | died | Sept 25, 1850 | Æ 54 |

Selima Clark | died | Nov 25, 1877 | Æ 84 |

In Memory | of Shelden son | of Mr. Champion | and Mrs Lois | Clark who | Departed this Life sept 1st A D 1793 | In the 7 year of | his age |

Mary A. Griswold | wife of | Samuel Catlin | died | July 6, 1880 | Aged 78 |

Asleep in Jesus, blessed sleep.

Samuel Catlin | died | Jan 17, 1860 | Aged 56 | Lucy Cat- lin | his wife- | died | June 27, 1842 | Aged 40 |

Walter Cleaver | died | Feb 26, 1861 | Aged 84 Years |

Orpah | wife of | Walter Cleaver | died | Dec 23, 1851 | Æ 78 |

Philena P. | 2nd | wife of | T. S. Canfield | died | Jan 15, 1871 | Æ 38 |

Orson Curtis | died | Oct 29, 1879 | Æ 73 |

Hepzibah | Wife of | Orson Curtis | died | Feb 11, 1888 | Æ 85 |

Ephraim E. | Son of | Elizabeth Doolittle | Died | March 13, 1840 | Æt 16 |

I must bid you all a long farewell
To seek the world where angels dwell

Jesse Derby | died | Aug 10, 1882 | Aged 84 Y'rs | 2 Mo's & 12 D's |

In Memory of | Samuel | Son of Enos & | Sally Emmons | who died Feb | 24th 1809 | Æ 1 year 9 Mo |

Enos Emmons | died | Feb 24, 1861 | Æ 81 | Sarah | his Wife | died | Mar. 1844, | Æ 62 |

Samuel Emmons | died | Feb 10, 1862 | Æ 52 |

Ethiel Emmons | born | July 7, 1802 | died Feb 8, 1873 | his wife | Almira Smith | born May 13, 1804 | died Feb 2, 1875 |

This monument is | erected to the Memory | of | Mr Timothy Foot | & Mrs. Sarah Foot | His Consort | The Former Died May the 8 | 1799 Aged 64 | The Latter Died October 22 | 1777 Aged 41 |

The soul's the only thing we have
Worth an important thought.

Timothy Foot | died | Oct 11, 1849 | Aged 82 | Abigail | Wife of Timothy Foot | died | Aug 25, 1851 | Aged 83 |

In | memory of | Sarah G. Foot | who died | Nov 7, 1851 | Æt 43 |

An Infant | daughter of | Timothy & | Abigail Foot | died December | 21, 1807 | aged 2 Months |

Mr | Wm S. Foot | died | Sept 9, 1848 | Aged 38 |

Mrs | Adaline T. | Wife of | William S. Foot | died | March 22, 1840 | Æt 25 |

Adaline E. Foot | died Sept 14, 1865 | Aged 24 |

| Here is the common lot |

Mr. | Andrew French | Died | Nov 3, 1843 | aged 55 |

> This body rests in hopes to rise
> When the glad trump is waking;
> His soul with Jesus in the skies
> Of endless joy partaking.

Jonathan Griswold | died | March 27, 1861 | Aged 86 | Betsey | his wife | died Sept 29, 1846 | Aged 66 |

Franklin | son of | Lyman L & Rachel | Griswold | died | March 7, 1861 | Æ 2 Y'rs & 5 Mo |

> Sleep on sweet one & take thy rest

In Memory of | David who died April 1st 1775 | aged 4 months | Patience who died May 12th | 1783 in the 5th Year of her age | Anne who died Octr 17th 1790 | aged 1 month | children of Judson Gitteau & | Patience his wife |

Thomas J. Gunn | died | Jan 16, 1868 | Æ 69 |

Phebe | wife of | Thomas J. Gunn | died | Aug 4, 1855 | Æ 55 |

John C. Gunn | died | Oct 8, 1859 | Æ 23 |

John C | son of Thomas J. | & Phebe Gunn | died April 17, 1825 | Æt 8 months |

Samuel N. son of | Samuel & | Betsey Gunn | died March 22, 1822 | Æt 24 |

Mr | Samuel Gunn | died Nov 3, 1826 | Æt 57 |

> Precious in the sight of the Lord
> Is the death of his saints.

Betsey | wife of | Ezra Hoyt | died Jan 1, 1823 | Æ 39 |

William Lucius Hall | 1820-1885 | HALL ||

David L. Hall | died | Jan 6, 1863 | Aged 41 || My Husband |

> Sweet be thy rest
> Till He bid thee arise
> To Hail him in triumph
> Descending the skies.

In | Memory of | William Hall | who died | Nov 25, 1777 | in his 39 year | Mary his relict | died March 1, 1796 | in her 57 year |

David Hall | died | Dec 31, 1831 | Æ 55 | Phebe | wife of |
David Hall | died | April 25, 1853 | Æ 73 |

In | Memory of | Sarah | Wife of E. S. Hall | Who died |
Aug 7, 1844 | aged 80 |

In | Memory of | Ephraim S. Hall | Who died | Jan 28,
1841 | in the 79 year | of his age |

> Gone to the resting place of man
> His long his silent home
> Whare ages past have gone before
> Where future ages come.

Mr | Amos Hine | Died Oct 17, 1831 | In his 78 year Mrs |
Eunice Hine | Died Aug 2, 1829 | In her 70 year |
Amos B. | Son of Amos & | Minerva Hawkins | Died Oct 6,
1830 | Æ 7 mo-s |

Mary J. Hayes | died | July 2, 1870 | Æ 31 |

William L. | son of | Sabrie & | Alice Ives | Feb 12, 1855 |
Æt 5 weeks |

In | Memory of Mrs | Lydia Linsly | wife of Mr Edward
Linsly | who departed this | Life May 14, A D | 1777 in the
28th | Year of her Age |

In Memory of Mr | Edward Lindsley | Who departed this
Life | March the 7, 1804 in | the 60th Year of His Age |

Charles Loomis | died | Apr 11, 1846 | Æ 48 |

Fanny B. Loomis | wife of | Charles G. Loomis | died |
Dec 23, 1849 | aged 46 |

Lucretia | Daughter of | Grandison & | Fanny Loomis |
Died | June 13, 1840 | Æt 4 yr-s |

Charles G. | Son of Grandison | & Fanny Loomis | Died |
June 13, 1840 | Æt 4 yr-s |

Ellen M. | daughter of | Leavitt & | Anthea | Munson died |
Apr 24, 1844 | Æ 1 y'r 9 mo | & 14 d's |

Orson Moss | died | Dec 6, 1860 | Æ 50 |

Laura | wife of | Orson Moss | died | Sept 2, 1848 | Æ 44 |
Elizabeth | their daughter | died | Sept 2, 1848 | Æ 8 |

Eliza | wife of | Orson Moss | Died Oct 15, 1883 | Aged 77
Years |

In memory of | Miss Betsey Munn | who died | Oct 27, 1834 | In the 40<sup>th</sup> year | of her age |

Aubrey C. | son of | Charles W. & | Bertie Noble | died | Mar 26, 1881 | Aged 7 W'ks |

Henry J. Peck | died | May 14, 1869 | Æ 33 | Dearest friend, we miss thee |

Mary | Widow of | John Peck | died | Aug 29, 1861 | Aged 97 | Blessed are the dead that die in the Lord |

In | Memory of | John Peck | who died | Dec 2, 1831 | aged 67 years |

Died | Sept 8, 1831 | an infant | daughter of | Marquis & | Hannah Peck |

Elizabeth Ann | daughter of | Marcus & | Hannah Peck | died | April 28, 1828 | Æt 3 years | & 18 days |

Marquis D. Peck | died | Apr 12, 1849 | Æ 58 | Hannah J. his wife died | May 22, 1876 | Æ 82 | Prepare to meet thy God.

George W. Peck | died | Apr 9, 1856 | Æ 28 |

> No marble can his worth impart
> Tis written on my bleding heart
> Inscribed with more than human skill
> In memory lives his virtue still.
> A mother.

In | Memory of Isaac Parish | who died | Aug 16, 1813 | Æ 63 |

Alfred | Son of Curtis S | & Abigail W. Potter | Who died | Aug 6, 1838 | Æ 2 yr. & 2 mo-s |

Polly B. | wife of | John Parish | died | Nov 23, 1825 | Æ 31 |

Rebecca Pickett | died | June 29, 1850 | Æt 74 |

Jasper Stoddard | died | Feb 5, 1873 | Æ 80 | Sophia | his wife | died | Aug 4, 1861 | Æ 64 |

Mr | Moses Stoddard | Died | Dec 21, 1831 | Æ 91 |

> The Almighty from his throne, on airth
> Surveys nought greater
> than an Honest Human Heart.

Mrs | Abigail Stoddard | Died | Nov 5, 1815 | Æ 67 |

> Th' aspiring Soul ardent and tremulo
> us like flame ascend - Zeal and
> humility her wings to Heaven.

In Memory of | Herman son of | Moses & Abigail | Stoddard who | died Sept 27th | 1793 aged 13 |

Mary P. | Daughter of | Nathan & Percy | Smedley Died | Sept 9, 1829 | aged 4 y'rs |

To the memory of | Nathan & Percy | Smedley. The former | died May 28, 1828 : Æ 42 | The latter, wife of Nathan | Smedley died Sept 10, 1827 | Æ 38 |

> Slow waves the willow oe'r the stone,
> That points where sleep my parents dear !
> Oft have I sought the spot alone
> To shed at ease the filial tear.

In memory of | Mr Nathan Smedley | who died the 12th of | March A D 1809 | In the 60th year | of his age |

> Let each who have a soul to save
> Extend his views beyond the grave
> And while salvation still is nigh
> To Christ the friend of sinners fly.

Frederick Smedley | died | Aug 1, 1855 | Æ 77 |

......mory of | .... Nelson | Wife of | John Stone | Who Died | Nov 3, 1835 | Æ 31 |

Enos Stoddard Esq. | died | June 23, 1850 | Aged 73 |

Mrs. | Amelia Stoddard | Wife of | Enos Stoddard, Esq. | Died Sept 23, 1830 | Æ 50 |

> No warning given : Unceremonious fate :

Mr | Charles Stoddard | died | May 23, 1844 | Æ 26 |

> Call'd not away when time had loos'd each hold
> On the fond heart & each desire grows cold
> But when to all that knit us to our kind
> He fell, fast bound as charity can bind

Catharine C. | wife of | Enos Stoddard | died | June 27, 1852 | Æ 38 |

In Memory of | Anne, wife of Chester Smedley | and Daughter of John Landon | who died April 14, 1809 in | the 23 year of her age, | And Also in Memory of Edward son | of Chester & Anne Smedley born | July 22, A D 1807 and died Dec the | 6th 1808 |

> When Christ the Resurection shall appear,
> He'll wipe from all faces every tear
> Nor sin nor death shall leave a stain
> O Come Lord Jesus quickly Come
> And call thy Blessed children home
> Nor let the grave victorious reign.

Mr. | David Smith | died | April 21, 1805 | Æ 51 |
Mary Smith | wife of | David Smith | died | March 3, 1848 | aged 86 |

Susan, wife of | Charles Smith | died | Oct 17, 1845 | aged 18 yrs |

Bateman Smith | died | Feb 17, 1869 | Æ 77 |

Julia B. | wife of | Bateman Smith | died | Jan 25, 1853 | Æ 55 |

Julia E. | wife of | George Stoddar | died Dec 15, 1887 | Aged 55 Y'rs |

This monument is erec | ted in Memory of Mr | Joseph Throop who | Departed this life | Oct - | 4th 1799 | in the 84th | Year of his age |

A daughter of | Dan & Olive | Throop died | Dec 22, 1822 | Æt 5 months |

Mr | Benjamin Throop | Died Oct 8, 1833 | Æ 81 | Mrs | Mary Throop | Died May 26, 1813 | Æ 57 |

In memory of | Mrs. | Deborah Throop | Wife of Mr Joseph Throop | who Died February 14 | 1811 Aged 94 years |

In Memory | of Mary an | daughter of | Mr William | and Mrs. Eunice | Throop who | died august 26th | 1793 aged 3 years |

In Memory of Lemon son | of Mr William and Mrs | Eunice Throop who | Departed this Life Oct | 28th A D 1793 in the 14 | year of his age |

In Memory of | Donald Treat | who died March | 24th 1803 in the 63d | year of his age |

> Beneath these clods my body lies
> Yealded to death a sacrifice

Eli Treat | died | Mar 17, 1854 | Æ 80 | Maria | his wife died | Aug 17 1854 | Æ 76 |

Caroline M. | wife of | Abel C. Tracy | died | June 2, 1858 | Aged 34 |

> Her days of affliction are oe'r
> Her days and her nights of distress
> We see her in anguish no more
> She has gained a happy release.

Edward | Son of | Abel C. & Caroline | Tracy | died | Jan 10, 1861 | Aged 11 |

Dan Throop | died Mar 31, 1878 | aged 82 | Olive Smith | his wife | died Sept 4, 1894 | aged 97 | THROOP || Charles Throop | died Mar 30, 1859 | aged 32 | Morris B. Throop | died Jan 15, 1863 | aged 27 |

Mr | James Wickwire | Died Sept 4, 1822 Æ 63 | Sally Wickwire | Died Oct 11, 1793 | Æ 13 y-rs | Asa Wickwire | Died Dec 11, 1793 | Æ 5 y-rs | Susan Wickwire | Died Aug 7, 1801 | Æ 6 mo-s | Mrs Sarah Wickwire | died July 22, 1848 | Æ 89 |

Waugh |
To the memory of | Mr Thomas & Mrs Rosannah |

Thomas Waugh | died feb || Rosannah Waugh | died 24th 1801 | in the 76th year | || Aug 4th 1789 | in the 60th of his Age | || year | of her Age |

In Memory of | Mr John Watson | who died Nov the 9th 1781 | in the 74th Year of his age | And of | Mrs Bethyah his wife | who died June the 24th 1792 | in the 87th Year of her age | This Monument is respectfully | erected | By James Watson Their youngest son |

In | memory of | Elizabeth | Wife of | Capt Samuel Waugh | Who died | July 3, 1850 | Æ 87 |

> Safely landed on that peaceful shore
> Where pilgrims meet to part no more

In | Memory of | Capt Samuel Waugh | Who died | Oct 12, 1838 | Aged 80 |

How transient is that life of man :
At most a brief contracted span
It blooms, it fades and serves to show
How vain how frail are things below.

Loudon | Baley Waugh | son of Samuel and | Elizabeth | Waugh who de | parted this Life | sept$^r$ the 12$^{th}$, 1796 | in the 3$^{rd}$ year of | his age |

Here lies interd A hum
an frame Resigned to
Earth and food for worms.

Chloe C. | Daughter of | Samuel & | Elizabeth Waugh | died | Jan 18, 1808 | Æt 1 year |

Charles Belden Carroll Wright | son of | Jonathan and Betsey Griswold Wright | born 22 October 1831 | died 22 September 1844 |

In memory of | Abigail Weeks | Died | Oct 24, 1822 | Æ 84 |

Nancy M. | only daughter of | Orson & | Matilda Weed | died | June 13, 1845 | aged 18 years.

This marble is erected as a
mark in the sod where sleeps
our only daughter till God
doth her call.

In Memory of | Samuel Weeks | who died | August | 18, 1821 | Aged 80 | Years |

Esther | wife of | Ezra Weeks | died | Sept 21, 1849 | Æ 69|

In | memory of | Ezra Weeks | who died | Feb 4, 1851 | Æ 74 |

Mr John Waugh | Died | April 21, 1813 | Æ 57 | Mrs Olive Waugh | Wife of John Waugh | Died | Jan 6, 1812 | Æ 45 |

In | Memory of | the widow | Ruth Waugh | wife of | Mr Robert Waugh | who departed this | life June 8$^{th}$ 1816 | aged 88 years |

Mr. Robbart Waugh | died Oct 6$^{th}$ 1802 | in the 78$^{th}$ year | of his age |

In | Memory of | Miss Margaret Waugh | Who died | March 24, 1844 | aged 78 |

Mrs Rhoda Waugh | Daughter of Mr Robert | and Mrs Ruth Waugh | Died January 8th A D 1805 | In the 43rd year of her | age |

In | Memory of | Christian Waugh | an adopted daughter of | Robert and Ruth | Waugh who died | April 27, 1815 | Æt 39 |

In | Memory of | Mrs Hannah Waugh | wife of | Mr. James Waugh | who died | Aug 26th 1824 | Æt 59 |

James Waugh | died | Mar 13, 1852 | Æt 88 y'rs |

He has gone where ransomed spirits
With Christ in glory shine
A mansion to inherit
Where joys are all divine.

In | memory of | Thomas Waugh | who died | Jan 1, 1841 | aged 74 y'rs |

In Memory of | Dr Thaddeus Waugh | Who died | Nov 9, 1810 | aged 52 | Ruth his wife died | Dec 13, 1843 | aged 78 | Their Son | Marquis M. Waugh | died Dec. 21, 1839 | aged 52 |

Grace Deeming | Wife of | Samuel W. Waugh | died | Sept 6, 1895 | Æ 69 |

Samuel W. Waugh | died | Apr 18, 1869 | Æ 67 |

Francis | Son of Samuel | W. & Caroline B. | Waugh | Died | March 17, 1840 | Æ 2 yr-s & 5 m's |

James B. | Son of William | & Lydia B. | Williams | Died | March 20, 1838 | Æ 10 mo-s |

Sleep on sweet babe
& thou art blest
for Christ hath died
For thee a rest.

Cynthia | wife of | Benj. Wickwire | Died Oct 9, 1879 | Aged 56 |

Benjamin Wickwire | died | May 23, 1854 | Æt 35 |

Sheldon Wickwire | died | June 4, 1852 | Æ 58 |

Celinda | Wife of | Sheldon Wickwire | died | Aug 29, 1883 | Æ 80 yrs |

In | memory of | Abigail | Wife of | Soul Warner | who died | July 30, 1835 | aged 77 |

Harvey Waugh | died | Apr 11, 1886 | Æt 58 |

Leverett J. Waugh | died | Feb 21, 1879 | Aged 62 |

Lucy B. | wife of | Leverett Waugh | died | April 15, 1866 | Æ 48 |

Horace Waugh | Died July 12, 1854 | Æ 63 | Anah | his wife | Died Mar 14, 1870 | Æ 76 |

Lucy J. | daughter of | Ruth C. & | David P. Wetmore | died | Mar 24, 1866 | Æ 1 y'r & 7 mo |

Franklin L. Wickwire | of Co C. 13 C. V. | Died at New Orleans | June 26, 1862 | Æ 18 |

Charles Wickwire | born 16 July 1810 | died 20 August 1887 | his wife Melinda | daughter of | John Griswold | born 16 June 1810 | died 20 August 1890 |

Luman Watrous | died | June 5, 1895 | Aged 62 |

Hattie B. | adopted | daughter of | Luman & | Harriet J. Watrous | died | Apr 26, 1879 | Æ 13 y'rs |

Andreas Weik | Feb 6, 1820 | Dec 18, 1896 | Christina | his wife | Oct 21, 1823 | Feb 7, 1897 || Auf | weidersehen |

Jakob K. Weik | died | Oct 7, 1895 | Aged 28 |

Edgar A. | died | Apr 12, 1883 | Æ 6 W'ks | Elmer B. | died | Dec 27, 1883 | Æ 10 Mo's | Walter F. | died | Sept 1, 1884 | Æ 5" 2 Mo's | Children of | Theron & Alice | Waugh |

# STONE BURIAL GROUND

In Memory of | Mr Stephen Stone | Who departed this |
Life July 30<sup>th</sup> 1794 | Aged 73 years |

Eliza Stone |

In Memory of | Mrs. | Rebekah Stone | wife to Mr Stephen |
Stone who departed | this life Nov 29<sup>th</sup> A D | 1767 in the 47<sup>th</sup>
year | of her age |

# Private Burial Ground in East Litchfield

Lucretia Clark | died | Dec 19, 1858 | Aged 85 |

Sally Griswold | died | Feb 14, 1858 | Æ 81 |

Betsey | wife of | Eli Norton | Died Aug 20, 1873 | Æ 77 |

Salley J. | wife of | Samuel M. Roberts | died | Jan 16,
1863 | Aged 38 |

> Dearest Sister, thou hast left us
> Peaceful in the grave so low
> Yet again we hope to meet thee
> Where no farewell tears shall flow.
>
> ———
>
> My flesh shall slumber in the ground
> Till the last trumpet's joyful sound
> Then burst the chains with sweet surprise
> And in my Saviour's image rise.

Lucy E. | wife of | Edward A. Smith | died | Oct 21, 1853 |
in the 25, year | of her age |

> Friend after friend departs,
> Who hath not lost a friend?
> There is no union here of hearts
> But it will have an end.

Howard L. | only son of | Edward A. & Lucy E. Smith |
died | Feb 18, 1854 | aged 4 years | & 6 mo |

> Sleep on, sweet child, the time is short
> The grave can't hold thee long
> Thou soon will rise in heavenly guise
> And join the bloodwashed throng

# CATHOLIC CEMETERY

Michael Bray | died | Nov 21, 1881 | Aged 48 Y'rs | Born in Fedamore, | Co. of Limerick | Ireland | (*footstone*) | Co A 2, Regt | Art'y C. V. |

Edward Burk | died | Mar. 18, 1873 | Æ 65 | Native of Grange | Parish of. Killaun | Co. Wexford, Ireland |

William Brahen | died Mar 2, 1895, aged 80 yrs | BRAHEN |

John Brennan | died | Oct 12, 1872 | Æ 43 | Native of Grange, Parish | of Killaun, Co. Wexford | Ireland |

Mary Ann | daughter of | John & Cathrine | Brennan died | Nov 22, 1860 | Æ 6 y'rs & 4 mo. |

Thomas | son of Patrick & Mary | Birmingham | died | Aug 5, 1870 | Æ 1 Y'r & 2 M. |

Patrick Birmingham | died | Aug 19, 1889 | aged 52 | BIR-MINGHAM |

Thomas Cahill | died | Mar 9, 1888 | aged 100 Y'rs | Margaret Cahill | his wife | died Mar 17, 1881 | age 75 Y'rs | CAHILL || Margaret A | daughter of | Joseph & Catherine | Cahill | died Jan 31, 1886 | age 20 y'rs |

CONLON || Katie | died | April 9, 1883 | aged 22 | Felix Died | Dec. 28, 1884 | Aged 26 | Rosa Died | Jan 7, 1885 | Aged 19 | Children of James And Margaret Conlon |

Michael Dempsey | —— | Catharine | his wife | died | June 8, 1895 | age 72 | DEMPSEY || Kate Gleason | died in New York | Jan 22, 1895 | age 36 |

Our Mother | Bridget | wife of John Donahue | Died July 13, 1884 | Aged 39 | .

In memory of | James Doyle | born | in the Parish of Borcis | Carlow Co. Ireland | died Mar. 24, 1879 Æ 76 |

Anthony Dwyer | Born in Cooneen Parish | of Templederry, County | Tipperary, Ireland | Died Sept 28, 1884 Æ 65 | Ellen Conway | his wife | Died Jan 12, 1892 | Æ 75 |

Maria | daughter of | Anthony & Ellen O Dwyer | Born in Cooneen Parish of | Templederry | Co. Tipperary Ireland | Died June 12, 1873 | aged 22 |

Patrick J. | son of | John & | Bridget Doyle | died | July 25, 1884 | Æ 22 |

Margaret Doyle | Died Mar 25, 1858 | Aged 18 | Mary Doyle | wife of | David Brown | Died Apr 10, 1864 | Aged 25 |

John Flynn | died | July 5 1879 | aged 60 yrs | Bridget | his wife | died Oct 23, 1888 | aged 71 yrs | FLYNN || Our sons | John Flynn | died March 12, 1859 | aged 11 yrs & 4 mos | Michael Flynn | of the 1, Conn. | Cavalry was killed | at Reams Station | June 29, 1864 | aged 18 yrs & 4 mos |

In | memorium | Joseph Fanning | died | Feb 2, 1879 | Aged 56 | Ann wife of | Joseph Fanning | Died Feb 25, 1895 | Aged 72 | FANNING |

John Herbert | born in Parish of Fedamore | County Limerick, Ireland | Jan 1, 1829 | died Aug 22, 1890 | HERBERT || John | died May 4, 1872 | aged 3 | Anne died May 13, 1872 aged 5 |

Philip E. | son of | Michael & Bridget | Harrigan | died | Feb 7, 1882 | Aged 14 |

Ellen | wife of | Moses Harris | died | Jan 30, 1893 | Æ 74 |

Bridget | wife of | Patrick Herbert | died | Aug 29, 1871 | Aged 37 | Erected by her Husband |

In memory of | William Kelley | Died | March 26, 1864 | Æ 35 | James | Son of Wm & Mary Kelley | Died March 22, 1864 | Æ 4 Yrs. 7 Mo's |

Mathew | son of | Wm & Mary | Kelley died | Sept 12, 1860 | Æ 3 y's & 2 mo |

Peter | son of | Patrick & | Bridget Kelley | died | Dec 5, 1881 | Æ 3 Y'rs 4 Mo | & 11 D's |

Thomas | Apr 19, 1894 | age 16 y'rs | Kate | Oct 19, 1880 | Age 5 Y'rs | Ellen | Sept 22, 1874 | Age 1 Y'r | John | Dec 27, 1879 | Age 1 Day | Children of B. & | John Kenny | KENNY || Mary Kenny | 1807-1895 |

Michael Kennedy | died | Apr 8, 1891 | Æ 76 Yrs | native of Borrisleigh | Co. Tipperary, Ireland | KENNEDY || Nora Kennedy | wife of Edward Welch | died July 15, 1892 | Æ 24 yrs & 8 mos ||

Willie | died | Dec 12, 1866 | Æ 8 y'r & 5 mo. || Son of | Michael & Catharine | Kennedy |

Mary Kirwin | wife of | Patrick Kirwin | died | Dec 13, 1884 | aged 64 Y'rs | Born in Clonocody | Co. Tipperary | Ireland |

Michael Lavin | died Jan. 16 1879 age 76 yrs | Bridget his wife | died Feb 18, 1890 age 78 yrs | LAVIN || Catherine T. Lavin | died Feb. 1, 1879 age 25 yrs | John Lavin | died Jan 11, 1880 age 45 yrs || Winifred Lavin | — |

Katie | daughter of | Bartley & | Margaret Lavin | died | Feb 24, 1883 | Aged 3 Y'rs |

Patrick Lavin | born | Mar 17, 1856 | died Oct 24, 1892 |

In | Memory of Mary Molloy | who died | Dec 1, 1877 | Aged 27 |

MOORE || William H. Moore | died | Aug 11, 1887 | Aged 27 |

Mary McCarthy | died | Feb 28, 1886 | Aged 18 | Margaret | died | Aug 20, 1878 | aged 3 m's | Patrick | died | Aug 8, 1880 | Aged 4 m's | Children of Patrick & Ann | Murphy |

Ann McGuff | died | June 24, 1880 | Aged 42 |

Catharine | Madden | died Oct 5, 1878 | Aged 11 d's |

Michael Joseph Madden | Jan 12, 1862—June 25, 1889 | MADDDEN |

Thomas E. | son of | Timothy — | Catherine Meagher | died | May 3, 1869 | Æ 3 Y'rs & 2 Mo |

Bridget | wife of | Darby McCarthy | died | March 10, 1870| Aged 77 | Born in Co. Clare, Ireland |

Mary | wife of | John McCarthy | died | March 1, 1884 | Aged 71 |

Francis O'Brien | died | Oct 17, 1884 | Aged 68 |

Catharine | wife of | Francis O'Brien | Died Jan 16, 1888 | Aged 67 | Native of County | Wexford, Ireland |

Patrick O'Sullivan | Son of | Patrick & Johanna | O'Sullivan | Native of the Parish of Tralee | County Kerry, Ireland | Died Sept 14, 1878 | Aged 50 |

Bridget Powers | died | July 13, 1891 | Aged 95 | Erected by her Son | Michael Powers |

Bridget Quigley | died | March 17, 1880 | Aged 35 Y'rs |

John Ryan | born June 22, 1800 | died Sept 26, 1880 | RYAN |

RYAN || Martin J. Ryan | son of | Michael & Catherine | Ryan | Died May 2, 1885 | Aged 21 | Katie Ryan | daughter of | Michael & Catherine | Ryan | Died June 22, 1882 | Aged 15 | James Ryan | Died Apr 30, 1887 | Aged 16 |

Willie | son of | John & | Johanna | Rourke | died | July 25, 1880 | Aged 8 Mo's | & 14 D's |

James | son of John & | Marcella Scanlan | died | Jan 10, 1881 | Æ 8 mo & 2 we. |

Johannah | daughter of | Patrick & | Henrietta | Shough-nessy | Born Aug 18, 1884 | Died Feb 21, 1885 |

Michael Sepple | died | Feb 21, 1889 | Aged 75 | a native of Ireland | Parish of Killworth | Co. Cork |

Ellen | wife of | Michael Sepple | Died Dec 12, 1881 | Aged 69 Yr's | Native of Ireland, Parish of | Killworth Co. of Cork |

Mary Welsh | Daughter of | John & Bridget Welsh | Born in Spring Mount | Co. Tipperary, Ireland, 1806 | Died Jan 31, 1885 | Æ 79 |

# Burial Ground of the Beach Family

This ground is on a slight eminence in a meadow nearly three miles northwest of the borough of Litchfield, adjacent to the road called for many years, "Beach Street," after the family who lived in the neighborhood and were buried here.

Most of the stones have been removed, according to the best information which can be gotten.

## INSCRIPTIONS

.......... | Memory of | David Beach | This Stone is erected | who departed this life | July 29th AD 1806 | aged Sixty three years | and four months | He was the first person | Buried in this ground | and at his request. |

.......... and of God.

IN memory | of | Laban Beach | Who Died | APril 15th | 1819 | Æ 74 |

1827 | Olive Beach. |

David | Beach | Who died | Feb | 11 | 1809 |

In Memory | of Naomi Wife | of L B who | Died Sept | 25th 1814 | Æ 48 |

M. B. |

Clarisa, wife of | Heman Beach | died Sept. 20, 1818. | aged 42 years. | James, son of Heman | & Clarisa Beach | died Sept. 1807 | aged 2 years | Clarisa | daughter of Heman | & Clarisa Beach | died March 7, 1822 | aged 13 years |

Abner Gilbert | died Dec. 11, 1822 | aged 59 |

# SOLDIERS' LOT, WEST CEMETERY

The Town of Litchfield several years ago voted to give a section of the West Cemetery for the burial of soldiers not having lots of their own, and in 1894 the citizens dedicated thereon a small monument, "IN MEMORIAM."

A few veterans have from time to time been interred on the lot, and in 1903 the State erected twenty-three headstones on it for those accredited to Litchfield quota in the Rebellion, who were buried in unknown graves on Southern soil.

The illustration shows this lot and the stones erected thereon.

## INSCRIPTIONS

William Baker, Co. I. 13. Regt. Conn. Vols. Died Sept 2, 1862.

Corp Franklin M. Bunnell Co. A. 2. Regt Hvy Arty C V Died Oct. 25, 1864.

George W Baldwin Co E. 8. Regt. Conn. Vols. Died Mar. 18, 1862

William Bradshaw C. A 14 Regt Conn. Vols Killed June 16, 1864 Petersburg Va

Charles Catlin Co I 13 Regt Conn Vols Died Sept 2 1863.

Corp. Sylvanus M Clark Co E 8 Regt Conn Vols Died Mar. 14, 1862

Alonzo Chapel Co I 13 Regt Conn Vols Died Feby 28, 1863

Mus. Thomas Dixon Co. D 29 Regt Conn Vols Died Aug 20, 1864

Jacob Forfe Co C 1 Regt Hvy Arty C V Died Mar 16, 1865

Mus. John Gutteman Co E. 1 Regt Cav. C. V. Died July 26, 1864 Andersonville Prison

John Handel Co. B. 2 Regt Hvy Regt C. V. Killed June 1, 1864 Cold Harbor Va

Henry W Hotchkiss Co A 2 Regt Hvy Arty C V Died Jan 23, 1896.

WEST CEMETERY—SOLDIERS' LOT

John Iffland Co A 2 Regt Hvy Arty C V. Killed June 1, 1864 Cold Harbor Va

Jacob Kearn Co A 14 Regt Conn Vols. Killed May 24 1864 North Anna River Va

Jerry Kerrier Co I 14 Regt Conn Vols Died July 1862

Amos W. Kilbourn 25 Batty Ohio Vols. Died Mar 14, 1901 Æ 65

Henry Mayo Co I 13 Regt Conn Vols. Died Apr 27, 1903 Æ 65

William H Norville Co C 2d Regt Hvy Arty C V Died Nov 10, 1863

Jerome Nichols Co E 8 Regt Conn Vols Died Oct 17, 1863.

Francis A Newcomb Co E. 8 Regt Conn Vols Died Mar 14, 1862

Watson Parmalee Co A 2 Regt Hvy Arty C V. Died Nov 25, 1862

Willard H Parmalee Co A 2 Regt Hvy Arty C V Killed June 1, 1864 Cold Harbor Va

Albert A Peck Co G 2 Regt Hvy Arty C V Died Sept 22, 1864

Patrick Ryan Co A 2 Regt Hvy Arty C V Killed June 1, 1864 Cold Harbor Va

Amos H Stilson Co A 2 Regt Hvy Arty C V Died June 20, 1864 .

Caralf Volusen Co B 2 Regt Hvy Arty C V Died Feby 27, 1864

Geo C Weed Co K 91 Regt N. Y. Vols Died May 7, 1891.

# MEMORANDA

## SOLDIERS' MONUMENTS

A beautiful soldier's monument, erected by the citizens of Litchfield, stands in the Center Park, of Litchfield. It is of white marble and of elegant design. Another soldier's monument is standing in the center of Northfield. Is of brown sandstone, and was erected by the citizens of Northfield directly after the end of the War of the Rebellion, and is said to have been the first of the soldier's monuments erected in the country.

*The inscriptions appear in other parts of this book.*

---

## CARE OF CEMETERIES

In Litchfield an association has been formed to care for the West Cemetery. By payment of a small annual due the subscriber can have his lot and monument taken care of.

The East Cemetery is of two divisons, the old part, which is taken care of by the town, if at all, and the northern part, which belongs to the Litchfield Cemetery Association, and is taken care of by it at a charge of two dollars per year to the lot owners.

The other yards in the town are uncared for.

In Morris an association has been lately formed to restore and care for the East Yard there. Generous subscriptions have been given, and the work has been well begun.

All of the cemeteries, in both Litchfield and Morris, are in a pretty respectable condition.

---

## REVOLUTIONARY DEAD

In the southeast corner of the East Cemetery at Litchfield are the remains of a large number of Revolutionary heroes. They were buried here, in trenches side by side without coffins —and there is nothing to mark their resting places.

## ACADIANS

In the Morris Cemetery are also the unmarked and unknown graves of many of the Acadian prisoners who were quartered upon Litchfield at the close of that war—1755.

(*Authority, traditions of old people, and grave diggers' statements*).

## THE TOWN POOR

The present farm of L. and S. Whittlesey, on the east side of Bantam Lake, in Morris, was for a long period the Town Farm of Litchfield, where it kept its poor. There was an inclosure on it in which were interred fifty-one of the inmates. There are a number of interments on the present Litchfield Town Farm with no inscriptions. Until recently no record whatever was made of deaths of the Town poor.

# INDEX

**KILBORN**
Abigail, 29
Anna, 128
Anna B., 128
Charles P., 128
Diadama, 128
David, 128, 30
Edith L., 221
Freeman J., 127
Hannah, 29, 30
Harrict, 127
Hiram, 127
Hobart, 127
Huldah, 160
Jacob, 115
James, 29
Jesse, 128
Jeremiah, 127, 128
Joseph, 29
Levi, 128
Lewis, 29
Lucretia, 128
Lucy Bradley, 115
Lucy Peck, 115
Maria, 128
Mary, 29, 30
Noah, 128
Norman, 215
Putnam, 127
Rollin F., 127
Riley P., 127
Thalia O., 128
Whitman, 128

**KILBOURN**
Amanda, 29
Amos W., 256
Ann, 29
Benjamin, 29
Caroline A. Canfield, 115
Catherine, 127
Charles, 29 (2)
Charles Catlin, 82
Charles J., 127
Charles M., 139
Chauncey, 30 (2)
Clarissa A., 30
Cloe, 30
Dwight C., 115
Eliada, 129
Elizabeth Cone, 28
Elizabeth D., 127
Emeline Coe, 127
Ethan, 186
George I. Gilbert, 122
Gertrude, 29
Giles, 29
Harry, 30
Henry, 127

Homer, 127
Julia Maria, 30
Laura J., 30
Lelia Kenyon, 28
Lois, 30
Lois S., 30
Lucretia, 139
Mary, 30
Mary Ann Dudley, 139
Mehala, 30
Payne Kenyon, 28
Sabra, 30
Samuel, 128
Sarah M. Hopkins, 115
Solomon, 29
Thankful, 186
Thirza, 30
Truman, 127
William P., 115

**KIMBERLY**
Edward, 186
Mary Jane Clark, 186

**KING**
Edward E., 29
Henry E., 29
Julia Rebecca, 28
Rebecca, 29

**KIRBY**
Harriot, 81
Roger, 186
Ruth, 81

**KIRCHBERGER**
Catherine Ruth, 221
Charles G., 221

**KIRWIN**
Mary, 253

**KNICKERBOCKER**
Laura A., 128
Laura, 129

**KOEHLER**
Aurelia, 82

**LAIRE**
William H., 221

**LANE**
Catherine R. Smith, 221
Edgar H., 130
Georgie H., 130
Henry A., 130
Lenora M., 130
Mary, 221
Mary E. Blakeman, 221
Thomas A., 130

**LAMPMAN**
Robert, 31

www.ingramcontent.com/pod-product-compliance
Lightning Source LLC
Chambersburg PA
CBHW050458270326
41927CB00009B/1803